MW01087463

Education as Preventive Medicine

A Salutogenic Approach

Michaela Glöckler

The Work of the School Physician at Waldorf/Rudolf Steiner Schools
Rudolf Steiner's Insights into Promoting Health for Children
Salutogenesis: Seeking the Source of Health

With contributions by:
Johannes Bockemühl
Ernst Bücher
Wolfgang Göbel
Wolfgang Kersten
Daniela Greif
Marina Kayser-Springorum
Armin Husemann
Gisbert Husemann
Helmut v. Kügelgen
Karl-Reinhard Kummer
Hans Müller-Wiedemann
Maria Theresia Pehm

RUDOLF STEINER COLLEGE PRESS

This publication has been made possible by grants from the Waldorf Curriculum Fund and the Medical Section of the Goetheanum.

Most of this book was originally published in German as *Gesundheit und Schule*, ISBN 3-7235-1007-8, © 1998 Verlag am Goetheanum, CH–4143 Dornach.

The English language edition is translated by Maria St. Goar.
The chapter on salutogenesis is translated by Uwe Stave.

Cover design: Claude Julien
Artistic technical advice: Theodore Mahle

Cover photographs: Sherry Hirssig
Our thanks go to the parents of the Sacramento Waldorf School for granting permission to use these photos of their children.

© 2002 Michaela Glöckler and Rudolf Steiner College Press

ISBN 0-945803-63-X

The content of this book represents the views of the author and in no way should be taken as the official opinion or policy of Rudolf Steiner College or Rudolf Steiner College Press.

All rights reserved. No part of this book may be copied in any form without the written consent of the author and the publisher.

Book orders may be made through Rudolf Steiner College Bookstore:
Tel. 916-961-8729, FAX 916-961-3032.
Catalog and online orders: www.steinercollege.edu.
Questions or comments, E-mail: bookstore@steinercollege.edu.

Rudolf Steiner College Press
9200 Fair Oaks Boulevard
Fair Oaks, CA 95628, U.S.A.

Table of Contents

Acknowledgments 5

Foreword to the English edition by Astrid Schmitt-Stegmann 7

Chapter 1   The School Physician as Preventive Medicine Specialist 11

Chapter 2   Sense Activity and Experience of Self 23

Chapter 3   The Arts in Relation to the Human Components 27

Chapter 4   Metamorphosis of Growth Forces into Thought Activity 33

Chapter 5   Rudolf Steiner's Description of a School Physician's Tasks 45

     A child should be able to develop sound in body, free in soul, and lucid in spirit. 45

     Classroom instruction based on insight into the human components .. 49

     Child study in faculty meetings: psychological insight into the individual child 58

     Pedagogical-constitutional classification 76

     The large-headed chiild and the small-headed child 76

     The earthly child and the cosmic child 82

     The fantasy-rich child and the fantasy-poor child 85

     Treatment of left-handedness 87

     Left-handers learning to write with the right hand 90
     Maria Theresia Pehm

     Educating practical life experience through dexterity exercises 100

     Nutrition—Interest—Consciousness 103

     Homework: whom does it serve? 106

     Education between preexistence and postexistence 109

Chapter 6   Weekly Schedules and Results of Research on Rhythm 115

     Nurturing the daily rhythm, including the night 119

     Weekly rhythm 135

     Monthly rhythm 141

     Yearly rhythm and care of the physical body 146

Chapter 7   Physiological Effects of Education 153

Medical and pedagogical questions in the preschool
and nursery years 153

About Elementary Eurythmy in the First Seven Years 154
Helmut von Kügelgen

We are Participants in the Creation of the Human Being 158
Helmut von Kügelgen

Treating children according to their temperaments 160

Proper breathing 163

Proper sleeping 166

Chapter 8   Rudolf Steiner's Comments on Subject Areas 171

Forming mental images 171

History, geography, geology: finding oneself through experiencing
the world 172

Artistic instruction and developing the faculty of judgment 179

Lifting unconscious questions into consciousness 181

The effect of instruction on the ego 183

Stimulation of intelligence 186

Speech instruction 187

Reading and observing 190

Zoology 192

On the differentiation of the sexes 193

Music and singing 201

Eurythmy 207

Eurythmy and singing 211

Arithmetic and morality 212

Physics and intellectuality 215

Threefoldness of the human organism and the interaction of science,
art, and religion 220

Chapter 9   School Physicians' Reports 225

Child Study

Methods of Child Study 227
Johannes Bockemühl

Child Study in Education and Therapeutic Education 238
Wolfgang Goebel

Bringing the ideas into practice

Description of the School Doctor's Work in Engelberg 245
Wolfgang Kersten

The Physician and Therapeutic Education 261
Hans Müller-Wiedemann

Important themes for the school physician

The Public Work of a School Physician 265
Marina Kayser-Springorum

Medical Examination for Entry into a Waldorf School 269
Karl-Reinhard Kummer

Effects of Soccer on the Developing Human Being 281
Karl-Reinhard Kummer

Dyslexia in the Waldorf School: a case report 290
Armin Husemann/ Daniela Greif/ Ernst Bücher

Anorexia nervosa 304
Gisbert Husemann

Glimpse into the Work of a Child Psychiatrist
and School Physician 311
Johannes Bockemühl

Chapter 10   Salutogenesis:: Seeking the Source of Health 325

Notes 347

Bibliography 355

Index 365

Acknowledgments

I would like to thank many people for their contributions in making this book possible.

First, of course, all of us who work with ideas from Rudolf Steiner thank him for his lifetime dedication to the future development of all humanity.

To my many colleagues in the medical and teaching professions, those whose work is represented directly in this book and all the others who are diligently working for children, I give my deepest appreciation.

My grateful thanks also go to all the people who have worked hard to present the contents of this book in a clear way to the English reader: Maria St. Goar, Astrid Schmitt-Stegmann, Dr. Uwe Stave, Rev. Richard Lewis, Deborah Brandow, Claude Julien, Judith Blatchford, and Hallie Wootan.

Lastly, but perhaps most importantly, we all owe our thanks to the children, the representatives of the next generation, who awaken our questions and lead us forward.

Michaela Glöckler
Spring 2002

Foreword to the English Edition

The purpose of this book is to give physicians, teachers, and parents an understanding of Waldorf education as preventive medicine, for what we teach children exerts a strong formative influence on their growing bodies and can therefore promote either health or illness. For this reason, from the beginning of his working with teachers and doctors, Rudolf Steiner pointed out that education must proceed from a consciousness of the child's health. *How* and *when* something is taught affects a child's disposition towards health or illness for life.

This awareness underlies Waldorf education. The whole curriculum is built on an understanding of the physiological and soul development of the child. It is the teacher's constant task to penetrate every subject to such an extent that its effect on the physical constitution of the child becomes clear. We must strive to do this work with ever greater consciousness, for the healthy development of the physical body is the basis for a healthy unfolding of the soul-spiritual individuality of the child. Therefore it is of great importance that doctors and teachers work together.

To address this need, Dr. Michaela Glöckler has established conferences the world over to foster collaboration between doctors and teachers. She is uniquely qualified to promote this cooperative working as she stands solidly in both the medical and pedagogical fields. As a medical doctor, she also grasps anthroposophical medicine in depth; as a school doctor for ten years at the Marburg and Witten Waldorf

Schools, she worked her way into all aspects of Waldorf pedagogy, including teaching young children and teenagers herself.

This collaboration between doctors and teachers that is so near and dear to Dr. Glöckler's heart was emphasized by Rudolf Steiner already in 1921, at the first Waldorf school in Stuttgart, Germany, when he spoke about the necessity of having a doctor who would be part of the school life, know all the children, teach certain subjects, and be concerned about the health and well-being of the whole student body.

Even though this book presumes basic knowledge of Rudolf Steiner's view of the human being, it is written in such a manner that anyone interested will find the way into what is presented. It not only gives insight into the growing child, but also addresses many of the problems that surface in children today and challenge both doctors and teachers: difficulties in concentration, dyslexia, lefthandedness, anorexia, lack of interest and motivation, to name just a few. The role of sensory development, an understanding of the arts as one way of addressing and healing the human being, the healthy development of thinking, feeling, and willing underlie much of the presentation.

The reports and experiences from the school doctors shed light on their working within a Waldorf school and also bring valuable understanding and new viewpoints or perspectives that can expand and enrich the teachers' work. Invaluable also are the chapters that bring us up to date with the research on the phenomena of rhythm. Every living organism is embedded in a rhythmic time structure. Life proceeds out of the dynamic interplay of various rhythms; many of these have their origin in cosmic rhythms. In addition to the rhythms of the physical organism, the human being experiences psychological and spiritual rhythms, as well as external rhythms in the cultural, social, and economic realms. Rhythm research is, therefore, an essential task of both medicine and education.

In Waldorf Education all *doing* is embedded in rhythm as a hygienic measure. The daily and weekly schedules of classes affect the health and well-being of the children. The day-night rhythm is a fundamental part of the teacher's understanding of how learning becomes capacity in the growing child. Careful consideration of the healthy breathing rhythm in *all* teaching supports the physiological as well as psychological breathing of the child.

Another matter of primary importance is tackled in the chapters that address the physiological effect of the different subject areas on the growing human being. This insight brings depth and consciousness into the educational task that make teaching profoundly meaningful. Dr. Glöckler points out that here is a field where further research is welcomed and collaboration of doctors and teachers is essential.

This book is primarily a translation of the author's *Gesundheit und Schule*, published in 1998. Some of the physicians' and art therapists' reports have not been included as their frame of reference was not germane to the current conditions in the English-speaking world. Also, some material on therapeutic eurythmy are not included here as German language examples would need to be completely rewritten for English. Perhaps this can become the subject of a separate publication. However, it is fortunate that a recent lecture by Dr. Glöckler on salutogenesis has been added as the last chapter.

Salutogenesis gives a modern mainstream name to the perspective from which Rudolf Steiner spoke nearly one hundred years ago. It is especially encouraging that these ideas are "coming of age" and can help to reorient doctors and the general public to a new understanding of the nature of the human being and of the conditions necessary to raise healthy children.

Dr. Glöckler has brought together in this book an invaluable collection of material that can serve as a reference book for generations. In addition to being a great support for the work of individual teach-

ers and doctors, we hope, with her, that it will also inspire further collaboration of doctors, teachers, and parents for the benefit of the
healthy development of children.

Astrid Schmitt-Stegmann
Spring 2002

CHAPTER 1

The School Physician as Preventive Medicine Specialist

The title of this chapter refers to a new job description, namely, that of the specialist for promotion of health and disease prevention at school. This task includes the following ten demands listed by Peter Paulig[1] as early as 1984 for establishing a humane school:

The child has the right to be a child even in school.

"Millions of children suffer at school, particularly the approximately 25% of those who fail or are threatened by failure. This holds true despite the fact that many teachers make the effort—often with great devotion—to help students to the extent that the school institution allows this," stated Professor Bärsch, president of the German Association for Child Protection, on the occasion of Child Protection Day in 1983.

Since nobody who is familiar with school conditions disputes this observation, we call on all discerning, responsible-minded people to become involved with still greater determination in combating the ills manifested in school: being sick of school, refusal to achieve, pessimism, escape into drugs, and aggression. Parents in particular must side with their children, and in the interest of all children and teachers, take a strong stand in favor of humanization of schools. We shall succeed in this only if, together, we stand for enforcement of the following ten demands:

10 Demands

1. Children want to learn! Therefore the demand has to be: We do not constantly require new bureaucratic measurements; we require

new goals for schools! The essential goal for a school must be the young people's developmental needs and expectations. Schools must say: Children are not barrels asking to be filled but fires to be kindled! (Rabelais)

2. Teachers require freedom in education and classroom instruction. The traditional control over teachers amounts to near incapacitation. The dangerous tendency to regiment everything and everybody allows individual pedagogical responsibility only within the framework of established boundaries. Because of this, the teacher's willingness to be responsibly involved with the individual student and the school in general is defined, narrowed down, and destroyed by diverse constrictions. Professional frustration and resignation are the results. How can discouraged and humiliated teachers educate our children to become responsible, productive, involved, helpful, happy human beings?

3. Teachers, the professional educators, must above all be trained better in a practical approach to education and developmental psychology. In continuing education courses, more importance should be attached to teaching methodology.

   Parents, the natural educators, must be given more genuine rights to participate in school affairs. As advocates for their children, they must be given and they must take the opportunity to share in forming the school.

4. A performance-oriented school must be a student-oriented school as well. (Regional Bishop Hanselmann). We want young people to be eager for accomplishment! We want the emphasis to be on what the individual child can achieve! We therefore demand a student-oriented school in which the individual young person is given the opportunity to learn enthusiastically whatever is of special interest and for which he/she is particularly gifted.

5. The main purpose of school is not merely to convey knowledge, to develop abilities, and to impart skills. Young people are not learning machines that can be programmed. What is important above all is to awaken their interest to learn something independently and persistently under their own motivation.

12

6. What has been practiced successfully for decades in private schools—such as those following Maria Montessori, Peter Petersen, Rudolf Steiner, and Freinet—must be introduced into public schools: reports on what has been learned rather than subjective number grades; unsupervised or free work; block-instruction; more pedagogical freedom for the individual teacher ,as well as increased rights of the staff to make decisions for a given school; and so on.

7. We need more model schools that are supervised scientifically. The positive experiences of such schools must be adopted by regular schools.

8. Schools must not be learning factories, but they must offer living space for young people, a space they like to seek out for nine to thirteen years. For that reason, classrooms and schools should be designed so that young people feel comfortable in them. Student-appropriate, appealing, and richly diverse surroundings offer a sense of security. They moreover stimulate the student's willingness to learn.

9. Collaboration with school physicians, school psychologists, and child guidance clinics must be increased to meet the young people with more understanding of their specific developmental needs, as well as of their life situation in school and at home.

10. In particular, we challenge all educators, psychologists, sociologists, and medical doctors to become involved in what happens daily in our schools. If, as has been ascertained by Professor Bärtsch, millions of children suffer in school, we summon these members of academia to leave their offices and lecterns. Based on their sense of responsibility to future generations, they should make contributions so that students and parents will no longer remain exposed helplessly, without any defense against the rotation of half-baked concepts. They must make their knowledge and abilities available and side with the children in our schools if further calamities are to be avoided.

School physicians can be of great help in putting such demands into practice. They can mediate in the triangle of parents, teachers, and students. They can make direct contact with government agencies and academic institutions and discuss health-related aspects of their concerns.

In a teachers' meeting on January 16, 1921 (*Faculty Meetings with Rudolf Steiner*), Rudolf Steiner made the following request:

This custom of having a school physician should be developed in such a way that it could be generally accepted. We should create a separate school doctor position. A physician, who in my view should be available, ought to know all the children in the school and keep an eye on them. Basically, he or she should not be required to offer specific instruction but to remain involved, as needed, with the children of all the different grades. He or she should be familiar with each child's state of health. Much could be said about this. I have often emphasized that people say: There are numerous illnesses but only one condition of health. But there are as many states of health as there are illnesses. This institution of a school physician who knows all the students and keeps an eye on them would amount to a full-time position. Such a physician would have to devote his or her services fully to us. I don't think we can do this. We are not financially affluent enough to afford it. It would have to be carried out on strict guidelines. Only that would make it acceptable. It would have to be somebody who is fully a part of the school.

A short while later, the idea of a school physician became a reality. In the Austrian physician, Dr. Eugen Kolisko, a person was found who was willing to become fully associated with the eighteen-month-old school still under development. He adjusted his fees to what the school could afford.

The special contribution of this school physician concept is that it is not merely a matter of general hygienic measures—such as medical checkups in school and insight into one or another subject—but it creates a new specialty in the medical field. The school physician as specialist in the development and learning of children and adolescents is envisioned as *the preventive medicine specialist in a form of education that intends not merely to convey knowledge but to teach all that is worth knowing in a way that produces, promotes, and cultivates health.* After all, good health is always the result of appropriate learning processes, of exertion, of overcoming pathological tendencies and inclinations. And depending on how the processes of learning and development are followed, good health can be fostered, or dispositions for illness can be promoted.

Any physician who deals with children and young people can observe daily how everything that occurs in infancy, in young children, in primary school age, and in the teens has an influence on the bodily and soul-spiritual development. Every organ attains its maturity based on the way it is utilized by the child. This implies that the organ reaches full development of its functions only during the teens—that it becomes stunted or remains insufficiently developed if it does not have the necessary stimulating activity and exercise. From the beginning of his work with teachers and physicians, Rudolf Steiner always stressed that educating is simultaneously healing, a subtle healing. The curriculum of the Waldorf school is therefore built exclusively on physiological aspects of learning and child development. Each subject is considered, above all, with respect to its effect on physical development.

Soul Economy is the title of a group of lectures by Rudolf Steiner that deal with an education whose goal is well-being. There, Rudolf Steiner outlines the course of healthy development from birth to adulthood and how it can be supported with suitable educational measures. This calls for creation of a new approach to preventive medicine—perhaps we might even say, for a paradigm change in preventive medicine. Prevention was understood up until now as exploration of factors that cause illness. One thus arrived at specific suggestions regarding hygiene: inoculation programs, instructions for keeping water and air pure, improvement of the quality of food, or reduction of harmful substances emitted by industrial complexes. There are also many recommendations of a psycho-hygienic nature on ways to protect children and young people exposed to environmental factors detrimental to their development. Up until now, therefore, prevention was directed at avoiding damaging influences. Likewise, so-called primary prophylaxis, which aims at preventing the appearance of certain diseases in the first place, can only be utilized in the case of diseases whose causes are known and can thus be eliminated as pathogenic.[2]

In contrast to this, Rudolf Steiner develops a concept which, in the sense of modern health research, is a salutogenic or hygiogenic ['origin of health'] concept. He develops his pedagogical starting point from those principles and interconnections of laws that work throughout human life in the service of health and represent the system of forces that promote self-healing. It is *these forces* that need to be strengthened by educational and medical means so that the pathogenic processes and substances can be countered more easily. Decades after Rudolf Steiner, J. Bengel, a rehabilitation psychologist, formulated this sphere of tasks as follows:

> Health is negatively defined as the absence of illness. . . . Health, its maintenance, and prevention of illness have received a great deal of attention in social sciences and psychosomatic medicine in recent times. Alongside the pathogenic and curative viewpoint appears a perspective that is described as salutogenic. It seeks preventive factors, resistance, and other effective factors for maintenance of health.[3]

The medical views of Galen and Hippocrates still give us an understanding of health. But along with the ascent of modern medicine, oriented as it is to natural science, the ancient understanding of health has yielded to pathogenic conceptions that describe health as the absence of illness, and no longer make use of concepts that describe health *as such*.

Now, through anthroposophical knowledge of the human being inaugurated by Rudolf Steiner, a concept that looks for the origin of health is introduced. It can lead to a preventive medicine that is based on the principle of health. Steiner researched the principles of self-healing in the interaction of the human being's physical, soul, and spirit components. He described the collaboration of the four components of the human being in this threefold organism. As a start, this salutogenic concept is outlined briefly below. For an understanding of the four components of the human being, the reader is referred to Rudolf Steiner's basic works.[4]

The sketch on the next page shows the different connections and interactions. (See Rudolf Steiner's *Anthroposophical Spiritual Science and Medical Therapy*, lecture of April 11, 1921.) The body in its totality is the result of the metabolic processes that build it up and regenerate it. They in turn are regulated by the close interaction of the human components. On the other hand, soul functions and the possibility of spirit activity are based on the various interactions of body-free and body-linked activities of these components.

In the buildup of the human organism, physical body, etheric body, astral body, and ego-organization work closely together throughout life. Active in the metabolic processes, they restore and maintain the material composition and functioning of the organs. *In the limb system*, physical body, etheric body, and astral body are connected with each other, whereas the ego-organization can partially remove itself. However, the ego is the element that bestows personal quality to movement and to the expressions of will.

Soul activity becomes possible because the ego-organization and astral body are only loosely connected with the physical and etheric bodies through the rhythmic system. (See Rudolf Steiner, *The Case for Anthroposophy*.) The astral body submerges rhythmically—through inhalation and heart contraction (systole)—into the physical and etheric organism and is released from them once again through exhalation and heart-expansion (diastole). The astral body's alternating activity of connecting and disconnecting itself is the basis

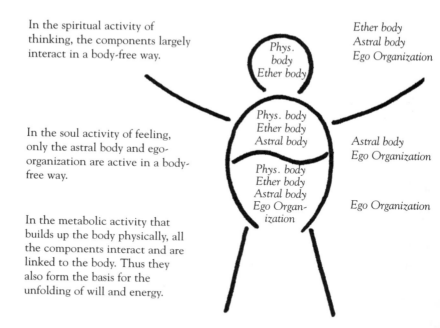

In the spiritual activity of thinking, the components largely interact in a body-free way.

In the soul activity of feeling, only the astral body and ego-organization are active in a body-free way.

In the metabolic activity that builds up the body physically, all the components interact and are linked to the body. Thus they also form the basis for the unfolding of will and energy.

Phys. body
Ether body

Phys. body
Ether body
Astral body

Phys. body
Ether body
Astral body
Ego Organ-ization

Ether body
Astral body
Ego Organization

Astral body
Ego Organization

Ego Organization

for the work of the rhythmic system as well as for the soul activity of feeling.

In *spiritual activity*, the ego-organization, astral body, and etheric body are free of the physical body while active in thinking. The etheric body is responsible for the central nervous system and the functions of the senses. During the day, that part of the ether body is available for body-free thought activity. At night, the etheric body enters once more into the physical body, regenerating the nerve-senses system which did not get enough attention during the course of the day. At night, the ego-organization and astral body are released completely from the nerve-sense system and commune with the beings of the spiritual world, as a rule unconsciously. (See chapter 7, Proper Sleeping.)

The foundation for the bodily activity of the ego is thus the metabolic-limb system; for the soul activity, it is the rhythmic system; for the spiritual activity, the nerve-sense system. In his spiritual research, Rudolf Steiner distinguishes the I or ego—the eternal core of the human being—from its earthly sheath, namely, the ego-organization's composite of laws. (See Rudolf Steiner, *An Outline of Esoteric Science*, chapter 2: The Nature of Humanity.)

As early as 1907, in his booklet, *Education in the light of Anthroposophy*[5,] Rudolf Steiner pointed out that the various components of the human being are not active in an individual concurrently. He therefore speaks of four so-called births. The expression "birth" illustrates that something comes to the fore and develops independence, something that formerly was active in the human organism in a dependent way. When the *physical body* of the child is born and its umbilical cord is severed from the mother, the child exists alone and must learn to maintain itself on its own. The functions of the organs most closely connected to the physical surroundings—sense organs and organs of digestion—begin an intense process of adaptation and development.[6]

When a child reaches the age of six to eight and the enamel crowns of the second teeth mature, the *birth of the etheric body* takes place. This refers to the release of those forces that have brought about growth and structuring of the organ systems up to the formation of the permanent teeth.[7] The release of the physical forces from the maternal organism enables the body to communicate with the physical environment via the senses as an individual. When the child is ready for first grade, the freed etheric forces now appear as cohesive thought activity. They then make possible arbitrarily recalled memories and inner communication with the surrounding world.

At the time the secondary gender characteristics appear, the *birth of the astral body* is in preparation. It occurs between the ages of twelve and sixteen and is characterized by the emancipation of the emotional life, which up until then had been firmly tied to and dependent on the body. The life of feelings and emotions increasingly links up with thinking and becomes autonomous. This is why young people can withdraw into their own soul world in quite another way than is possible for children whose astral body is still strongly tied to the physical and etheric body.

Between the ages of eighteen and twenty-four, when the physical organism has fully matured, the *ego organization* is the last to be born. Along with this—liberated from the body—purely spiritual will forces are freed for a person's own creative thought activity. The ego-organization (through which all the other now body-free interconnections of laws and processes can be integrated in thought) is of a will nature—meaning an intentional nature—as is the eternal core of the human being. Thus, for young adults, the birth of the ego-organization signifies their entering into will maturity and responsibility for themselves and others.

Human beings owe their *thinking* to the etheric forces and laws that are being freed from the body; they owe *feeling* to the body-free astral forces and laws; they owe their free *ability of willing* to the ego-organization's laws that are being loosened from the body. On the basis of this understanding of the human being as a starting point, the significance of all educational measures regarding physical development can also be considered and evaluated. The basis for a

school physician's work at a Waldorf school is the accurate knowledge of the constituion of the human being and its threefold nature, only briefly described here, and the Waldorf school curriculum based on it.[8]

Eugen Kolisko (1893-1939) exemplified the professional image of a school physician at a Waldorf school. He was familiar with the physical condition of all the students. He worked on a full-time basis in the school all morning. He himself taught first aid, biology, and chemistry in the upper grades. He attended classes, observed individual children, and discussed their state of health with teachers and parents. In the afternoons when he had his office hours, he would see students, teachers, or parents for medical treatment and counseling.

CHAPTER 2

Sense Activity and Experience of the Self [9]

Karl König wrote *Sinnesentwicklung und Leiberfahrung* [Development of the senses and experience of the body], a basic book based on his experience as a physician in schools for children in need of special care. A child's ability to control the body and be aware of him- or herself within it depends to a large degree on the use of the senses, especially in the earliest years of life. The senses transmit a sense of self to the ego, which is active in perception.

The *sense of touch* transmits self-experience at the body's periphery, promoting a feeling of security through body contact, a trust in existence.

The *life sense* transmits experiences of comfort and harmony and a feeling for whether the processes in one's own body and those in the environment harmonize or not.

The *sense of self-movement* transmits perception of one's own movements; an experience of freedom and self-control proceeds from the mastery of movement.

The *sense of balance* gives the experience of position in space, of balance and the capacity to sense the center of gravity, something that leads to an experience of inner calm. The ability to practice inner stillness and soul-balance has its basis in this sense.

The *sense of smell* conveys the experience of immediate closeness to aromatic substances.

The *sense of taste* transmits qualities of sweet, sour, salty, and bitter and, with the sense of smell, produces differentiations of taste as well as an experience of digestion and of transformation.

The *sense of sight* brings about the experiences of light and color.

The *sense of warmth* transmits experiences of warmth and cold.

The *sense of hearing* transmits experiences of tone and unlocks our experience of inner soul space.

The *word sense* transmits the experience of the form of a word, including the sound and its meaning. For example, *lyubov* expresses something quite different about the nature of love than *amour, amore,* or *love* do.

The *sense of thought* transmits comprehension of meaning concerning a thought or a thought-connection.

The *ego sense* transmits an experience of another ego's being. It opens up perception of the spiritual force-configuration of another human being and an experience of his/her essential nature.

The ego, as the personality's eternal nucleus of being, experiences itself in relation to the world through its sense impressions. Through the senses of taste, of life, of self-movement, and of balance, the ego is first of all tuned to its own body and the relationship of its body to the world. The characteristic qualities of this that lead to self-experience are: trust, harmony, and the feeling of freedom and inner calm. Through the senses of smell, taste, sight, and warmth, the ego experiences itself primarily as a being of soul. It feels enabled to perceive world polarities and their balance, namely: light, darkness and color; warmth, cold and temperateness; repelling and pleasant tastes and smells, with all the nuances in between. Through the sense of hearing, the word sense, the thought sense, and the ego sense, the ego finally experiences itself as an active spirit-being. This comes about through confrontation with the inner revelations of other human beings, of other creatures and things, in sound, word, thought, and quality of their being.

If the education of the senses is neglected, if no loving attention and understanding are paid to the world, to human beings, and to everyday activities, experience of self and the world will be seriously impeded. Already during the school years, this can lead to lack of interest and learning disabilities. This is also a major cause of increased drug consumption in our time. The deficiency of experience and the lack of self-experience resulting from undeveloped or wrongly developed functioning of the senses becomes unbearable for the ego, which then seeks alternate satisfaction in the intensity of experiences brought about by drugs.

CHAPTER 3

The Arts in Relation to
the Human Components

In connection with his lectures *Art in the Light of Mystery Wisdom* given in the first Goetheanum, Rudolf Steiner describes in a distinctive way how the intrinsic laws of the arts—of architecture, sculpture, painting, music, poetry, and eurythmy—are the expression of the human being who plays with the forces and laws of the components of his/her being. The human physical body is kept in check within the sphere of gravity upon earth, and the structure of bones and muscles reflects the contact with gravity as the most economical use of material substance for bearing and carrying the body's structure. So, too, architects freely deal with these laws of the physical realm. In a manner of speaking, they project the structural laws of their body into round, oval, or cubic construction projects. This even includes the organic style of architecture inaugurated by Rudolf Steiner, where the collarbone's double-arched surface and the forms of the trabecular structure of the thigh bone, as well as many other details, become visible.[10] The art of architecture deals creatively with the inherent laws of the physical body and its wisdom-imbued interchange with earth substances. Sculptors, on the other hand, play with the sculptural-pictorial lawfulness of their etheric organism. They creatively use any surplus forces in the etheric body, which is the bearer of growth, regeneration, and (in body-free function) the thought activity.

To be a true artist, one has to be born to it. Every human being has some artistic talent. Just think of children's pictures of houses and castles, the spontaneous capacity to model and form, to sing and dance. Artists have this at their disposal in greater measure and it is expressed not only during childhood and the teens but throughout an artist's entire life. In childhood and youth, all human beings can avail themselves of these surplus forces, because their being's components are not yet completely mature or fully "incarnated." These surplus forces are free for spontaneous artistic creation. Later on they can only be maintained by means of conscious cultivation and training. Due to the configuration of the various components of their being, artists possess a certain surplus of forces throughout their life, a dominance of forces in a particular component part of their being.

Wolfgang Schad has described in detail these relationships in regard to painting and drawing in his basic essay, *Zur Organologie und Physiologie des Lernens. Aspekte einer pädagogischen Theorie des Leibes* [Organology and physiology of learning. Aspects of a pedagogical theory of the body].[11] Some of the impressive examples of children's drawings typical of various ages [see Strauss, 1994] are reproduced here for clarification.

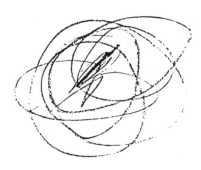

Picture 1 on left: Whirl Ball by a girl 1 year and 10 months old.

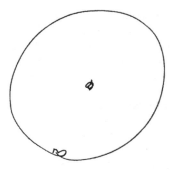

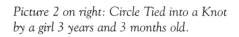

Picture 2 on right: Circle Tied into a Knot by a girl 3 years and 3 months old.

Picture 3 on left: The Head-Footers
by a boy 3 years and 9 months.

Picture 4 on right: Two "Ladder-People"
by a boy 4 years and 5 months.

Picture 5 on left: One of
the first scenes: Mothers
With Children and Baby
Carriage Taking a Walk.
Drawing by a girl age 5
years and 2 months.

If children *play* with their astral forces, independent of the pliable etheric forces, this comes to expression in their need for musical activity. If education does not meet the child's or teenager's need with intensive development of musical capacities, this artistic tendency will be lived out in a passive way by endlessly listening to recorded music. Through making music and listening to music, the ego experiences itself in the area of astral laws. For this reason, music always touches the essential core of the human personality.

By contrast, in the realm of poetry, the wisdom-filled laws of language are expressed through the formative force of the ego organization, which is the bearer of the self's core. In epic, lyric, and dramatic poetry, the ego formulates its experiences and actions through thinking, feeling, and willing.

In eurythmy, on the other hand, the lawfulness of the etheric is applied in a conscious way. In sculptural movements, particularly of arms and hands, but also of the entire body, verbal and musical works are presented.

A glance at the evolution of artistic creativity in the course of human history shows how architecture, sculpture, and painting went through extensive development before the art of poetry (in the narrowest sense) started with Homeric epics and Greek tragedies. Lyric poetry, as an expression of individual soul experience, belongs to a still later time. Eurythmy is an art of the twentieth century. It has only quite distant antecedents in temple dances of the Egyptian and Greek mysteries.

In *Art in the Light of Mystery Wisdom* (lecture of December 29, 1914), Rudolf Steiner outlines his artistically conceived knowledge of the human being as follows:

Laws of the physical body	→	used outside the body constructively: Architecture
Laws of the etheric body	→	used in physical matter (wood, clay, stone) creatively in pliable-pictorial forming: Sculpture
Laws of the astral body	→	applied artistically in the etheric order of laws: Painting
Laws of the ego or ego-organization, the bearer of the human core of being	→	creatively activated in the realm of astral laws: Music
Order of laws of the spirit-self (astral body purified through self discipline)	→	applied creatively in the realm of pure ego activity: Poetry
Order of laws of life body (etheric body consciously taken hold of by self-discipline)	→	freely applied in the realm of the purified astral body (spirit-self) taken hold of by the ego through self-discipline: Eurythmy

These few indications may suffice to make it clear why Rudolf Steiner recommended that teachers and physicians study the ways in which the human organism is an expression of the laws inherent in sculpture, music, and speech. Armin Husemann, formerly school physician at the Stuttgart Waldorf School, currently head of the medical seminar at Filder Clinic, has applied himself to the elaboration of this approach to the human being, particularly in the field of music. We are indebted to him for publishing a collection of excerpts from lectures by Rudolf Steiner on this theme in collaboration with his father, Gisbert Husemann.[12]

CHAPTER 4

Metamorphosis of Growth Forces
into Thought Activity[13]

On the basis of the knowledge of the human being and its relationship to the various arts briefly outlined in the last chapter, we can now work in two different directions. A physician will be interested in how the sculptural, musical, and linguistic laws form the body's architecture, its sculptural framework, its proportions and numerical relationships, and its integrated statement: This is I; this is my body through which I can express myself. A teacher, on the other hand, will be more interested in how the human being's components that are being emancipated from the body appear as constructive thought activity (etheric body), become evident in tension and repose, in harmony and disharmony of the emotional life (astral body), and are expressed as intentions through language and movement of the life of will (ego-organization). By working together, the physician and the teacher can increase their awareness of what must be done for the child's bodily and mental well-being.[14] Based on such an understanding of the human being, it becomes comprehensible why too strong a claim on the soul-spiritual forces can have a weakening effect on the bodily development, and why a claim on the developing soul-spiritual forces that is not appropriate for a given age likewise leads to tendencies toward illness. A medical history from Rudolf Steiner's *Introducing Anthroposophical Medicine* (lecture of March 30, 1920) throws light on this:

An eight-year-old boy is brought to a pediatrician's office. The referring family doctor asks for a diagnostic examination, particularly regarding the possible exclusion of a tumor, since for the last eight months the child has lost weight and stopped growing.

Initial examination shows a pale, well-proportioned, underweight boy with no other symptoms of disease. Likewise, a neurological examination is normal except for vigorous bilateral reflexes. In conversation, the child appears intelligent and alert. The blood profile indicates nothing particularly remarkable except for a somewhat lowered hemoglobin count.

Asked about conditions at school, the mother reports that the boy has an older brother and could hardly wait to attend school himself. He is eager to learn, pursues questions even after he comes home. In particular, he asks his father to explain everything to him. His father is a teacher and the boy is especially fond of him.

Following a detailed talk with the mother, the decision is made not to order further diagnostic examinations in the next four weeks but to excuse the boy for the time being from school. The father is asked to do something with his son in the afternoons (a game, a walk) but not to explain complicated subjects to him. A single medication is to be administered, a homeopathic distillation of the plant extract from chicory (Cichorium intybus). According to anthroposophical insight into the human being and into nature, this plant equally supports nutrition and the structure of the various systems of organs in the human being. The plant-forces that are active in their bitter, extracted substances stimulate the vital activities of the digestive organs. The forces of the plant's alkaline salts support the formation of blood. The forces of the silicic acid content work not only in a stimulating way on the organs of nerves and senses, but also in a formative way on the bones.

The conventional method of referral stated: Suspicion of tumor following loss of weight and suspension of growth. The additional spiritual-scientific diagnosis asserted: Suspicion of etheric body's weakening due to too much intellectual strain.

After four weeks, the boy's coloring had clearly improved. The weight gain, however, barely amounted to 2.2 pounds. The decision was made to suspend school attendance for two more months and to have him do light physical work in the house and garden. Success justified the measures taken. Weight increase proceeded more quickly, summer vacation started, and it was decided to begin with school again after vacation. However, the boy was to attend only the first two hours at school and then return home. For the time being, no homework was to be assigned. The teachers who witnessed the success of this treatment agreed with this idea, particularly because no significant decline in achievement had to be feared considering the boy's intelligence. Following a full year of treatment and resulting weight gain, growth commenced as well. Gradually, the demands of school could be increased, but as yet no homework was assigned in place of physical activity and play. Two years later, it was possible to conclude treatment. The boy had fully caught up with the developmental deficit of his body. The medical history outlined here can make it clear how important it is, especially in pediatrics, to consider both bodily and soul-spiritual processes(that is, processes of learning).[15]

To clarify this relationship still further, we need to go into what Rudolf Steiner termed "hygienic esotericism." The following passages are taken from the chapter, "Vom Tempelschlaf der ägyptischen Mysterien zum Hygienischen Okkultismus heute" [From temple-sleep in the Egyptian mysteries to hygienic esotericism today] in Michaela Glöckler, *Medizin an der Schwelle* [Medicine at the threshold], 19ff:

In his lectures, *Universe, Earth and Man*, Rudolf Steiner describes the deeper relationships between the ancient Egyptian and our present Fifth Post-Atlantean Cultural Epoch (also discussed in his *An Outline of Esoteric Science*). In a lecture on August 15, 1908, he first describes the Egyptian mummy-cult and its significance for the development of modern materialism. Then he turns to the characteristics and purpose of the temple-sleep and speaks of its correspondence in our present culture:

We must now call to mind the nature of the temple-sleep, one of the remedies employed by Egyptian priests. As a rule, anyone who in some way suffered from diminished health in those days was not treated with external remedies; there were only a few of these, and they were rarely used. Sufferers were in most cases taken to the temple and there put into a kind of sleep. It was no ordinary sleep, but a kind of somnambulistic sleep which was so intensified that the patient became capable of having not merely chaotic dreams but of seeing actual visions. During this sleep the patient perceived etheric forms in the spiritual world, and the priest-sages understood the art of influencing these etheric pictures which passed before the sleeper; they could control and guide them.

Let us suppose that a sick person was put into the temple-sleep. The priest, who was knowledgeable in healing, was at his side. He formed and shaped the etheric visions and entities in such a way that, as if through magic, there actually emerged before the sleeper the forms whom the ancient Atlanteans had looked upon as their gods long ago. These divine forms, especially certain figures connected with the healing principle, of whom the various peoples merely retained a memory, as in Germanic, Norse, and Greek mythologies, were now placed before the soul of the person who was in the temple-sleep. . . . The priest-sages guided this dream-life so that powerful forces were liberated during these etheric visions, and these forces affected the body's forces, which had fallen into disorder and discord, in an ordering, harmonizing way. . . .

In this process of being lifted up to the spiritual level, a healing element was present in ancient times, and it would be well if human beings were to learn to understand this again, for then they would learn to understand the great mission of the Anthroposophical movement. For what else is this mission but to lead human beings up to the spiritual world, so that they may again behold those worlds from which they have descended. It is true that in the future people will not be put into a somnambulistic condition; self-consciousness will be fully maintained. All the same, a strong spiritual force will become active in human beings, and the possession of wisdom and insight into higher worlds will then be an element that can influence human nature in harmonizing, healing ways. Today this connection between spirituality and the healing arts is so concealed that those who are not initiated in some form into the deeper wisdom of the Mysteries do not know much about it. They cannot observe the subtle facts that confront them. But one who has deeper insight knows the profound inner conditions on which a case of healing may depend. Let us suppose, for example, that a certain illness befalls a person and that it has an inner cause, not a fractured thigh-bone or an upset stomach, for these are external causes. Anyone wishing to go deeply into this will soon find that in the case of a person who frequently enjoys working with mathematical conceptions, the conditions of healing are very different from those in another person who does not care to be occupied with such matters. This fact attests to the remarkable connection between a person's mental life and the state of his or her external health. . . .

Take another example: We face completely different conditions of health in two people, of whom one is an atheist in the worst sense and the other is deeply religious. If both become afflicted with the same disease and you use the same remedies, you may cure the religious person but not the other one. These are things which to modern thinking—at least to the greater part of humanity—will seem absurd. Yet, it is so.

The observations made here by Rudolf Steiner in 1908 that seemed rather absurd to modern thinking then have become recognized now as scientific fact at the end of the twentieth century. The numerous investigations in immunological and psychoneuro-immunological fields have shown all too clearly that the functions of the immune system decisively depend on the soul and spiritual identity of the human being. Uncertainty, fear, and doubt as well as grief and resignation work in an immuno-suppressive manner on the human organism, whereas an idealistic approach to life, an active religious life, and a degree of joy in existence bring about exactly the opposite. They have an immunostimulant effect.[16] In many oncological centers, artistic and psychotherapeutic procedures are today standard concomitant treatments alongside surgery, chemotherapy, and radiation. Still, however interesting and stimulating the results of psychoneuroimmunology are, the bridge to concrete spirit knowledge has not been discovered. To be sure, the positive influences of soul and spiritual activities upon the body are established, but the inner connection is not discerned, and therefore the essentially materialistic attitude remains. This can be overcome by the anthroposophical study of the human being with its central paradigm of the metamorphosis of the body-shaping activity of the human components into body-free activity of soul and spirit. Rudolf Steiner and Ita Wegman described this metamorphosis in regard to the dual function of the etheric forces in the first chapter of their book, *Fundamentals of Therapy*, in the following way:

These forces that are effective in the etheric body are active at the beginning of human earthly life—most clearly during the embryonic period—as formative and growth forces. In the course of earthly life, a portion of these forces is liberated from the involvement in form and growth processes and turns into thought forces, the very forces that, for ordinary consciousness, bring forth the shadowy world of thought.

It is of the greatest significance to know that the ordinary thought forces of the human being are refined forces of form and growth. A spiritual element manifests in the forming and growing of the human organism and appears as spiritual thought force in the course of life.

Now this thought force is actually only a portion of the human formative and growth force weaving in the etheric dimension. The other portion remains true to the task it possessed at the beginning of human life. It is only because the human being continues to develop when his or her form and growth processes have advanced and, to a degree, are brought to a conclusion, that the etheric-spiritual element, living and weaving in the organism, is able to appear in further life as thought force.

In this way, the malleable sculpting power is revealed to imaginative spiritual vision as an etheric spiritual element from the one side, and from the other side it appears as the soul content of thinking.

On the threshold between unconscious and conscious thought life stands the ego with its everyday learning processes and considerations. Through them, it becomes conscious of its metamorphosed growth forces and formative forces as thoughts, the thoughts that have a concrete inner relationship to all the world phenomena. After all, there is no lawfulness that cannot be grasped in thought and does not participate in some way in the development and construction, the function and form of the human organism. And even as the etheric organism appears divided into a conscious and an unconscious life of thought and growth during the day, so, at night, the whole of the etheric body is dedicated to its task of regenerating and nurturing the life processes of the organism.

If, during the day, the ego was active in an enthusiastic, warm way in this thought organism, it carries along constructive life-furthering aftereffects out of the thought life into the nightly life of regeneration. But if, by day, thinking was dry, chilly, and unsatisfactory to the soul element or purely oriented to external facts of life, it bears with it the aftereffects of a thinking bound only to the physical world of existence, a thinking that has lost its kinship to the impulses of life, soul, and spirit. (See Rudolf Steiner's *The Search for the New Isis*.) Night after night, this can then affect the vitality of the organism in a hindering or a stimulating way. In turn, depending on destiny, the physical constitution, and life circumstances, it can lead by day to the development of one or another illness—or to the promotion of health. Thus, by day, the etheric body works in a polar manner as formative forces-body and thought body. At night, on the other hand, it is homogeneously active as the organism of formative forces.

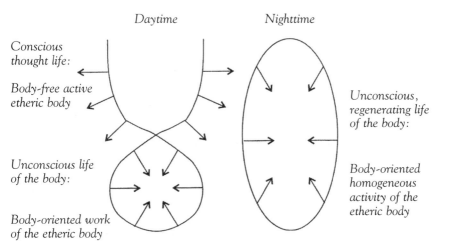

In *Universe, Earth and Man* (lecture of April 7, 1908), Rudolf Steiner describes to us the difference between the effects upon the body that proceed from pure thoughts (such as, for instance, in mathematics) and from thoughts bound to sense perception:

An entirely different influence is exercised upon human nature...by so-called sense-freee ideas, and by those filled with sense perception. Think for a moment of the difference between a person who loves and one who hates mathematics... It is of great use... to our innermost being to dwell on conceptions that we cannot see. It is equally useful to dwell on religious conceptions, for these likewise relate to things we cannot grasp with our hands, things that have no connection with outer, material things—in a word, things that are sense-free. These are matters that, one day when people will be more concerned again with spiritual things, will have a great influence on educational principles. . . .

People who have been trained from childhood to live with sense conceptions will not be cured as readily—because their nervous system lives under sickly conditions—as those who from early on have been accustomed to sense-free ideas. The more you accustom a person to think of something other than objects, the easier it is to cure him or her.

In ancient times when people were ill, it was customary to place before them all kinds of symbolic figures, triangles, and combinations of numbers. The purpose, besides any other value these things possessed, was to uplift these patients from mere perception of what was sketched. If I place a triangle before me and merely look at it, it is of no particular value. On the other hand, if I see in it the symbol of the higher triad of the human being, it becomes a healing conception for the spirit. . . .

Spiritual science will therefore become once more a great, comprehensive remedy, just as it was in the hands of the ancient Egyptian priests, who did, however, require a dimming of the patient's ego in the temple-sleep. The spiritual worldview is a healing worldview. . . . Oh, spiritual vision beholds a future where no inner causes of sickness will exist for those able to provide inner and outer conditions of spiritual wisdom. External causes will always exist. They can only be eradicated as a spiritual-scientific art of healing gains more and more ground. We realize that when we rightly understand the effect of the spirit, the temple-sleep is not a riddle to us.

This theme that spiritual science will be needed more and more for maintaining humanity's health in the future is taken up again by Rudolf Steiner in his lecture "Hygiene as a Social Question" in 1920 (in *Health Care as a Social Issue*, lecture of April 7). He confronts physicians with the great cultural task of increasingly becoming the hygienic teachers of their contemporaries and directing their own attention to preventive medicine in the salutogenic sense of the primary promotion of health.

At the end of the First World War, on December 1, 1918 in Dornach, Rudolf Steiner also described this basic thought from the point of view of the various talents of the peoples of the East, of the West, and of Central Europe (published as *In the Changed Conditions of the Times*).[17] He speaks here about the latent, hidden, spiritual capacities of the peoples of the East, the Center, and of the West, capacities that will increasingly develop in the future. He describes how genetic esotericism will develop in the East, meaning, an intimate knowledge of the processes of reproduction and the spiritual conditions that lie at the basis of incarnation. Conversely, in the West, a mechanical esoteric faculty will develop by means of which human beings will form a deep connection with the life of machines. They will learn how to activate machines through soul and spiritual forces in an individual way. In regard to the esoteric capacity that will develop in Europe, he speaks (in the lecture of December 1, 1918) of a new hygienic capacity:

> This hygienic esoteric capacity is well on its way and will not be long in arriving, relatively speaking. This capacity will come to maturity simply through the insight that human life in its course from birth to death progresses in a manner identical with the process of an illness. Processes of illness are, in other words, only special and radical transmutations of the quite ordinary, normal life process taking its course between birth and death, except that we bear within ourselves not only the forces that create illness, but also those that heal. And these healing forces, as every esotericist knows, are precisely the same as those that are applied when a person acquires esoteric capacities, in which case these forces are transmuted into the forces of knowledge. Transformed into knowledge, the healing power innate in the human organism simply produces esoteric knowledge. . . . At the point when hygienic esoteric capacities develop, an outer material medicine will no longer be needed. The possibility will exist to treat illnesses not arising due to karmic causes—karmically caused illnesses would be untreatable—by psychic means prophylactically and prevent them. Everything will change in this regard. Today, this still appears to be sheer fantasy, but it is something that will come very soon.

The pursuit of a conscious path of inner discipline is the health source that any physician and therapist must be familiar with today (see Steiner, *How to Know Higher Worlds*). In *Education for Special Needs* (in the lecture on June 26, 1924), we discover basic indications on how self-discipline and the teacher's inner schooling can affect the activity of the inner component of the student's being. Here, Rudolf Steiner demonstrates how the reciprocal effects between teacher and student are subject to certain laws. The quality that lives in the spirit-presence of the teacher's ego has a direct influence on the student's astral body. The activities taking place in the soul (astral body) of the teacher affect the configuration of the student's etheric body. And the effects that appear from the teacher's habits, his/her line of thoughts, the whole of the etheric constitution and behavior, make a lasting impression on the student's physical body:

What does this mean? If you find that the etheric body of a child is in some way weakened or deficient, you must modify your own astral body in such a way that it can work upon the child's etheric body, correcting and amending it. We could, in fact, make a diagram to demonstrate how this principle works in education:

Child:	physical body	Teacher:	etheric body
	etheric body		astral body
	astral body		ego
	ego		spirit-self

The teacher's own etheric body (and this should follow quite naturally as a result of his or her training) must be able to influence the physical body of the child. The teacher's astral body has to be able to work on the child's etheric body. The ego of the teacher must be able to influence the child's astral body. And now you will be rather taken aback, for next we come to the spirit-self of the teacher, and you will think that surely the spirit-self is not yet developed. Nevertheless, such is the law. The teacher's spirit-self must work upon the ego of the child. And I will show you how, in fact, not only in the ideal teacher but often in the very worst possible teacher, the teacher's spirit-self—of which he or she is not yet in the least aware—influences the child's ego. Education is indeed veiled in many mysteries.

But now it dawns on us that the teacher's health-giving astral body must influence the stunted etheric body of the child. How can an educator's astral body be educated—self-educated, that is, which still has to be the case today—in regard to these issues? For at present, anthroposophy can do no more than give an incentive; we cannot set up seminars immediately for all that is needed. The teacher's own astral body must have such a constitution that it has an instinctive understanding for the debilities in the etheric body of the child. Let's assume that the child's etheric body is deficient in the region of the liver. As a result, the child stops short at intentions, always has the will to do something, but the will-impulse comes to a standstill before the actual deed. If teachers can feel their way right into this situation (that the child's will ought to push through to action), if they are able to feel this stoppage that the child feels, and are able at the same time out of their own energy to evoke in their soul a deep compassion for the child's experience, then they will develop an understanding in their own astral body for the situation the child is in. Gradually, such teachers will succeed in eliminating in themselves all subjective sympathy or antipathy when faced with this phenomenon in the child. By ridding themselves of sympathy and antipathy, teachers work on the discipline of their own astral body.

So long as one reacts with sympathy or antipathy to such a characteristic in a child (for example, that he or she wants to walk, but cannot, something that can become a conspicuous and pathological condition, one that even leads to the conclusion that the child is incapable of learning to walk), when this condition appears to a slight degree and the teacher reacts to it with irritation, so long will he or she be in fact ineffective as an educator. Not until the point has been reached where such a phenomenon becomes an objective picture and can be taken with a certain composure as an objective picture for which nothing but compassion is felt—not until then is the necessary mood of soul present in the astral body of the teacher. Then, he or she will do everything else more or less correctly. You have no idea how little it basically matters what educators superficially say or do not say, but how much it matters what they themselves are as teachers.

Now this law applies not only to the relationship between teacher and student. In individual human life, we are familiar with the fact that it depends to a large degree on the ego's presence of mind—how we experience ourselves in our soul, whether we manage to maintain good humor or let ourselves go. Likewise, the essential mood of our astral body, the way we think, our interaction with emotions, and the manner in which we handle our will in alternating between work and rest strongly affect the configuration of our etheric body and the development of habits. In contrast to this, the physical body is a result of the vitalizing processes that occur in the etheric body. The state of our constitution can thus be directly influenced by the given facts of physical reality, on the one hand, and by our soul-spiritual conduct on the other. In the lectures, *The Theosophy of the Rosicrucians*, Rudolf Steiner describes how this law is even effective throughout repeated earth lives. As an example, something that could not properly be worked out in the soul in one life affects the constitution of the etheric organization of the following life and can also lead to a functional cause of illness.

CHAPTER 5

Rudolf Steiner's Description of a School Physician's Task

A child should be able to develop sound in body, free in soul, and lucid in spirit.

On August 24, 1922, Rudolf Steiner spoke in Oxford about the basic soul-spiritual forces involved in the art of education [lectures published as *The Spiritual Ground of Education*]. These indications make clear the critical importance Rudolf Steiner attached to those educational endeavors by teachers that are directed toward the age-related bodily development in the child. The school physician was also introduced as an absolutely necessary partner for the teacher.

From the things I have already said it may perhaps be clear to you what all educating and teaching in the Waldorf school should strive for. The aim is to bring up children to be human beings strong and sound in body, free in soul, and lucid in spirit. Physical health and strength, freedom of soul, and clarity of spirit are things humankind will require in the future more than anything else, particularly in social life. But in order to educate and teach in this way, it is necessary for the teacher to acquire thorough mastery of those things I have attempted to describe.

Educators must have complete discernment of the child's organism, and it must be a discernment of the organism enabling them to judge physical health. For those who are in a position to judge physical health and who can then bring it into harmony with the soul can say to themselves: This is to be done with this child, with that child, something else.

Many people today are of the opinion that a physician should be assigned to a school. They would like to develop the system of school physicians more widely. But, just as it is not good when different branches of instruction, different subjects, are given to different teachers who make no contact with one another, neither is it good to place the charge of physical health in the hands of a person who is not a member of the staff, not a member of the faculty. The situation presents a certain difficulty, of which the following incident will give you an example.

During a guided tour of the Waldorf School, a gentleman who, in his official capacity, was a school inspector, visited our school. I spoke of what can be observed in regard to the physical health and organization of the children; I told him about one child who has a certain heart disorder, and about another with some other disability etc., and the man exclaimed in astonishment: Why, teachers would have to be medically knowledgeable for this to have any validity in a school!

Indeed, if it is necessary for wholesome education that teachers should have a certain degree of medical knowledge, then they must have it, must acquire it. Life cannot be twisted to suit the idiosyncrasies of human beings. We must structure the institutions in accordance with life's demands. Just as we must learn something before we can do something in other areas, so must teachers learn something before they can do something in education.

Thus, for instance, it is necessary for a teacher to acquire precise insight, particularly into a very young child in connection with what the child expresses while playing. Play involves a whole complex of activities of soul—joy, sometimes also pain, sympathy, antipathy, and particularly curiosity and the desire for knowledge. A child wants to examine the objects he or she plays with and tries to see what they contain. And in what emerges from this free activity of the child's soul—an activity as yet unconstrained into any form of work—we must be able to observe how it comes out of feeling, how it satisfies or does not satisfy. For if we guide the child's play so that the child experiences a certain satisfaction, we mainly promote that activity in regard to health that is connected with the human digestive system. And whether or not a person will be subject in old age to obstructions in his or her blood circulation and digestive system depends on how his or her play was guided in childhood. There is a fine, a delicate connection between the way a child plays and the growth and development of his or her physical organism.

You should not say that the physical organism is a thing of little account, that you are an idealist and cannot concern yourself with such a lowly thing as the physical organism. This physical organism has been placed into the world by the divine spiritual powers of the world; it is a divine creation, and we must be aware that we as educators are called upon to cooperate in this spiritual creation. I would rather express what I mean by a concrete example than in abstract sentences.

Suppose children exhibit an extreme form, a pathological form, of what we call the melancholic disposition; or suppose you confront a pathological form of the sanguine temperament. Now, a teacher must be able to know where the borderline is between the simply physical and the pathological. If you observe that a melancholic child is tending to become pathological—and this is far more often the case than one would think— you must try to contact the child's parents and learn from them what the child's diet is like at home. You will then discover a connection between this diet and the child's pathological melancholy. You will probably find— to give a concrete example, though there might be other causes—that the child has been given too little sugar in the food served at home. Owing to a lack of sugar in the food, the activity of the liver is not regulated properly. For the peculiarity of the melancholic child is that a certain substance that is otherwise produced in plants—we call it starch—is formed in the liver, yet something is wrong. All human beings form starch in the liver, but it differs from plant starch; it is an animal starch that in the liver is immediately transformed into sugar. This transformation of animal starch into sugar is a very important part of the liver's activity. This is out of order in the melancholic child, and one must advise the mother to put more sugar into the child's diet; in this way one can regulate the glycogenic activity of the liver, as it is called. And you will see how much can be achieved with this purely hygienic measure. Education must indeed be extended to include the totality of the human being.

In the sanguine child you will find precisely the opposite. Frequently, such a child is being turned into a sugar addict. He or she is given too much candy; too many sweets are served. Now, precisely the opposite activity comes about. The liver is an infinitely important organ, but it is an organ that resembles a sense organ much more closely than one would imagine. The purpose of the liver is to observe and understand the whole human being from within. The liver has a sensitivity for the whole human being. Hence its organization differs from that of other organs. In other organs, a certain amount of arterial blood flows in and a certain quantity of venous blood flows out. The liver has a different arrangement. A special vein enters it and supplies it with special venous blood. This has the effect of making the liver a kind of outer world within the human being. This enables human beings to perceive themselves by means of the liver, that is, to perceive what affects their organism. The liver is an extraordinarily fine barometer for sensing the kind of relation human beings have to the outer world. If you advise the mother to reduce the amount of sugar she feeds to a pathologically sanguine child—a skittish child who skims nervously from one impression to the next—you will help bring about an extraordinary improvement in such a case.

Thus, if you are a good teacher, you can give children such guidance as shall make them truly healthy, strong, and active in all their physical functions through what you do, not in school, but at other times as well. And you will notice what enormous importance this has for the whole development of these children as human beings.

Some of the most impressive experiences we have had with children at the Waldorf School have been with those of age fifteen or sixteen. We started the Waldorf School with eight elementary grades, but then added on, grade by grade, a ninth, tenth, and now an eleventh grade. These upper grades—which are of course advanced grades, not elementary grades—have the boys and girls who are fifteen and sixteen years old. There, we face special difficulties. Some of these difficulties are of a physical and moral nature. I will speak of these later. But, even in the physical respect, one finds that human nature tends continuously to become pathological and has to be shielded from this condition.

Among the girls, under certain circumstances, you will find a slight tendency to chlorosis, to anemia, in the whole developing organism. The blood in the girl's organism becomes deficient; she becomes pale, anemic. This is due to the fact that during age fourteen, fifteen, and sixteen the spiritual nature is separated out from the total organism; this spiritual nature, which formerly worked within the whole being, regulated the blood. Now the blood is left to itself. It must be rightly prepared so that its own power may accomplish this larger task. Girls are apt, then, to become pale, anemic, and one must know that this anemia comes about when one has failed to arouse the girl's interest in the things one has earlier been teaching or telling her. Where attention and interest are kept alive, the whole physical organism participates in the activity which is engaging the inmost self of the human being, and then anemia does not arise in the same way.

The opposite is the case with boys. In boys, a kind of neuritis comes about, a form of having too much venous blood in the brain. Hence, during these years, the brain behaves as though it were congested with blood. In girls we find a lack of blood in the body; in boys we deal with a slight form of profusion of blood, a wrong form of venous and arterial blood, particularly in the head. This is because the boys have been given too many sensations, they have been over-stimulated, and have had to hurry from sensation to sensation without pause or proper rest. And you will see that

48

the troublesome behavior of fourteen-, fifteen-, and sixteen-year-olds does appear in this way and is connected with the whole physical development. When one can view the nature of the human being in this way, not disdaining the physical aspects, one can do a great deal in pointing the way to public health as a teacher and educator.

Classroom instruction based on insight into the human components

In a lecture on April 15, 1924 for the teachers in Bern entitled "Anthroposophical Pedagogy and its Preconditions" [published in *The Roots of Education*], Rudolf Steiner explained:

These four components are entirely different from each other, but ordinary observation does not distinguish between them because they play into one another. Ordinary observation never goes so far as to recognize the revelation of human nature in the etheric body, the astral body, or the ego. But it is not really possible to teach and educate without a knowledge of these things. . . .

Now the way in which human nature works through the etheric, astral, and ego organization is quite remarkable and of significance for education and teaching. As you know, we become acquainted with the physical body when we make observations on the living human being, as we are accustomed to do, or even on the corpse. In so doing, we use our brain-bound intellect, and with it we interpret our sense perceptions. But with this kind of observation we never come to know the higher members of human nature. They elude mere sense-perception and the intellect. If you think only in terms of natural laws, for instance, you will never understand the etheric body. Training at colleges and universities would therefore have to include more than just the methods enabling us to observe the physical body and study it with our brain-bound intellect.

Quite a different university training would be needed to enable us to perceive, for example, how the etheric body manifests in the human being. This would really be a necessity, not only for teachers of all subjects, but especially for physicians. Such training would initially consist of learning to model like a sculptor, truly model from within based on the unfolding of human nature, so that one could reach the point of creating forms out of their own inner laws. You see, the form of a muscle or of a bone cannot be comprehended by the methods of present-day anatomy and physiology. Forms will only be understood when you grasp them based on the sense of form. Now something comes up immediately to which people of the present age react as if it were sheer insanity. But after all, Copernican theories were considered pure madness in their day, and until the year 1828 a certain church viewed Copernican teachings to be madness and forbade the faithful to believe in them.

Now, this is what I mean. Consider the physical body. It is heavy; it has weight and is subject to the laws of gravity. The etheric is not subject to gravity, on the contrary it is always trying to be gone, to disperse into the far spaces of the universe. And it does do that immediately following death. The first experience after death is to live through the dispersal of the etheric body. One experiences that the physical corpse follows the laws of the earth when it is lowered into the grave; if it is cremated it burns according to physical laws just like any other physical object. This is not the case with the etheric body. It tends away from the earth just as much as the physical body tends toward the earth. But the etheric body does not tend away equally in all directions, nor does it tend away from the earth in a uniform manner. Here comes something that seems grotesque but is true; it is a true perception of the observation of which I have spoken.

Take the earth's surroundings. Up there in the heavens we find groupings of stars, one here and another one there, and all these groupings

are different from each other. And these groups of stars attract the human etheric body; they draw it out into the far spaces. Assume that a human being is here in the center (circle in middle of diagram). The etheric body is then attracted by this group of stars which has a strong effect; from the other grouping of stars it is less strongly attracted. From yet another group it is again attracted in another way. The etheric body is not equally drawn in all directions, rather, it is attracted in varying degrees to the different directions of space. The result is not a spreading globe. But inasmuch as the etheric body wants to stretch out, this gives rise to what can be shaped through the cosmic forces working down from the stars on a certain form of the human being so long as we live on earth and bear an etheric body within us. We see how, in the upper part of the thigh, the forming forces shaping the muscle come from the stars. Likewise, what forms the bone comes from the stars. We need to discover how different forms can originate from all directions of cosmic space. We must try to model these varying forms out of clay, and then we shall find that in one particular form the cosmic forces work to produce length; in another, the form is rounded off sooner. Examples of the latter are the round bones; examples of the former, the tubular bones.

So we must be sculptors and develop a feeling for the world. This feeling was present in the humanity of olden times as a sort of instinctive consciousness. It was clearly expressed in the Orient of prehistoric millennia, but we can still trace it in Greek culture. Just think how materialistic artists of today are often baffled by the human forms of Greek sculptures. Why are they baffled? Because they believe that the Greeks worked from models. Our modern artists have the impression that the Greeks observed the human being from all sides. But the Greeks still possessed a feeling for how the human being is born out of the cosmos, and how the cosmos itself forms us. When the Greeks created a sculpture like their Venus de Milo (which is the despair of modern sculptors), they took what streams out of the cosmos and is merely a bit distorted by earthly forming, and placed it, at least partly, into the human organization. The point is: You have to realize that if you try to sculpt a human form according to nature, you cannot possibly do so by slavishly adhering to models that nowadays are placed in studios. You must be able to turn to the great cosmic sculptor who creates the human being out of what you can aspire to as the feeling for space. This has to be developed first: the feeling for space!

People imagine that they can gauge the human form by drawing a line through it like this, another through the outstretched arms and another like this [Rudolf Steiner is drawing]. These are the three dimensions of space.

One draws the human being slavishly into the three dimensions. This is pure abstraction. If I draw a straight line through a human form in the right way, I deal with quite different forces of attraction, this way or that, in all directions of space. This geometric space that turned into Kantian space (concerning which Kant produced such unfortunate definitions and abstract theories, a purely concocted illusion) is in reality an organism that has different forces in all directions . Merely having developed our coarser physical senses, we do not develop this delicate feeling for space. But it can be experienced in all directions. If we allow it to hold sway in us, then the true image of the human being will arise. Out of an inner feeling and sensitivity for space, the sculptured human form will arise. And if you have a feeling for this handling of the soft plastic substance, you will find in this approach the right conditions for an understanding of the etheric body, just as the conditions for an understanding of the physical body are contained in your brain-bound intelligence.

We have to create a new method of acquiring knowledge, namely, a kind of plastic perception that is always linked somewhat with inward plastic activity. Otherwise, knowledge of the human being stops short at the physical body, for the etheric body can only be grasped through pictures, not through concepts. We can only understand these etheric images if we are able to re-fashion them in some way, in imitation of the cosmic fashioning.

Now we go on to the next highest component of the human being. How do matters stand today? On the one hand, we have the prevailing views of natural science and their exponents who authoritatively convey the right knowledge to humanity today. On the other hand, we find anthroposophists with twisted, isolated minds, who additionally speak of the existence of an etheric and astral body. Now those who are used to scientific thinking try to understand the description of the astral body with the same methods of thought they apply to an understanding of the physical body. This cannot be done. True, the astral body expresses itself in the physical body; its physical expression can be comprehended according to natural laws. But the astral body itself in its true inner being and function cannot be grasped by natural laws. It can be comprehended if one has not only an outward but an inner understanding of music, such as could be found in the Orient, an understanding that was still present to a lesser degree in Greek culture; in modern times it has disappeared altogether. Just as the etheric body works out of cosmic sculpture, so the astral body works out of cosmic music, cosmic melodies. The only thing that is earthly about the astral body is time, the musical measure. Rhythm and melody work directly out of the cosmos, and the astral body consists of rhythm and melody. It is of no use to approach the astral body with what we know of the laws of natural science. We must approach it with what we have acquired for ourselves out of an inner understanding of music. Then you will find, for example, that when the interval of a third is played it can be felt and experienced in the inner human nature. You can have a major and minor third, and considerable variations in human feelings can be aroused by this division of the scale. This is still an inner human experience. When we come to the fifth, we experience this on the surface, on the boundary of ourselves, as though with the fifth we were only just inside ourselves. The sixth and seventh we experience as if they want to take their course outside us. We pass out of ourselves with the fifth, and as we enter into the sixth and the seventh, we experience them as something external, whereas we feel the third to be an eminently inward experience. This is the effect of the astral body. It is a musician in every human being, a musician who imitates the music of the cosmos. And everything in the human being is, in turn, active in him or her and finds expression in the human form. If we can really come close to such a thought in an effort to comprehend the world, it can be a profoundly moving experience for us.

You see, we are speaking now of something we can study quite objectively—something that flows out of the astral body into the human form, arising, in this case, not out of cosmic sculpture, but out of the fact that the impulse of music streams into us from our astral body. Here again, we must take our start from an understanding of music, just as a plastic understanding was necessary earlier for studying the activities of the etheric body. If you take that part of our organism that goes from the shoulder-blades to the arms, it is an effect of the prime that indwells the human being. In the upper arm, we find the interval of the second (all this comes to expression through eurythmy), and in the lower arm, the third (major and minor as we have it in music). When we advance to the interval of the third, we find two bones in the lower arm; and this continues right down into the fingers. This sounds like mere words and phrases, but one can behold these things through real spiritual-scientific observation of the human being just as exactly as mathematicians get to the bottom of their mathematical problems. You cannot arrive at this through an inferior kind of mysticism; you must investigate it with exactitude. In order to comprehend all this, universities offering training in medicine and education should really have to begin with an inner understanding of music, an understanding of music that, in full inner awareness, must lead one back to the musical understanding of Oriental times, even before Greek culture began. Oriental architecture can only be comprehended if we understand how religious perception flashed into form. As music only finds expression in experiences of time, so does architecture in experiences of space. Likewise, human beings must be studied in accordance with their astral and etheric bodies. And the life of feeling and passions cannot be understood if it is merely comprehended psychologically, as we say today, in accordance with natural laws. We can only do so if we approach the human being with the same soul-forms we observe in music. A time will come when an unsound emotion will not be described as is done today by psychologists. Instead, when confronted with a defective emotion, one will speak of it in musical terms as one would speak, for instance, of a piano that is out of tune. . . .

Now we come to the ego organization. As the astral body can be studied in music, so the true nature of the ego-organization can be studied in language. Hence one says that everyone, even physicians and teachers— and this is admitted already in the case of teachers—has to stop at today's form of language. But can they then understand the inner configuration of language? No, they can only do so if they regard language not as the product of our modern mechanism, but as something in which the genius of language works in a living and spiritual way. You can do it if you train yourself to understand the ways and means in which a word is configured. Untold wisdom lies in words, wisdom far beyond the grasp of human beings. All human characteristics are expressed in the way in which people form their words. The peculiarities of any nation can be recognized in its language. Take, for instance, the German word *Kopf* 'head'. This is originally connected with the rounded form of the head that you also find in the word *Kohl* 'cabbage' and in the expression *Kohlkopf* 'head of cabbage.' The word arises out of a feeling for the form of the head. Here, the ego has a quite different conception of the head from what we find, for instance, in *testa*, the word for head in the Romance languages, which comes from testifying, bearing witness. In this case, the feeling out of which the word was formed comes from quite a different source.

If you understand language in this inward way, you will see how the ego-organization works. There are German-speaking regions where lightning is not called *Blitz* but *Himmlitzer*. People there do not think of the single flashes of lightning so much as the snake-like form. Those who say *Blitz* picture the single flash, and those who say *Himmlitzer* picture the zigzag form. This is how human beings really live in language, as far as their ego is concerned, although in today's civilization they have lost their connection to language, for language has become abstract. I do not mean to imply that if you have this understanding of language, you will already have attained inner clairvoyant consciousness, whereby you will have insight into beings who are identical to the human ego organization. But you will be on the way to such a perception if you follow your speaking with inner understanding.

Medical schools and teacher training colleges should foster an education in the direction of what is required if one is inwardly aspiring to work in a pliable way with an inner feeling for space, an inner relationship to music, and an inner understanding of language. Now you will say: The lecture halls are even now so empty, and in the end the teachers' training colleges will be just as empty if you include all the things you have mentioned. What would we come to?

There are constant efforts to extend medical training. If that is continued in the method as is done today, a person will not be qualified till age sixty. This is not due to inner conditions, but to the fact that these inner conditions are not fulfilled. If you fail to move on from abstract conceptions to conceiving things plastically and musically and to an understanding of the cosmic word, that is, if you stop at abstract ideas, your horizon will be endless. You will go on and on and never come to a boundary from which you can survey the whole. The understanding that will arise from an inward comprehension of modeling and music will make human beings inwardly more rational, and then, believe me, their training will in fact be accelerated rather than delayed. And such an inner course of development will be the right method of training for educators, and not only for them, but for those who have so much to contribute to modern education—the physicians.

Having seen from the introductory lectures how the physical health of human beings is linked with the manner in which they are educated and trained, it will be clear that true education cannot possibly be developed without having regard for true medicine. It is quite impossible. Educators and instructors must be able to judge the conditions of health and illness in the human being. Otherwise the need for a physician in the school arises, but the doctor is brought in from outside, something that is the worst possible method that could be adopted. For what is such a physician's relationship to the children? He does not know them, nor does he know, for example, what mistakes the teacher has made with them, and so on. The only possibility is to cultivate an art of education that embodies so much therapy that the teacher will constantly be able to see whether his or her measures are having a good or bad influence on the children's health. But no reform is brought about by bringing a doctor into the school from outside, necessary though this may appear to be. With the kind of training given to physicians at the present, they do not know what to do when they are sent into the schools. We must simply become familiar with the sort of training that is provided when we aim at an art of education based on a knowledge of the human being,

One hesitates to say these things because they are so difficult to grasp. But it is an error to believe that the ideas which have arisen from natural science can give us an understanding of the human being. And to discern this error is one of the vital conditions in the development of the art of education.

It is only when we look at the child from this point of view that we can see, for example, what radical and far-reaching changes occur with the coming of the second teeth, when memory actually becomes a pictorial memory and is no longer attached to the physical body, but to the etheric body. What factor really brings forth the permanent teeth? It is that up to this time the etheric body was completely, tightly bound up with the physical body, but then it separates a bit. If it did not do so, we would get new teeth every seven years. (As people's teeth decay so rapidly nowadays, this would be quite a good thing, and dentists would have to look for another job!) When the etheric body has separated, its effects that formerly worked in the physical body now work in the realm of the soul. If you have a perception for these things and can examine a child's mouth without his/her knowledge, you will see for yourself that it is so.

It is always better for a child not to know that he or she is being observed. This is why experimental psychology is so unsuccessful, because the child notices what is being done. You examine the child's second teeth; they have been formed by the etheric body and then become a modeled image of memory. One can observe by the configuration of the teeth what sort of memory the etheric body has set up. With the exception of slight alterations here or there, you cannot change the second teeth. Something could be done even after they have formed, if medicine were to develop in the way described by Professor Römer in his book on dentistry that is based on anthroposophical insights he adopted. But this need not concern us here. When the etheric body is loosened and stands alone, the development of memory is separated off from the physical and remains almost entirely in the element of soul, a fact that can really put a teacher on the right track. For until the change of teeth occurs, the soul-spiritual formed a unity with the physical-etheric. After this, the physical, which formerly worked together with the soul, is expressed in the form of the second teeth, and what collaborated with the physical in this process is separated off and is revealed as an increase in the power of forming ideas, and in the formation and reliability of memory.

If you acquire this kind of insight into human nature, you will acquire a great deal that will help in education and instruction. And when you are

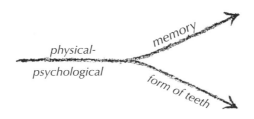

physical-
psychological

memory

form of teeth

filled with this spiritual knowledge of the human being in a living way and then observe people, you will acquire ideas and methods of teaching that will truly fill you as educators with inner inspiration and enthusiasm, something that passes over into your practical work. The rules laid down in introductory books on education only produce an abstract activity of the soul, whereas what arises out of an anthroposophical knowledge penetrates the teacher's activity and will, and becomes the impulse for all they do in the classroom.

You become organized in your soul as a teacher through a living knowledge of the human being. If, on the other hand, you merely study methods that arise out of natural science, you may arrive at some clever ideas of what to do with a child, but you will not be able to carry them out; for your skill and practical handling of the child must arise out of the living spirit within you, the physical teacher. Now, if you can enliven such insight in yourself through a true knowledge of the human being, you will notice how, when the etheric body really is freed during the change of teeth, children have an inner urge to receive everything in the form of pictures; in their own inner being they want to become pictures. In the first period of life before the change of the teeth, impressions do not try to become pictures, but habit and skill. Memory itself was habit and skill. With their movements, children want to imitate what they have seen. They have no desire to form a picture. But then you can observe how perception changes, how children want to sense in themselves that pictures are arising in their soul. Now, you must bring everything into a pictorial element in your lessons. You yourself as teacher must understand how to create pictures of everything.

In his newest book about the change of teeth in the child,[18] Armin Husemann has published far-reaching Goethean research about the connection of the changing of teeth with the soul-spiritual development. This book is strongly recommended. The following impression from observation of a first grade class illustrates the facts described above by Rudolf Steiner:

This first grade had already been in progress for about three months. The class teacher announced the title of the story he now wanted to relate. He said: At the close of our main lesson today, I want to tell you the story of Faithful John. A number of the children in the class were familiar with this—admittedly not so well-known—fairy tale by the Brothers Grimm. The children had conflicting reactions. Whereas the eyes of many lit up with enthusiasm that they were allowed to hear this wonderful story, a rather bold boy called out to the class, expressing the sentiment of some of his classmates: Oh, I already know that story; can't you tell another one? From this polar reaction, one can figure out in which of the children the enamel at the crowns of the teeth had matured sufficiently (something that as a rule correlates with the beginning of the change of teeth) and where it had not. Where this has occurred (it takes place between the ages of six and eight),[19] the formative activity of these most solid of bodily forms has by this time been freed for thinking and seeks work. Spiritually speaking, it wants to "bite into something" and, in so doing, to hang on to what has already been heard. With this, abstract memory is born, as is the capacity to create an afterimage in one's own thinking of what one has heard and seen without necessarily having to imitate it immediately—something that younger children do as a matter of course. So, those children, whose eyes were gleaming because they wanted so much to hear the story again, could as yet not avail themselves of their abstract memory sufficiently. They would remember what they were looking forward to when they heard the story again.

Child study in faculty meetings: psychological insights into the individual child

In July 1924 Rudolf Steiner gave education lectures in Arnhem, Holland (published as *Human Values in Education*). By then, he had participated in a large number of faculty meetings at the Stuttgart Waldorf School. He reported some of these experiences to his listeners on July 21, 1924:

First, I should like to make it clear that the soul of all instruction and education in the Waldorf School is the faculty meeting These meetings are held regularly and I attend them whenever I can manage to be in Stuttgart. They are not only concerned with external matters of school organization, with drawing up the timetable, with the structure of classes, and so on, but they deal in a far-reaching way with everything on which the life and soul of the school depends. Now, the aim of the school is to offer instruction and education based on a knowledge of the human being, meaning, on the basis of insight into each individual child. This is why psychological observation of each child is a fundamental part of the whole development of instruction in all its concrete details. In a discussion of a given child in a faculty meeting, the teachers attempt to grasp the nature of the human being as it comes to expression in the particular individuality of that child. You can imagine that one is confronted there with all levels and types of children's talents and qualities of soul. We are confronted with every variation of what is present in the young human being, from the psychologically and physically poorly endowed ones to those gifted to the point of genius—and one hopes life will confirm this.

If you want to observe the true inner nature of children, you must acquire psychological insight into them. This kind of insight not only includes a general form of observing the capacities of individual children, but above all the ability to appraise these capacities correctly. You need only consider the following: You can have a child in class who appears to be extraordinarily gifted in learning to read and write, or seems to be gifted in learning arithmetic or languages. But it is psychologically superficial to stop here and say that this child is gifted, because he or she easily learns languages, arithmetic, and so on. In childhood, say around the ages of seven, eight, or nine, the ease with which a child learns can be a sign that later on he or she will become a genius; it can equally well be a sign that sooner or later such a child will become neurotic or in some other way turn into a sick person. We can gain the insight that a human being consists not only of the physical body, which is perceptible to the eye, but that he or she likewise possesses an etheric body, the source of the forces of growth and nourishment that cause the child to grow taller. Moreover, we can reflect on the fact that the human being contains an astral body, the laws of which have nothing whatever to do with what is being physically built up, but, on the contrary, work to diminish the physical and destroy it in order to make room for the spiritual. In addition, we can consider the ego-organization that is bound up with the human being. Now, we know that the three higher organizations—etheric body, astral body, ego-organization—must be heeded in the same way that we pay attention to the perceptible physical body. Then we will be able to form an idea of how complicated a human being is, and how each of these components of the human being can be the cause of a talent, or a lack thereof in any particular area, or can show a deceptive talent that is transient and pathological. We must develop the insight to determine whether a talent is of the kind that has a healthy tendency or one that tends toward the unhealthy.

If, as a teacher and educator, you represent the knowledge of the human being described here in these lectures with the necessary love, devotion, and selflessness, something quite remarkable ensues. In associating with the children you become—do not misunderstand the word, it is not meant in a bragging sense—you become wiser and wiser. As it were, you yourself discover how to evaluate a given faculty or achievement of the child. You learn fully to enter in a living way into the child's nature and to do so comparatively quickly.

I know that some will say: If you assert that the human being, in addition to the physical body, consists of supersensible components— etheric body, astral body, and ego-organization—it follows that only someone who is clairvoyant and able to perceive these supersensible members of human nature can be a teacher. This is not the case. Everything perceived through imagination, inspiration, and intuition as described in my books, can be evaluated by observing the physical organization of the child, because it comes to expression everywhere in this physical organization.

It is therefore entirely possible for teachers or educators, who simply carry out their profession in a loving manner based on a comprehensive knowledge of the human being, to speak as follows about a particular case: Here, we face the fact that the child is quite well in regard to the ego, the astral body, and even the etheric body. But the physical body shows signs of hardening, of stiffening, so that the child is unable to develop the faculties potentially present spiritually, because the physical body is a hindrance. Or imagine another case. It is possible to observe that certain precocious attributes are appearing in a particular seven- or eight-year-old child; it is surprising that, early on, the child learns this or that subject. But we should watch out; the physical body is too soft and has the tendency to run to fat eventually. For if the physical body is too soft, if the fluid element outweighs the solid element, so to speak, this particular tendency causes the soul-spiritual to push forward—and then we have a precocious child. During the further development of the physical body, this precocity is pushed back again and, under certain conditions, everything may well change once more. The same child can then turn out to be just average or even below average as an adult. In short, the point is that what external observation reveals in the child must first be evaluated inwardly. Nothing whatever is really determined if one merely speaks of faculties or the lack thereof.

Biographies of all sorts of different persons can teach you what I am now saying. In following the course of humanity's cultural development, one could cite a great number of distinguished individuals who as adults achieved great things but as children were regarded as almost completely lacking in any aptitudes; at school some even had to repeat grades. Indeed, one comes across the most remarkable examples. There is a poet, for instance, who until the age of eighteen, nineteen, and even twenty, was considered to be so incapable by all his teachers that they advised him not to engage in academic studies. But he did not allow himself to be put off and continued his studies. Not so long afterwards, he was appointed inspector of the very same schools into which it had not been thought advisable for him to seek admittance as a young man.

We have an Austrian poet, Robert Hamerling, who studied with the purpose of becoming a teacher in a secondary school [*gymnasium*]. In the examination, he obtained excellent marks for Greek and Latin; on the other hand, he did not receive certification for teaching German, because his essays were considered inadequate. This notwithstanding, he became a famous poet.

I could go on with such examples and you would see everywhere that it is indeed hard to perceive in the growing child what is in fact potentially present in a young person. Yet this has to happen in a school where the goal is to educate and teach correctly. This is why the greatest value is placed on studying the children in faculty meetings at the Waldorf School. This is done in order that the whole body of teachers is always informed about how matters stand in the individual case of a child. Naturally, this is becoming a more and more demanding task. The Waldorf School was established a few years ago with about 150 children. Today, along with all the parallel classes that had to be added, it numbers about 800 students in over 20 classes with far more than 40 teachers. This can show you that the possibility to proceed in the way I described can only be realized if, at the same time, there develops in you a perception for knowing which specific child you must start out with. A child can possess a nature that, once you understand this child, can shed light on many other children. Again, some children can be such that understanding is almost of no help. Still, all this can be overcome by loving devotion for what is present here in the way of insight into the human being. . . .

In your observation of the soul-spiritual and the physical-corporeal, the important thing is to remain aware of their unity in your whole way of thinking. People find it hard to understand that this is a necessity in education and teaching. Once, a man, who was quite intelligent and was directly engaged in matters pertaining to schools, visited the Waldorf School. I myself took him around for several days. He showed great interest in everything. But after I had told him all I could about one child or another—we spoke mostly about the children, not about abstract educational principles, our education being based on insight into the human being—he finally said: Well and good, but then all teachers would have to be medical doctors. I replied: That is not necessary, but they should certainly have some knowledge concerning health and illness in the child's constitution, as much as teachers need to know for their educational work.

For where will it end if it we say that provision cannot be made for some reason, or that the teachers cannot learn this or that because we cannot institute it? Provision simply must be made for what is required and the teachers must learn what is necessary. This is the only possible standpoint.

The so-called normal faculties that a human being develops, capacities that are present in every human being, are best studied by observing pathological conditions. And if one has learned to know a sick organism from various points of view, then the foundation is laid for understanding a soul endowed with genius. It is not as though I were taking the standpoint of a Lombroso or someone holding similar views; this is not the case. I do not assert that genius is always a condition of sickness, but one does actually learn to know the soul-spiritual in learning to know the sick body of a child. In studying the difficulties that the soul- spiritual has in coming to expression in a sick body, one can learn to understand how the soul seizes hold of the organism when it has something special to express.

Thus, pedagogy not only comes up against slightly pathological conditions such as exist in children of limited capacity, it encounters the element of pathology in the widest sense of the word. This is why we have introduced medical treatment for the children in our school. But we do not have a doctor who merely practices medicine and is quite outside the sphere of education. Our school physician, Dr. Kolisko, is a class teacher at the same time. He stands completely within the whole system of education in the school; he is acquainted with all the children and is therefore in a position to know the particular direction from which a pathological symptom may appear in a child he is familiar with. This is altogether different from what is possible for a school physician who visits the school only on certain rare occasions and judges a child's state of health based on a checkup lasting only a few minutes.

Quite apart from this, no hard and fast line is drawn in the faculty meetings between the soul-spiritual and physical-corporeal when considering the case of any particular child. The natural consequence of this is that teachers gradually have to acquire insight into the whole human being, so that they are just as interested in every detail connected with physical health and sickness as they are in what is spiritually sound or unsound.

This is what we try to achieve in our school. Each teacher should have the deepest interest in, and pay the greatest attention to, the whole human being. It follows from this that our teachers are not specialists in the ordinary sense of the word. In effect, the point is not so much whether a history teacher is more or less master of his or her subject, but whether he or she on the whole has a personality that can affect the children in the way that has been described and has an awareness of how the child develops under his/her care.

From the time I was fourteen or fifteen years old, I myself was obliged to teach, to give private lessons, simply in order to survive. I had to acquire this pedagogy through direct experience in the practice of education and teaching. For instance, when I was a very young man, only twenty-one, a family asked me to undertake the education of their four boys. Among them was one —he was then eleven years old when I became the private tutor in that family—who was extremely hydrocephalic. He had most peculiar habits. He disliked eating at table, and would leave the dining room and go into the kitchen where the garbage bins were. There he would eat potato peelings, but along with them the dirt in the bins. At age eleven he hardly knew anything. An attempt had been made on the basis of earlier instruction that he had received, to let him take an entrance examination to a class at a primary school. But when he handed in the results of his examination, there was nothing but a notebook with one large hole where he had erased something. He had produced absolutely nothing else whatever, even though he was already eleven. The parents were distressed. They belonged to the cultured upper-middle class, and everybody said: The boy is abnormal. Naturally, when such things are said about a child, people feel prejudice against him. The general opinion was that this boy should learn a trade, for he was capable of nothing else. I came into the family, but nobody really understood me when I stated what I was prepared to do. I said: If I am given full responsibility for the boy I can promise nothing except that I will try to draw out of the boy what is in him. Nobody understood this except the mother with her instinctive perception, and the excellent family physician. He was the same doctor who later on, together with Dr. Freud, established psychoanalysis. When, at a later stage, psychoanalysis became decadent, he severed his connection with it. It was possible to speak with this man, and our conversation led to the decision that I should be entrusted with the boy's education and training.

Within eighteen months his head had become noticeably smaller, and the boy was now sufficiently advanced to enter a secondary school. I continued on with him further for he needed extra help; nevertheless, after eighteen months, he was accepted as a pupil in a secondary school. To be sure, his education had to be carried on in such a way that there were times when I needed one and a half hours in order to prepare what I wanted the boy to learn in fifteen minutes. It was essential to exercise the greatest economy when teaching him and never to spend more time on a subject than was absolutely necessary. It was moreover a question of arranging the day's schedule with great exactitude. I arranged a set amount of time for the practice of music, a time for gymnastics, for going on a walk and so on. If this is done, I told myself, it will be possible to draw out of the boy what is latent within him. Now there were times when things went quite badly with my efforts in this direction. The boy became pale. With the exception of his mother and the family doctor, everybody said: That fellow is ruining the boy's health! To this I replied: Naturally I cannot continue with his education if there is any interference. Things must be allowed to go on according to our agreement. And go on they did.

The boy finished secondary school, attended university, and became a physician. The only reason he died young was that, when he was called up and served as a physician during the World War, he caught an infection and died of the effects of the ensuing illness. But he carried out the duties of his medical profession in an admirable way. I only bring this example up in order to show how necessary it is in education to consider all things as a whole. It shows, for instance, how, with certain treatment, it is possible in the long run to reduce a hydrocephalic condition week by week.

Now you will say: Certainly, something of this kind can happen when it is a case of private tutoring. But it can equally well happen with comparatively large classes. For anyone who enters lovingly into the knowledge of the human being put forward here, will quickly acquire the possibility of observing each individual student with the attention he or she requires, and this will be possible even in a class with many students. But this psychological perception is not so easily acquired if you, a single individual, go through the world and have no interest whatsoever in other people. I can truly say that I am aware of what I owe to the fact that I really never found any human being uninteresting. Even as a child, no human being was ever uninteresting to me. And I know that I should never have been able to educate that boy if I had not found all human beings interesting.

It is this expanding of interest that pervades the faculty meetings at the Waldorf School like an atmosphere, so that—if I may say so—a psychological mood prevails there. These faculty meetings then really turn into a lofty school of psychology. It is interesting to see how, from year to year, the body of teachers as a whole is able to deepen its faculty of psychological perception.

In addition to all that I have described, the following must be considered when one reflects on a given class. We do not go in for statistics in the ordinary sense of the word, and not only the individual students, but also the classes are living beings for us. You can take a particular class and study it by itself, and it is extraordinarily interesting to observe the imponderable forces that then come to light. When one class is studied, and when the teachers of the different classes discuss the special characteristics of each class in their meeting, it is interesting, for instance, to discover that a class that has more girls than boys—for ours is a co-educational school—is a completely different entity from a class with more boys than girls; and a class consisting of an equal number of boys and girls is yet another completely different entity. All this becomes extremely interesting, not just on account of the words that are exchanged between students, nor because of the romances that always occur in the upper grades. Here too, the required perception is attained, a perception that sees what needs to be seen and does not see where it is not necessary to do so. Quite apart from this, the inner imponderable entity composed of the various male and female individualities gives the class a quite definite spiritual structure. In this way you get to know the class individuality. And if, as is the case here in the Waldorf School, there are parallel classes, it is possible when necessary—it is rarely necessary—to change the seating arrangements in the classes a little.

In turn, studies such as the composition of classes as such represent the content of faculty meetings. Thus, the content of these meetings not only deals with school administration but provides a living continuation of education itself within the school so that the teachers are always learning. In this way the meetings become the soul of the whole school. Then you learn to evaluate trivialities rightly, to give due weight to what has real importance, and so on. Then there will be no outcry when a child commits a minor misdemeanor. But there will be an awareness when something happens that might endanger the further development of the school. So the overall picture of our Waldorf School, which has only come about in the course of the years, is an interesting one. By and large, our children in the upper grades are more advanced in grasping what students are supposed to learn in school than those of other schools. On the other hand, as I said, in the lower classes they remain somewhat behind in reading and writing, because we use different methods that are extended over several years. But between the ages of thirteen and fifteen, our children begin to excel over students of other schools in regard to the ease and skill of comprehension with which they can enter into subjects, and so on.

Now a great difficulty arises. It is remarkable that where there is light, shadows are thrown by objects. Where there is weak light, there are weak shadows; where there is strong light, there are strong shadows. Likewise, in regard to certain qualities of soul, the following may be observed. If insufficient care is taken by teachers to establish contact with their students in every possible way so that they are models on which the children truly base their own behavior, then moral deviations can occur that are counter-images of a lack of contact. About this we must have no illusions whatever. It is so. This is why so much depends on a complete convergence of the teachers' individualities with the students' individualities, so that through this strong inner attachment of the children to the teachers, further development on the one side corresponds fully with the ongoing development on the other.

In the further course of the lecture, Rudolf Steiner deals with questions concerning the structure of the daily schedule and then goes on to report with remarkable, encouraging openness on difficulties of the school's everyday operation:

In this connection I must say that it is possible to have teachers in the Waldorf School who prove to be inadequate; I will not describe them, but a dissonance can occur. On entering a classroom, one can experience that one fourth of the class is lying under the benches, a quarter is on top, and the rest are continually running out of the room and making noise outside. We must not let these things baffle us. The situation can be straightened out if one knows how to deal with the children. They should be allowed to satisfy their urge for movement; one should not fall back on punishment but undertake to put these things right in other ways. We are not at all in favor of issuing commands; on the contrary, everything must be allowed to develop on its own. But it develops by itself through what I have described as the teacher's inner life. Certainly, children sometimes are awfully noisy, but this is only a sign of their vitality. They can likewise be lively in doing what they should, provided the teacher knows how to arouse their interest. Of course, we must make use of the good qualities of a so-called good child, so that he or she learns something; with a naughty child we must even make use of the naughty qualities, so that such a child makes progress too. We do not get anywhere if we are only able to develop the good qualities. We must occasionally develop the so-called naughty qualities, but must be capable of giving them direction. Frequently, these so-called naughty qualities of a child are precisely those which signify strength in the grown-up human being; they are qualities which, rightly handled, can culminate in what is most excellent in the adult person.

Again, one has to determine whether a child gives little trouble because he or she is well-behaved or is ill. It is easy, if you only consider your own convenience, to be as pleased with a sick child who sits still and does not misbehave as with good children, because they do not require much attention. But if you truly have insight into human nature, you often find that you have to devote much more attention to such a child than to a so-called naughty one. Here too, it is a matter of psychological insight and manner of treatment, naturally from the soul-spiritual point of view.

Another point is that, in the Waldorf School, the essential part of instruction is the responsibility of the school itself. Homework that burdens the children so much is assigned to the smallest extent possible. Because all the work is done together with the teachers, the children's attitude is quite unusual. Something quite characteristic can happen in the Waldorf School, as the following example demonstrates. Certain pupils have really been up to some mischief. A teacher who is not yet imbued with the Waldorf school approach wants to punish these children in an especially clever way. He says: You must stay after school and do some arithmetic. These children are quite unable to understand that doing arithmetic could be regarded as punishment, for this is something they do with greatest pleasure. And the whole class—this actually happened—asks: Can't we stay too?

Now, was that punishment? As you can see, the whole attitude of mind changes completely, and it should never happen that children feel they are being punished when they have to do something they actually do with dedication, satisfaction, and joy. Our teachers discover all sorts of ways of getting rid of wrong behavior. Our Dr. Stein, who is particularly inventive in this regard, once noticed that during his lesson in an upper grade the children were writing letters and passing them around. Now what did he do in order to put the matter right? He began to speak about the postal service, explaining it in some detail and in such a way that the writing of letters gradually ceased. The description of the postal service, the history of the origin of correspondence, apparently had nothing to do with the misdemeanor noticed by the teacher, nevertheless it had something to do with it.

These comments are supplemented by observations Rudolf Steiner made on August 16, 1923 at Ilkely in England in connection with lectures published as *A Modern Art of Education.*

A gentleman whose thinking was wholly concerned with education once came to visit the Waldorf School, and I tried to explain the spirit underlying the teaching there. After a while, having listened to me and having looked at things, he commented: But if you work along these lines, the teachers will have to know a great deal about medicine. From the start, it seemed to him quite impossible that they would understand medicine to the extent required for such instruction. I said that since this arises out of insight into human nature, a certain amount of medical instruction ought to form part of any course for teachers.

There is no doubt; we can never say that questions concerned with health ought to be left merely to the school physician. I think we are particularly fortunate at the Waldorf School in that our school physician is himself part of our staff of teachers. Dr. Kolisko is a medical doctor by profession and, besides looking after the children's health, is also a member of the teaching staff. In this way everything connected with the bodily health of the children can proceed in fullest harmony with their education.

This, in effect, is necessary: Something must be included in our teacher training that relates to health and sickness in children. To give an example: A teacher notices a child growing paler and paler. Another child changes his or her natural color because the face turns noticeably red. If the teacher observes accurately, he or she will find that the reddening child furthermore shows signs of restlessness and sudden anger. The teacher must be able to relate all such symptoms properly to the nature of soul and spirit. Abnormal pallor—or even the tendency to it—is the result of overexertion of memory. The memory of such a child has been overstrained and one must put a stop to this. In the case of the child with an abnormally red coloring, memory has not been engaged sufficiently. This child must be given assignments to memorize this or that and then has to demonstrate that the subject matter has been retained in memory. Hence, a child that becomes pale must be relieved of too much memorization; a child with excessive red coloring must be allowed to develop in the direction of memory.

We approach the whole human being only when we can deal harmoniously in such detail with the soul-spiritual and the physical. Thus, in our Waldorf School, the growing human being, that is, the child, is treated in accordance with his or her potentials of spirit, soul, and body, above all, the potentials of the temperament.

In the classoom itself, we seat the children in a way that enables them to express their various temperaments—choleric, sanguine, melancholic or phlegmatic—amongst themselves. If the choleric children are seated together, they tone each other down. The same goes for the melancholic children. Of course, the teachers must be capable of observing these temperaments. In turn, dealing with these temperaments deeply affects bodily development.

Assume you have a sanguine child who is inattentive to what he or she is supposed to learn. Every impression from the outer world immediately engages the attention but passes away again just as quickly. The right treatment for such a child will be to reduce the quantity of sugar in the food—not unduly, of course. The less sugar is absorbed, the more will the excessively sanguine qualities be modified and a harmonized temperament take their place.

In the case of a melancholic child who is always brooding, just the opposite treatment is necessary. More sugar must be added to the food. In this way we work down into the physical constitution of the liver, for the action of the liver differs essentially according to whether a large or small quantity of sugar is consumed. In effect, every activity of outer life penetrates deeply into the physical organism of the human being.

In this regard, we take the greatest care at the Waldorf School that there will be close contact between the teaching staff and the children's parents. A really close contact, of course, is only possible to a certain degree, for it depends on the amount of understanding possessed by the parents. We try, however, to the greatest possible extent, for the parents to turn with comprehension to the class teacher in question in order to obtain advice as to the most suitable diet for the individual child. This is just as important as what is taught in the classroom.

We must not imagine in a materialistic way that the body does everything, although a child with no hands obviously cannot be taught to play the piano. The body's role is to be a suitable instrument. Just as you cannot teach a child with no hands to play the piano, you cannot rid a child whose liver is overactive, of melancholy—no matter what psychological measures are employed by the abstract systems of education. If, however, the action of the liver is regulated by sweetening the diet, such a child will be able to use that bodily organ as a fit instrument. Only then, the soul-spiritual measures you take will be effective. . . .

True knowledge of human nature shows us the following: It is really nonsensical to speak of abnormalities or, worse, diseases of the spiritual part of the human being —although, of course, in colloquial language and for the purposes of everyday life there is no need to be fanatical and pedantic, and such terminology can indeed be used. But fundamentally speaking, spirit and soul are never ill. Illness can only occur in the bodily foundation and then pass over from body to soul. Since the human being in earthly existence can only be dealt with by approaching his or her nature of spirit and soul through the body, it is essential in the treatment of so-called abnormal children to realize that the body, because of its abnormality, is making it impossible to approach the being of soul and spirit. The difficulty lies in the body. As soon as we overcome a bodily defect or a defect of body and soul in the child and are able to approach its nature of soul and spirit, we have done what is necessary. In this connection, therefore, our constant aim must be to understand and recognize the delicate, intimate qualities and forces of the bodily nature of the human being.

If we observe that a child does not grasp things normally, that something hampers him or her from connecting concepts and perceptions, we shall have to conclude that there is some irregularity in the nervous system. Individual treatment will do much in such a case, perhaps by slowing down class instructions, or by special stimulation of the functions of will, and so forth. In a given case, especially when a child is abnormal, treatment must always be individual, and we shall be able to accomplish much good either by slowing down the teaching, or fitting in an element of will. Great attention must of course be paid to bodily training and physical care in the case of such a child. Let me explain the basic principles by giving you a simple example.

Suppose it is difficult for a child to link up ideas in his or her mind. We shall achieve much, for example, by giving the child physical exercises which, from out of the soul, bring the body, the whole organic human system into coordinating movement. We tell the child: Touch the lobe of your left ear with the third finger of the right hand! Make the child do the exercise quickly. In turn, we can say: Touch the top of your head with the little finger of the left hand! Then we can tell the child to alternate quickly between the first and the second exercise. Thus we cause the organism to be brought into movement in such a way that the child's thoughts must flow swiftly into the movements. Consequently, by causing the nervous system to become more skillful, we make it in the proper way into the foundation for the faculty that the child is supposed to exercise when it is a question of connecting or separating perceptions and concepts.

In this regard, one can gain really wonderful experiences about the ways in which the child's spiritual nature can be improved by cultivating the bodily nature. Suppose, for example, a child returns again and again to some fixed idea. This is readily noticed and is viewed as a weakness of soul. The child simply cannot help repeating certain words or returning over and over again to certain concepts or views. They take a hold of his/her being; the child cannot get rid of them. Observe such a child closely. Of course, these symptoms assume an individual form in each child and that is why a true knowledge of the human being, one that can make individual distinctions, is so necessary. You will generally find that the child does not step forward with the toes and front part of the foot, but places weight too much on the heels. Now try, as far as possible, to make the child do these movements so that he or she must first pay attention to every step taken until such an attentive gait slowly becomes habit. And then, if it is not too late—as a matter of fact, a great deal can be achieved in this direction between the seventh and twelfth year—the child will show extraordinary improvement in regard to such defects of soul. However, we must understand the way in which, let us say, the movement of the fingers of the right hand works on the speech-organism; how a movement of the fingers of the left hand work on what proceeds from the faculty of thinking and can come to the assistance of the speech-organism. We must know how walking on the toes or walking on the heels reacts on the faculties of speech and thought, and especially on the faculty of will. The art of eurythmy, working as it does with normal forces, teaches us a great deal when we deal with the abnormal. The movements of eurythmy—which, for the normal human being, are of course primarily formed in an artistic direction—are then modified so that they have a therapeutic effect. They are brought out of the human organism. Soul-spiritual ability, which can still be aroused during the period of growth, is thus stimulated through the bodily nature. This clearly demonstrates how important it is to observe the accord between spirit, soul, and body when we have to deal with the abnormal aspect of children at school.

Rudolf Steiner speaks repeatedly about the faculty meeting of the Waldorf School as being the very heart organ of the school organism.

This should not merely be the place where administrative matters, changes in the schedule, or administrative and disciplinary questions are negotiated. To a much greater extent, this should be the place where one learns from the children by describing and dealing with their one-sidedness, particularly their developmental problems and pathological symptoms. The pedagogically valuable insights thus gained can be made useful for work in the class. This should moreover be the place where teachers can speak openly and freely among themselves about their concerns, indeed, even about their failures—where they can help one another learn from their own mistakes and one-sidedness, and how to contribute something to the welfare of the whole. Here, week after week, practical educational research should occur when the teachers, together with the school doctor, the therapeutic eurythmist, and the remedial teacher meet together. Rudolf Steiner summed up this concern as follows in his lecture of August 23, 1922 at Oxford [published in *The Spiritual Ground of Education*]:

It is not a question of constructing the school on the lines of some clever, sudden fancy—for then a construction, not an organization, would ensue. It is truly a case of studying, week after week, the organism that is already in existence. For an observer of human nature—and this includes the child's nature—the most concrete educational measures will emerge from month to month. Just as a physician who examines a person for the first time cannot immediately say what all has to be done for the patient, but has to keep him or her under observation, since the human being is an organism, even more does an organism such as a school have to be studied continuously. It can well happen that, compared to the nature of the staff and children in 1920, you have to proceed quite differently with the staff and children you encounter in 1924, perhaps the faculty has increased, and the children will certainly be quite different. In face of this, paragraphs 1 through 12 could be as well defined as possible, but they would be of no use. Experience is only of use if it is gained day by day in the classroom.

For this reason, if I speak of the Waldorf School organization, the teachers' meeting is the very heart of the school. These faculty meetings are held periodically. When I can be in Stuttgart they are conducted under my guidance but they are otherwise held at frequent intervals. Here, before the assembled teachers, everything is discussed down to the last detail concerning the whole school and what the individual teachers have experienced in their classes. These ongoing faculty meetings tend to form the school into an organism in the same way that the human body is an organism by virtue of its heart. And what matters in these faculty meetings is not so much any abstract principles, but the readiness of all teachers to work together in good will, and abstention from any form of rivalry. It is of supreme importance that a suggestion made to another teacher is only presented when one has the right love for every single child. By this I do not mean the kind of love that is often spoken about, but the love possessed by an artistic teacher.

Now this love has a different nuance from ordinary love. It is, in turn, another nuance, but still, if you can have profound empathy for sick people as human beings, you possess a love of humanity. But in order to treat a sick person, you must likewise be able—please do not misunderstand this, but it is so—to have love for the illness. Furthermore, you must be able to speak of a beautiful illness. Such illness is naturally quite serious for the patient, but for the one who has to treat it is a beautiful illness. Under certain circumstances, it can even be a splendid illness. It may be bad indeed for the patient, but for the one who has to become involved in it, who has to be able to treat it with love, it can be a splendid illness. Similarly, a boy who is full of mischief can by his very rascality, his way of being bad, of being a ne'er-do-well, sometimes be so extraordinarily interesting that one can love him extraordinarily. Here in the Waldorf School, for instance, we have a very interesting case, a boy who is quite abnormal. He has been at the Waldorf School from the beginning; he came straight into first grade. He had the peculiar habit of running up to the teacher as soon as the latter had turned his back and hitting him. The teacher treated this little rascal with extraordinary love and interest. He stroked him, led him back to his seat and gave no sign of having noticed that he had been hit from behind. This child can only be treated by taking into consideration his whole background. One has to know the parental environment in which he has grown up, and one must be familiar with his pathology. Then, in spite of his misconduct, one can make progress with him, especially if one can love this form of misconduct. There is something lovable about a person who is exceptionally naughty.

A teacher has to look at these matters quite differently from the way a person looks at them more from the outside. Indeed, it is very important to develop this special love I have mentioned now. Then one knows what to say accordingly in the faculty meeting. In dealing with normal children nothing helps as much as what you can observe in abnormal children.

Healthy children are comparatively hard to study, for in them every characteristic is toned down. One does not readily see how it stands with a certain characteristic and what relation it has to others. In a sick child, where a character complex is present, you soon discover how to treat this particular character complex even pathologically. This can subsequently be applied to normal children.

The following are a few more pertinent examples concerning discussions of children in teachers' meetings with Rudolf Steiner [from *Faculty Meetings with Rudolf Steiner*, January 16, 1921]:

Dr. Steiner: There is young T. L. in grade 6b who has difficulty with his writing, running one stroke into another. In cases like this, where a slight tendency exists for cramps in the central nervous system that do not emerge, something that later might lead to writer's cramp, we should try to counteract it early on. This boy should do eurythmy with dumbbells. These need not be particularly heavy, but he should do the eurythmy movements holding dumbbells. You will notice that his writing will be corrected.

There are other things you could do in addition. You could try giving him a pen that slants in a different direction. There is a type of nib, though I don't know whether these have been available since the war, that is fixed on the pen holder at an angle. A boy like this would first have to get used to the new position. If he brings awareness into the way he holds his fingers that will be good for him too.

Moreover, the axes of his eyes converge too closely. You would have to try to make him keep his eyes a little further away from the paper, so that the ocular axes do not converge so much. We should wait and see how his writing changes under the influence of these more organic methods. If you see that he is really making an effort and that he manages to write something neatly, he can be taken in hand and his conscious will can participate. . . .

A teacher (speaking of another boy): He cannot concentrate.

Dr. Steiner: If you can deal with children from the pathological point of view, you could get somewhere with that boy if you would bleed him several times. Eventually, that ought to be a part of pedagogical measures. But at present we would encounter fearful objections.

Besides, you could get somewhere with him if you would persuade him to develop the habit of carrying something out from beginning to end absolutely consistently. If he does something wrong in the course of one of these tasks he would have to write it down. In his case you must somehow manage to carry the thing through clearly to its final conclusion. You can achieve a great deal if you get him to carry on with a thing until he has absolutely finished it. His main trouble is an overactivity in the blood. He is terribly tense, and he is what I would call a physical bully. He wants to swagger. His body swaggers. That would be substantially changed by treating his blood.

A number of children could be greatly helped if we set about it properly. I will select a few in each class who ought to have physical treatment. It is obvious that K.R. ought to have proper treatment. He ought to be given a diet, in accordance with things I have spoken to you about.

We ought to institute the position of a school physician, and it must be run in a way that would be acceptable to public opinion. We ought to create this special position of the school physician. . . .

A teacher: May I ask whether you recall the case of D. R.?

Dr. Steiner: The boy has remained physically small. He looks very inquisitive. I believe he needs the security of constant reassurance that you like him. He doesn't experience much love at home, even though his mother does go around talking cleverly. He should be given some love at school. You should often do things like talking to him, which is difficult because he makes an unpleasant impression. Talk to him a lot and ask him about one thing and another. He really looks as though this is how he ought to be tackled. The boy is just a bit frozen.

Pedagogical-constitutional classification

The descriptions given here of a pedagogical-constitutional typology of children are contained in my book, *Das Schulkind: gemeinsame Aufgaben von Arzt und Lehrer* [The school-age child: common tasks of physician and teacher] along with explanations and indications. In this book, the original descriptions by Rudolf Steiner in faculty meetings and in educational lectures are quoted. Steiner depicts essential and one-sided faculties of children in a larger constitutional context; this creates starting points for educational measures.

The large-headed child and the small-headed child

from the Faculty Meeting of February 6, 1923

Dr. Steiner: Today we shall discuss questions concerning hygienic measures in the school as was planned with Dr. Kolisko. Here, right at the beginning, I shall not actually be able to give any details of treatment, because I shall need to introduce a few principles first. But this will create a good basis for our further study which ought to take the form of typical examples that might well arise through your bringing questions you would wish to have answered.

First, I would like to draw your attention to the fact that our whole Waldorf School pedagogy has a therapeutic character. The whole system of instruction and education is aimed at having a healing effect on children. That is to say, if education is set up in such a way that the right thing is done at each stage in the child's development, a healing quality will permeate education and the treatment of children. For, if prior to the change of teeth, the child is turned into an imitative being in the right way, and if authority then takes over in the proper manner and prepares for the development of judgment in a corresponding way, all this has a really healing effect on the child's organism.

But by far the most important thing to aim for in our whole cultivation of school health is for the teachers to absorb right into their very flesh and blood a feeling for the threefold nature of the human organism. In the case of each child, the teacher ought to have an instinctive feeling, as it were, for whether the activity of one of these three systems predominates, the nerve-sense system, the rhythmic system, or the metabolic-limb system, and whether he or she ought to do something to counteract this predominance by stimulating one of the other systems.

Let us take a look at this threefold human being today, particularly from the teacher's point of view. We have the nerve-sense system. We only understand this system rightly if we are conscious of the fact that laws prevail there which are not the physical-chemical laws of earthly matter, but that in their nerve-sense system human beings lift themselves above the laws of earthly matter. In its whole formation, the nerve-sense system is the result of life prior to birth. Human beings receive the kind of nerve-sense system that conforms with their pre-earthly life. And it is just because the nerve-sense system's whole constitution has actually been raised above earthly matter that this system is suited to develop all the activity related to soul and spirit with detachment.

Exactly the opposite is true of the metabolic-limb system. Of all the three systems in the human being, this one is the most dependent on letting the natural processes continue in it, so that if we learn in physics and chemistry about the processes taking place on earth, we likewise learn about the processes that continue on into the human being insofar as he or she has a metabolic-limb system. But these processes tell us nothing about the laws governing the human nerve-sense system.

The rhythmic system lies between the two and brings about a natural balance, as it were, between the two extremes.

The fact is, however, that these things vary from individual to individual, particularly in children. The activity of one system always predominates over the others, and you have to do what is necessary to restore the balance. For that, you have to develop a potential for noticing how children express themselves, so that this reveals to you what you have to do with children to bring their health into complete balance.

In this regard, it is important to realize that you can produce a good effect on the nerve-sense system if you know the right amount of cooking salt that must be added to the children's food. If you notice, for instance, that a child is easily inclined to being inattentive and takes only a momentary interest in what you are teaching, in other words if this child is too sanguine or phlegmatic, you must see to it that sufficient formative forces are stimulated to enable him or her to pay more attention to the outside world. This is accomplished by the addition of salt. If you have children at school who are inattentive and only show a fleeting interest, you will be able to follow it up and find that their organism is not digesting salt properly.

If it is a severe case, it will often not suffice to advise that salt be added to the dishes. You will notice that either through ignorance or carelessness the child's parents put too little salt in the food, and you can be ready with advice. But it may also be that the organism as such rejects salt. This can be helped by giving lead compound in very low potency, for it is lead that stimulates the human organism to digest salt properly up to a certain level. If it goes beyond this level, it can make the organism ill, of course. It is a matter of bringing things to the right level, and to notice whether a child has, let me say, the first indications of a tendency to craniotabes [softness of the skull]. Many children have this. Then you know that the whole healing process must be brought into the directions I have just indicated.

It is a fact that many educational systems pay insufficient attention to things like this, for example, not even to the children's outer appearance. You could stand in front of a school and notice that some school children have large heads and others have small heads. As a rule the large-headed children are the ones who ought to be treated in the way I outlined above. The small-headed children will be treated differently, as I shall explain. A particularly large physical development of the head is a sign that indicates the defects of inattentive, phlegmatic characteristics. Then you have children with the opposite disposition, whose metabolic-limb system does not become involved strongly enough in the activity of the whole human being. Their metabolism functions organically, but these children do not spread their metabolic activity sufficiently throughout their whole organism. If you observe them outwardly, you notice that they like to brood, but that in turn they are irritated too much by external impressions and react to them too strongly. These children's whole organic system is improved if you see to it that they are given the proper amount of sugar.

Just have a look at the way children are brought up in the following direction: You find parents who, so long as their children are little, overfeed them with all sorts of candy and sweets. When they come to school these children will always be the sort who are preoccupied with themselves, psychologically, mentally, and therefore also physically; they begin to brood if they do not feel sufficient sweetness in their organism and become nervous and irritable when they do not receive enough sugar. You have to watch this, for if such children continuously receive too little sugar, their organism gradually goes to pieces. It becomes brittle, the tissues grow inflexible, and the organism eventually even loses the ability to digest sugar in the foods properly. You then have to see to it that sugar is added to the foods in the right way. It may happen, moreover, that the organism in a sense refuses to digest sweet things properly. Then you must come to its aid by administering minute dosages of silver.

Actually, for a teacher or educator, the child's whole life of mind and soul can become an indication of the proper or improper organization of the body. If a child shows too little inclination for discriminating ideation, if he or she muddles everything up and cannot distinguish properly, the nerve-sense system does not function properly. The trouble you have getting such a child to discriminate may at the same time be a symptom that the nerve-sense system is not functioning correctly, and you have to proceed with what I just said.

If children do not have sufficient ability for synthesized or constructive thinking, if they cannot form mental pictures of things, and if, particularly where art is concerned, they lack any skills, as is the case with lots of children nowadays, that is a symptom of the metabolic-limb system's being out of order, and one must help in the other direction, with sugar. It is indeed important that, even in the hygienic and therapeutic regard, you notice whether a child lacks either discriminating ideation or synthesizing, artistic ideation.

Now let's look at something else: Imagine you have a child who is obviously lacking in discriminating perception. This can be a sign that such a child diverts the astral body and ego too much from the nerve-sense organization. Then you have to see to it that the child in some way has his or her head cooled down, for instance, by giving it a cold sponge-bath every morning.

If the opposite is the case and the child is inartistic, lacks the synthesizing constructive element of perception, and does not react warmly to what you wish to teach, the astral body refuses to intervene properly in the metabolic-limb system. You must try to rectify this by seeing to it that at a suitable time the abdomen is thoroughly warmed through.

You cannot underestimate such things. They are extremely important. If a child has no ability at all for painting or for music, you should not regard it as a deviation into materialism to advise the parents to place a warm compress on the child's abdomen two or three times a week at bedtime, so that he or she stays warm during the night.

People nowadays are far too inclined to scorn measures taken on the material level and overestimate abstract, intellectual measures. But we should correct this false view by keeping in mind that divine powers make use of their spirit-minds in regard to earth by achieving all their aims in a material way. The divine spiritual powers cause it to be warm in summer and cold in winter. These are spiritual measures achieved through material means by divine-spiritual powers. If the gods tried, by means of education, intellectual or moral instruction, to achieve what they do achieve by making humankind sweat in summer and freeze in winter, it would be wrong. So you must not underestimate the effect of material means on children. We must keep these things constantly in mind.

Another symptom for the same organic defect, as I would like to call it, is that where synthesized thinking is lacking, children are pale. Children turn pale at school, and their paleness should be treated similarly to the way you treat the astral body that will not enter the metabolic-limb system properly. By the same means of applying warm compresses on the abdomen, you will produce a lessening of pallor, because you can actually cause the child's whole metabolic-limb system to get going, so that it then works more actively through all the systems of the organism.

If the metabolism develops too actively throughout the system, so that you only have to say some trifling thing and the child gets a red face and becomes very annoyed, that should be treated in exactly the same way as when the astral body and ego do not want to enter the nerve-sense system properly, and it is necessary to have the child's head washed in cold water in the mornings.

It is of utmost importance for the teacher to foresee the state of the child's health to a certain extent and to be able to take prophylactic steps. This is of course less rewarding than curing an actual illness, but in childhood it is far more important.

Under certain circumstances, it is important that, after having applied a healing process to the child's organism, you have to bring it to a halt again. You see, if you have been treating a child with lead for a while in the way I prescribed, you have to allow the whole process you have produced in the organism to heal over. So if you have administered lead to a child, and you have achieved your aim, it is a good thing to administer some copper compound for a short time, so that no residue of the process remains which had been produced by the lead.

If it has been necessary to treat the child with silver for a while, administer iron after that to allow the inner process to heal over.

I would like to add the following: If you notice that a child is losing herself in her organism, so to speak, it means that she does not have sufficient inner strength. Let us say the child has chronic diarrhea, or the movements of the limbs are clumsy; she flings her arms and legs around, and drops things when she tries to pick them up. These are the first signs of a process that will have a devastating effect on a person's health in later life. You should never disregard it if a child has diarrhea frequently or passes too much water, takes hold of things so awkwardly as to drop them, or shows any form of clumsiness in handling objects. Things like this should never be simply disregarded. A teacher should always keep a sharp lookout on whether the child holds a pen skillfully or unskillfully, or the chalk when writing on the blackboard. I could say, through such watchfulness the teacher works like a hygienic physician . I mention these things now because not much is gained by admonishing the child to do or not to do something. The only person who will have an effect is the one who constantly deals with his or her class.

On the other hand, you can achieve a lot by external therapeutic means. In a case like the above, give the child low doses of homeopathic phosphorus, and you will find that it will be comparatively easy for you to handle the child when you correct him or her in regard to clumsiness, indeed even the organic weakness I described. Administer phosphorus, or if the trouble lies deeper inside the organism and the child develops too much gas in the intestines, administer sulfur. If such a problem surfaces more externally, then the remedy should be a type of phosphorus. Advise the parents to add something that is found in the colored blossoms of plants to the child's food. Frankly speaking, if a child is a consistent bed-wetter, you will certainly achieve good results if you treat it with phosphorus, and, in regard to diet, suggest the addition of some mild paprika or pepper in the child's food for as long as it is necessary. This must be determined from the manner in which the child subsequently appears.

In matters of this kind it is really essential for teachers to cooperate in the right way. We are in the lucky position of having Dr. Kolisko as our physician in the faculty, and detailed indications should not be implemented without consulting him, for it is necessary to have had previous experiences in pharmaceutical-physiological matters if you are to arrive at a correct judgment. But it is necessary that every teacher should develop an eye for these things.

On occasions like this, dear friends, I must mention again and again that, above all, through instruction itself in the classes, you should see to it that the right relationship between nerve-sense system and metabolic-limb system is brought about. Any irregularity in the rhythmic system shows that the above are not properly related. If you notice the slightest irregularity in a child's breathing or circulation, you should pay attention to it at once, for the rhythmic system is an organic barometer for improper collaboration between head and metabolic-limb systems. As soon as something like this is noticed, you should immediately ask yourself what might be wrong in the two systems working together. Secondly—I won't go into the details of classroom therapy today, I would rather do that next time, today I will just say something on principle—you ought to realize clearly that in your lessons you must alternate in a suitable way between an element which draws children to the periphery of their bodies and an element that draws them into themselves.

A teacher who can instruct a class for two hours without once making the children laugh is a poor teacher, because he or she never causes the children to come to the surface of their bodies. A teacher who cannot, however gently, manage to touch the children's feelings so that they enter into themselves is also a bad teacher, for there must be an alternation between the one extreme of a humorous mood when the children laugh (they need not actually laugh, but be cheerful) and the other extreme of a mood of tragedy, emotion, and weeping (but they need not shed tears, just withdraw into themselves). It is necessary to bring ambience into the lessons. It is a therapeutic measure, this opportunity to bring atmosphere into teaching.

If you carry your own emotional weight into the lessons, however justified it may be in your private life, you really ought not to be a teacher. It is essential to bring children to the bodily periphery of experience. If you cannot do it in any other way, then at least try to tell them a funny story at the end of a lesson. If you have kept them hard at work in the most serious way throughout the whole lesson, so that they almost have a sort of skin cramp in their faces from having exerted their brains, at least tell them a joke at the end of the lesson. That is vital.

The earthly child and the cosmic child

from a lecture of June 13, 1921

published in *Education for Adolescents*

It is important to add the following to what we have by now observed in regard to an exploration of the nature of children. When studying children, we should try to see whether the cosmic organization predominates, something that becomes evident in the plastic forming of the head, or whether the earthly influence predominates, something that manifests in the plastic molding of the rest of the organism, notably the limbs. And then we will have to consider how best to treat the two types—the "cosmic" child and the "earthly" child.

In the case of the earthly children, we have to understand that much of the forces of heredity are present in them, and that these forces powerfully pervade the metabolic and limb system. We shall notice that, although these children may on the whole not be of a melancholic temperament, when we deal with them from a certain point of view and put questions to them, they frequently disclose a melancholic undertone beneath the surface of their general temperament. This melancholic undertone derives from the earthly element in their nature.

When we note this in children, we shall treat them appropriately if we try to introduce them to music that proceeds from the melancholic minor and passes over into the major—either by leading the minor into a major form or by presenting such a passage in an individual composition to the children. An earthly child can be spiritualized particularly by the demands made on the body by music and eurythmy. Especially where a general sanguine temperament prevails along with slight melancholic traits, painting can easily help the child. Even if such a child shows little talent for music and eurythmy, we must take the greatest pains to call forth the surely existing inclination for music and eurythmy.

In turn, when we deal with children with a clearly developed head organization, it is important to introduce them to reflective subjects such as history, geography, literature, and so forth. Here, we have to take into special consideration not to remain in the realm of mere contemplation. Instead, as I showed yesterday in another connection, we have to pass on to a presentation of the subject that can arouse certain moods of soul, such as tension and curiosity, that are then followed by relaxation or satisfaction, and so on.

Particularly in matters like these we must reacquire the habit to view the spiritual in harmony with the physical body. It is really true that the beautiful Greek conception that viewed the physical-corporeal in complete harmony with the soul-spiritual has been utterly lost. For the ancient Greeks, the influence of a work of art upon the human being was always something they observed as well from the bodily point of view. They spoke of the crisis of an illness, of "catharsis," in the same way they spoke of the effect of a work of art; they even spoke in the same terms of education. In fact, they observed the same process we referred to yesterday; and we shall really have to find our way back to such processes; we shall have to learn to bring together again in our thinking the soul-spiritual and the bodily-physical processes.

For this reason it is important for all of us to use all of the temperament qualities in ourselves in order to teach history to our children, imbuing our lessons with strong personal sympathies. The children will have time enough in later life for objectivity. To make our teaching entirely objective when we tell the children about Brutus and Julius Caesar, for instance, to refrain from showing any emotion in the picture we give of the contrasts, the difference between these two, is to teach history badly. We must certainly be involved, although there is no need to be excited and to rave about the situation, but openly exhibit a slight leaning toward sympathy or antipathy in regard to Brutus and Caesar when describing their story. Along with us, the children must be stimulated to feel what we feel. Above all, history, geography, geology, and subjects of this kind should be presented to the children with real feeling. Geology, for instance, becomes quite fascinating when the teacher has a deep, sympathetic understanding for the various rocks and stones he or she describes. In this connection one could recommend to all teachers to read Goethe's treatise on granite, entering into it with heart and soul. They would discover that, in entering into the world of nature not merely with thought but with their whole being, they are brought into a human relationship with that primordial patriarch, the sacred granite of remote antiquity. Of course, such an attitude must then be extended to other things.

If we develop this kind of approach to the subject in ourselves, we can reach the point of being able to let the children share in our experience. In many instances, such a method will naturally make things more difficult for us, and we shall have to work hard. But it is the only way to bring life into teaching and education. Fundamentally speaking, all that we impart by way of feelings fosters the growth of the children's own inner life, while what we give them merely in ideas is dead, and remains dead. Through conceptions, we give children nothing but reflected pictures; by teaching them conceptions, we work with the worthless human head, which, as we have seen, is of value only in relation to the prenatal past when it was in the spiritual world. In order to reach what is inherent in the blood and has significance here on earth, we need to teach children conceptions imbued with vibrant feeling.

The fantasy-rich child and the fantasy-poor child

from the lecture of June 15, 1921

published in *Education for Adolescents*

We can now carry these matters a little further. In our school, many different types of children are mixed together. We have children, for instance, who have little imagination, and others who have a great deal. We need not jump to the conclusion that half our children are poets and the other half are not. You notice this less through the actual unfolding of imagination than through the development of memory. Memory is closely related to the activity of fantasy. We deal with children—and we should observe that—who quickly forget the pictures of what they have experienced or have heard; the pictures disappear easily. We have other children for whom the pictures not only remain but acquire an independent power of their own; they keep coming up again and again, involuntarily. It is important to observe that these two types exist. Of course, there are all possible intermediate stages.

Suppose we deal with children who possess a wealth of imagination. This signifies simply that they have a memory that works so that pictures will arise again in transformed manner. More frequently, they do not arise in a transformed way but as reminiscences. In that case, the children are held captive, as it were, by what they have assimilated. And then there are those in whom it all disappears.

We need to know how to deal with these types of children in the right way. It is quite possible to occupy a group of children in various ways, if we acquire a routine in the best sense of the word, a routine in the spiritual sense. In children who have poor memory, children for whom the pictures do not readily arise, it is good to try to encourage them to be more observant while reading and to place greater value on listening to what has been narrated. In turn, when we see children who are captives of conceptions they have assimilated, so to speak, we should give greater consideration to writing, to what is outside, to what brings about movement. So, we should really try to occupy a larger group of children by giving about half of them who have little imagination the opportunity of cultivating reading and observation. (Of course this means only cultivating it a little more, for all this is relative.) In the case of children with abundant imagination, we should particularly cultivate painting and writing.

We can extend this still further. It is of particular importance that the following is observed—naturally, what I am suggesting can be implemented only gradually. Children who are poor in imagination, who do not easily bring up their memory-pictures, should preferably do eurythmy exercises standing still, meaning, with their arms. For those who are richer in imagination and liable to be tormented by their conceptions, it will be particularly beneficial to bring the whole body into motion through striding, treading, walking. Help can be given by these means, and it is most important that we truly observe such things.

We can furthermore add that eurythmy exercises with consonants are particularly helpful for children who are rather phlegmatic in bringing up their ideas; while for those who are bothered by their ideas, frequent eurythmy exercises with vowels are good. We can observe how vocalization of vowels by children calms the arising of ideas out of the organism, whereas that of consonants encourages the calling up of ideas. Thus, those children who are poor in imagination, who are not bothered by their conceptions and forget easily, should be made to do eurythmy exercises with consonants. Those who are plagued by ideas should do the eurythmy vowel exercises. When you pay heed to such things, you can introduce a lot to a group of children.

Here, I would like to add that in regard to music it is likewise of great benefit to gain an idea of the children's dispositions in respect of imagination—whether they have little or a great deal, and how this works over into memory. Where children are poor in imagination and find it hard to bring up their ideas, they should be occupied more with instrumental music; whereas children who are rich in imagination and are readily plagued by their conceptions, even to an extreme degree, should be involved in singing. The ideal plan would be, if only we had the necessary space, to have music lessons and singing lessons going on at the same time. A wonderfully harmonizing effect could be produced in children through the dual experiences of listening to music and making music. It might even come to the point were we could alternate between the two. It would be most significant, for instance, if we could let one half of the class sing while the other listens, and again, the other way round. This is something that would be exceedingly desirable and should be cultivated. For, when listening to music, a healing, therapeutic influence is exerted upon what the head is supposed to do to the organism; while when singing, this has a healing influence upon what the body is supposed to do for the head. Human beings would become far healthier if all that we should do in instruction could be done.

We are not at all sufficiently aware of the fact that in the course of evolution humanity has regressed. Once, human beings were so advanced that there was no particular need for instruction. The freedom of human beings was not interfered with in the way we do today. Nowadays, as soon as children are six years old, we begin to make inroads on their freedom. Having committed this offense against their freedom, we ought to make up for it by educating them in the right manner. We must clearly understand that we must improve the way we educate, for otherwise we approach a terrible state. People may boast all they want of the high standard of culture, of how few illiterates there are, and so on. But these "literates" are still only mere copies, automatons of what was prepared for them in school.

Treatment of left-handedness

The treatment for left-handedness is an important, constantly recurring theme in many Waldorf schools. Every school physician should be concerned with this question. As basic reading for this, the collection of indications by Rudolf Steiner on this theme are recommended. They are published in an instruction booklet for curative eurythmists. Furthermore, this subject is described in detail in the book *Das Schulkind*. A presentation that can be recommend as an introduction to these problems for parents is found in the book, *A Guide to Child Health*. For an introduction of neurophysiological principles of hemispheric dominance, attention is called to *Left Brain—Right Brain* by Sally Springer and Georg Deutsch.

In contrast to the present-day practice of giving children a "free hand" in everything, learning to write with the right hand is recommended in Waldorf schools. For learning to write with the right hand—without otherwise trying to influence the spontaneous use of the hands—changes nothing in regard to the dominance but leads to a strengthening of the right hand.

In recent years, Barbara Sattler has once again brought this way of proceeding into question through her publications about left-handedness (*Der umgeschulte Linkshänder* [Reeducation of left-handed children] Donauwörth 1996). However, in her writings, no arguments are raised that in any way can fundamentally place the managing of left-handedness as recommended here into doubt. In a Waldorf school, it is not a question of reversing a child's left-handedness. This is an ever-recurring misunderstanding. The concern is purely directed toward accustoming the child to the right hand in scholastic matters, meaning, to manage writing and form drawing with the right hand. Nothing whatsoever is changed in regard to the dominance of one side over the other in the child's brain. The hemispheric dominance remains completely intact and, in the case where cross dominance is present, can be developed to clear right- or left-sidedness with the help of therapeutic eurythmy exercises and other training in skills. Just as little as the right hemispheric dominance is changed in a right-handed violin player, when he or she touches the strings on the violin's finger-board in a masterly way with the fingers of the left hand, just as little is the left dominance changed in a child who learns to write with the right hand. The reasons why learning to write with the right hand is a helpful therapeutic support for the left-handed child's entire constitution, in light of an understanding of the whole human being, are to be found in the before-mentioned chapter on left-handedness in the book A *Guide to Child Health*. -

It is crucial, however, that learning to write with the right hand should only be started when there is agreement by the child, the teacher, and the parents. It is wonderful if a school physician can foster this understanding in the interest of the child. If such agreement cannot be reached, the child should be left free.

In the faculty meeting in Stuttgart on May 25, 1923, Rudolf Steiner responded as follows to the question of whether one should wean children from being left-handed:

As a rule, yes! While they are young, prior to age nine, left-handed children can still be accustomed to do all their school work with the right hand. It would only be correct not to do this if it could have harmful effects, something that is rarely the case. Children are not a simple sum but a complicated power. . . .

The phenomenon of left-handedness is a decidedly karmic phenomenon. In regard to karma, it is a phenomenon of karmic weakness. As an example: In the previous incarnation, a person has overworked himself. He overstrained himself not only physically or intellectually in his work, but in his whole life of soul. He brings a pronounced weakness into his following incarnation. He is not capable of overcoming this karmic weakness, which is now in the lower part of his being. (The part that arises from life between death and a new birth in human beings in the new incarnation is concentrated particularly in the lower part of their organization, whereas the part that arises from the previous life appears more in the head region.) What would otherwise develop strongly becomes weak, and to compensate for this, the left leg and the left hand are engaged to help. The preponderance of the left hand leads to the right frontal convolution of the brain's being engaged in speech instead of the left side.

If we give in to this too much, this weakness may persist into the following, the third, incarnation. If we do not give in to it, the weakness will be offset.

In the faculty meeting of December 18, 1923, Dr. Steiner said:

If you have children who are distinctly left-handed, you would have to make up your mind. In truly left-handed children, the hands appear as if reversed; the left hand looks like a right hand and has more lines than the right.

You can use the eyes to combat this. Make truly left-handed children look with both eyes at the top of their right arm, then let the ocular axes of the eyes move down the arm as far as the hand, and up again. Then the arm should be stretched out. Do this three times.

Rudolf Steiner recommends activation of the right hand in scholastic matters, meaning, for writing letters and numbers, not at all for artistic, practical, or other spontaneous activities. It is therefore not a question of a changeover from left to right, but of acquiring the faculty of writing with the right hand.

In order to add a practical example from a school physician's everyday activities in recent times, three case histories are reproduced, which Waldorf teacher Maria Theresia Pehm kindly placed at our disposal.

Left-handers learning to write with the right hand: Experiences from the first two years of school
Maria Teresia Pehm

At the end of the 1994 school year, it was decided that I would take on the next First Grade. When I became acquainted with the parents of my children at the first parent evening, the mother of Tobias approached me and spoke to me about her son's left-handedness. Immediately I listened intently. Nine years earlier, I had worked with Patricia to acquire the ability to write with her right hand. This had been accomplished without too many difficulties, although Patricia was a headstrong girl. Here I was challenged once again to deal with left-handedness. But it was strange that—just as in the pioneer situation nine years ago—neither a school physician nor a therapeutic eurythmist was available at the school as a helpful supporter.

While making a house visit prior to the beginning of the school year, I found that the parents were responding openly and courageously to my willingness to train Tobias in right-handed writing. They had two children in the school and were somewhat familiar with the ideas of Waldorf education, so I had given them the booklet, "The Problem of Left-Handedness." We agreed that they should make an appointment for Tobias to be examined by the former school physician. On principle, the doctor discouraged the parents from a changeover, but he said that if they really stood behind such a procedure, one could perhaps try it.

Subsequently, it turned out that in my small class of twelve children I had two additional left-handed children: Eva and Matthias.

After visiting Eva's home, the father told me they had attempted to get Eva to write with the right hand and that this had been quite hard for Eva to do. They would rather not risk it again, especially since she was a delicate, melancholic child. And the doctor likewise tried to discourage it. Matthias's mother told me she wanted to accept her child the way he was, and not try anything else. No visit to a doctor took place.

With some regret I accepted the decisions and concentrated on Tobias. On the first and second day of school I waited, but on the third day I said to the children after the rhythmic part of the lesson:

"Some children in our class have come from heaven in such a way that they do many things with their left hand, things that most people do with their right hand. These children may learn to write, however, with the right hand if they want to. I know from Tobias that he wants to do it. He moreover has a Dad who, although he is left-handed, has likewise learned to write with his right hand. Now I will help Tobias with this and all the other children with me when he does a few special exercises every day. But Eva and Matthias will learn to write with the left hand."

I called Tobias to the back of the class where we had our space for movement. All the children were allowed to turn their chairs around and they watched us with great attention.

First Exercise:

Right arm and right hand stretched out to the front, take one step with the right foot, bring the left foot forward level with the right foot while I say the words: With the right hand I want to write. Then place the left arm and hand on the back; the right arm and hand remain [hanging down] at the side of the body. Take one step backward with the left foot, then bring the right foot back level with the left foot while I say, "With the left, I let it go."

To begin with, I alone said the sentence—as a sort of substitute ego —later, the child spoke along with me or even alone. I had this exercise done once.

Second Exercise:

Hopping on the right foot, the left foot lifted up at an angle, and the right arm stretched forward, Tobias approached me while I said in a rhythmical manner,

"That is the writing hand. Show me your writing hand." And then I lovingly grasped the hand he stretched out to me. I had this exercise done twice.

Third Exercise:

Right arm and hand is stretched out, the left hand moves forward along the back of the right arm, then back along the underside, lovingly caressing the arm and hand. I had this exercise done three times.

After a while the other children wanted to do this too and from then on I let all the children take part.

Fourth Exercise:

Prior to any activity (form drawing or writing), Tobias takes a little amethyst in his left hand.

Tobias's first forms done with the right hand,on the blackboard and on the paper, came out surprisingly well. In the course of the second week he made tremendous progress. With concentration and almost self-confidently he worked with his right hand, rarely did the piece of chalk or crayon slip into the left hand. I generously acknowledged and praised his efforts.

In the third week of form drawing, Tobias almost always drew well balanced forms. One day he suddenly said, "I don't need the gemstone anymore." From then on, he only had it in his left hand during the beginning of the work he was doing.

From my journal: Fifth school week. Tobias has succeeded in the adjustment to using his right hand as his writing hand. The initial two weeks with his first letters solidified his adjustment. With enthusiasm Tobias draws his letter pictures with his left hand, paints with the left and writes with his right hand. For his words, he can already stay on a straight line and he adjusts the size of small and large letters. In regard to the hopping exercise, Tobias definitely tries hard now to jump toward me while retaining a pleasing, upright posture and not getting into a rush. At first he always wanted to be the first but now no longer feels the need. Tobias is developing splendidly.

And now to Eva: On the third school day, I mentioned that she was among those children who could do the most with their left hand. Like all the other children, she watched as Tobias did his three exercises. When it was her turn to draw a vertical line on the board, I asked her whether she wanted to write with the right hand or with the left. She answered clearly and certainly, "With the right hand." "Really?" I asked. "Yes," she affirmed. "Well, in that case you will receive a gemstone for your left hand."

It soon became evident that Eva had a harder time than Tobias. As a rule, her forms on paper did not look beautiful. She was rarely able to finish drawing the form in its entirety, could not align her will in the direction of doing this, but was not unhappy about that. She needed a good deal of encouragement and objective recognition when she did make progress. Her parents felt that they were thrown off guard by this, but took note of their daughter's decision without any protest. They were aware of little Eva's willfulness. They even supported my efforts, because it was out of the question for them to vacillate back and forth. At the end of the third week I began a notebook of their own with each child. In it I had them draw forms on the left side with the left hand, on the right side with the right hand. In Eva's case it could clearly be noted that she had achieved more clarity and certainty with the right hand in tracing lines (despite her awkwardness). She herself critically took note of that.

In writing, Eva developed a delicate but rather clear line. Words began to look surprisingly uniform. In the fifth week, Eva told me she no longer needed the gemstone.

Eva had less difficulty than Tobias with the numbers. She rarely wrote them on the wrong side of the page.

When I asked Matthias on the third day of school which hand he preferred to write with, the clear reply was, "With the left one!" And so it remained until Monday of the second school week. He suddenly took the crayon into his right hand and, as if it were a matter of course, drew his vertical lines. My question of whether he now wanted to write with the right hand was answered with a mischievous smile in the affirmative.

From then on he joined Tobias and Eva in their exercises and did them with obvious pleasure. His mother, a primary schoolteacher, felt offended. It was difficult for her to accept all this. But she restrained herself so as not to disturb the process that was going on between me and the class and Matthias.

Matthias was the only child, who, during the testing that I did with him, carried out everything with the left hand or at most with both hands. Matthias was not really at home in his body, particularly not in his limbs. He lived in it as though in a glove that was much too big. I expected an improvement in his degree of incarnation from all these constant efforts of will. Matthias truly did not find it easy to write with his right hand; it obviously cost him a good deal of effort, but he himself wanted to do it. When I observed him writing with the left now and again, and called his attention to it, he never reacted with displeasure or annoyance. His mother began to support him in a loving way. Still, she was unsure of whether we were doing the right thing. After about half a year I consulted with Dr. Michaela Glöckler, giving her a detailed description of my pupil and copies of his work. I was definitely encouraged in my intentions.

Matthias's further development in the first and in the second school year was quite satisfactory. He received the following report-card verse:

My body is the house of my soul,

  it dwells within it, goes in and out.

My mouth is the gate of my soul,

  in words, my soul goes forth.

The eyes are two tiny windows.

Through the eyes the sun shines in.

Servants, strong I have four:

Two hands and two feet of my own.

They help me at the first command,

  they carry me anywhere in the land.

But he could only say his verse while twitching and swaying to and fro. In January of 1996 he became quite ill with chickenpox. Afterwards he could recite this verse with handsome composure. His handwriting progressed amazingly, both upper and lower case Roman letters in autumn, as well as cursive script after Easter.

In autumn of the second school year, all three children had initial difficulties with right-handed form drawing. The right-left symmetries were likewise rather difficult for them. But they got into the writing of the small letters very quickly and well. The thick wooden pencils were a great relief for these children. They got a big kick out of writing and showed themselves to be just as skilled at this as the right-handers. Learning to write in the cursive style was also no problem. Tobias had the most difficulty in acquiring smoothness, Matthias had it easiest, but this was perhaps due to their temperaments.

Now, at the end of the second school year, I make bold to say that the endeavor with all three children was successful. At Easter time of the first school year, I had been assigned another left-handed writer, who in the public school likewise had learned to write with the right hand without any particular support. But he has not yet achieved the same level as the other three children.

What actually motivated me to take on this challenge? When I think it over, only one indication held up, namely, the one of the karmic weakness that I as a teacher can help to balance out. To be sure, this demands a good deal of courage and persistence. For one does not have undivided support even from the staff or from the physicians. And even the media writes only about left-handed children who, when they had to learn to write with the right hand, sustained dramatic damage—something that is no surprise considering the fast-paced method of teaching writing in the public schools.

It is very important to me to make it clear that learning to write with the right hand is not a reversal, but in fact, the acquisition of a new capacity. The children still do all the other activities with their left hand as they are used to do. It is moreover important constantly to bear these children in mind in a loving way, to encourage them and not to be sparing in objective and heartfelt praise. Anxiety or passivity on the part of the teacher or parents, an attitude of "It isn't so bad" have their effect, just as much as do courage, carefulness, and the attitude of taking the process in which the child becomes involved absolutely seriously.

It goes without saying that one has to remain in constant contact with the parents in order to exchange observations concerning the physical and mental development of the child. I have not involved the parents of the school as a whole in this process so as to maintain a certain area of protection for the children. Even with all the courage I had, and aside from the idea of destiny, I was glad to have the support of Dr. Glöckler that backed me up. Her contributions in both *A Guide to Child Health* and *Das Schuldkind* [The schoolchild] have been a great help to me and the parents in developing an awareness for all this.

The question remains open as to what can be done so that resistance against the training of right-handed writing does not increase even more among school faculties, and indeed, even among school physicians.

❖   ❖   ❖

The form drawings and writing samples on the next two pages were all done with the right hand. They clearly demonstrate how different and individual the interplay was between parents, teachers, the school physician, and the child in each case. They furthermore demonstrate that courage, trust, and persistence are necessary. When these faculties receive support, the children's self-confidence grows. They achieve a victory that strengthens their forces of will and perseverance.

Left:
Tobias
First grade form drawing

Right:
Tobias
First grade writing

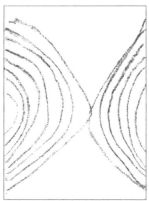

Left:
Tobias
Second grade
dynamic drawing

Right:
Tobias
Writing
End of second grade

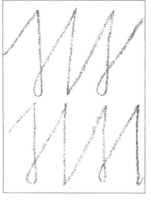
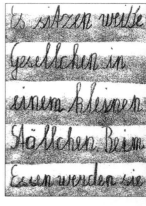

Left:
Eva
First grade form drawing

Right:
Eva
First grade writing

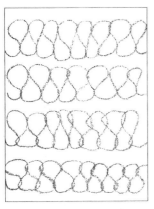

Left:
Eva
Second grade
Dynamic drawing

Right:
Eva
Writing
End of second grade

Left:
Matthias
First grade
Form drawing

Right:
Matthias
First grade
Writing the first word

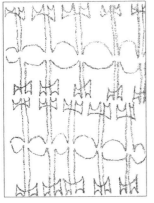

Left:
Matthias
Second grade
Dynamic form drawing

Right:
Matthias
Writing
End of second grade

Educating practical life experience
through dexterity exercises

Rudolf Steiner explains in the fourth lecture (August 15, 1924) of *The Kingdom of Childhood*:

One can moreover go on to allow children to become skillful through their own being in graphic imaginative thinking by saying: Touch your right eye with your left hand! Touch your right eye with your right hand! Touch your left eye with your right hand! Show me your left shoulder with your right hand from behind; your right shoulder with your left hand! Show me your left ear with your right hand! Show me your left ear with your left hand! Show me the big toe of your right foot with your right hand! and so on. You can thus have children do all kinds of funny exercises on themselves. Another example, "Make a circle with your right hand around the left! Make a circle with your left hand around the right! Make two circles formed by both hands into one another! Make two circles with one hand in one direction and the other hand in the other direction. Have the children do this faster and faster. Or: Quickly move the middle finger of your right hand! Quickly move the thumb of the right hand! Quickly move the little finger."

This is how one has children do all kinds of exercises on their own bodies with quick presence of mind. What is the result of such exercises? When children around the age of eight do them, they learn how to think— to think for the rest of their lives. Learning to think directly through the head is not the kind of thinking that will last for life. It makes you "tired of thinking" later on. If, on the other hand, with quick presence of mind, you have to do movements on your own body which require that you must think about them, you will become wise later on in life. One will be able to observe a connection between a person's wisdom at age thirty-five or thirty-six, and the exercises that person did as a child of six or seven. This is how different epochs of life are connected with each other.

In the decades after Rudolf Steiner gave this advice to the Waldorf teachers, a lot of research has been done in neurophysiology that confirms these recommendations exactly. Familiarization with the body's pattern and such activities as sensory integration exercises aim to support orientation in one's body, and simultaneously, orientation in space, as well as coordinated use of the sense functions. This is the basic prerequisite for a clear, mobile conceptual faculty. Here, too, the law of metamorphosis of growth forces into thought activity applies. The intelligent behavior that the body has acquired metamorphoses, along with the liberated formative forces, into the corresponding capacities of thought. Implementation of these exercises has especially far-reaching effects between the ages of seven and nine—just at the age when, along with the transformation in the body to that of school child and the onset of the change of teeth, the formative growth forces become free. If such exercises are carried out with the whole class in the rhythmic portion of the main lesson or at the beginning of speech instruction, less gifted children and those in need of special assistance do not constantly feel that they need something extra. They can do the necessary activities particularly directed at them along with all the other children for whom it is also an educational exercise appropriate for this age. When these exercises are carried on in remedial instruction in a more intensive and regular manner, this of course strengthens the effect.

With regard to this, Rudolf Steiner said the following at the June 14, 1920 faculty meeting in Stuttgart, in response to a question as to whether a certain child ought be transferred to the remedial class:

I don't think it is possible. Especially in first grade you should not go too far in segregating some children by placing them in a remedial class. I have seen it done—that is true—but on the other hand not so terribly much is lost if a child still writes badly in first grade. Of course, all children like this would benefit immensely, if you could manage to do the kind of exercises with them that I inaugurated originally.

If you do something like this with them (Dr. Steiner demonstrated an exercise): Pass the right hand over your head and grasp your left ear. Or they will gain a lot if you have them draw something like a spiral moving inward, a spiral moving to the right and a spiral moving to the left, exercises like these through which children have to move into thinking.

Regarding writing, there are a few who write very badly and a lot who are first-rate. The children will not gain much from your telling them they will learn to write better if they improve their handwriting. Make their fingers skillful! Then they will learn to write better.

I do not think that you can manage to improve a child's poor handwriting through efforts to write better. You have to make efforts to help children to become more skillful in form drawing. If they would play the piano they would learn to write better. It is a correct observation that truly bad handwriting arose at the same time as children's toys became so extraordinarily materialistic. It is really shocking that a large segment of toys consists of boxes of building blocks. This sort of thing should not be a toy at all because it is atomistic. If a child had a simple forge, the point would be to work at it. I should like to have moving toys for children. [This relates to movable picture books, where the child has to pull on threads or some other device in order to cause a change in the picture.]

That is mentioned in *Education of the Child*. Toys are awfully bad nowadays, and that is why children do not learn finger agility any longer and write poorly.

It would be sufficient if one were to prompt children who have bad handwriting to draw quite simple forms with their feet. Of course, this cannot be done at school. This has a good effect on the hand. Small circles, semi-circles and triangles should be drawn with the feet. They should hold a pencil with their big toe and the toe next to it and draw circles. It isn't easy to do it, but it is interesting. It is difficult to acquire a skill in this, but it is interesting to do it. It would be a good thing to have children draw figures with a stick outside in the sand with their toes; that has a strong effect on the hand. Or let a child pick something up with his foot. Picking up a handkerchief with the foot instead of the hand works quite strongly. I won't say that they must eat with their feet. But you must understand that you cannot do it systematically. You must try not to be directly concerned with correcting the writing, but by making them skillful in drawing artistic forms, achieving symmetry through a complicated form. (Turning to a teacher): Marking the beat is a good thing for developing rational and logical forms.

By now the close relationship between development of movement and development of intelligence has been thoroughly researched. It is all the more astounding that dealing with children in this regard in practice has been so inconsistent. Mechanical toys become more and more complex. Children are encouraged to be spectators or to do cognitive exercises on a computer. Movement continues to decrease so that exercises in movement and active play are considered therapy and no longer denote the normal life of a child. School physicians should view this as a challenge to speak up publicly for the right of children to experience healthy development in movement.

Nutrition—Interest—Consciousness

Ehrenfried Pfeiffer recalls Rudolf Steiner's telling him in conversation that the difficulty of attaining to a spiritual world conception encountered by humanity today is a question of nutrition:

> In this conversation Rudolf Steiner first referred to the necessity of a deepening of esoteric life, and in this connection indicated certain faults typically found in spiritual movements. Pfeiffer then asked: Why is it that despite your detailed and numerous indications, the spiritual impulse and particularly the inner path of schooling bear so little fruit in individuals? Why do the people concerned give so little evidence of spiritual experience despite all their efforts? Why, above all, in spite of theoretical insight, is the will for action, for successfully carrying out these spiritual impulses, so weak? Pfeiffer was especially anxious to receive an answer to the question as to how one could build a bridge to active participation and implementation of spiritual intentions without being pulled off the right path by personal ambition, illusions, and petty jealousies—for these were the three negative qualities Rudolf Steiner had named as the main inner hindrances. Then came the memorable and surprising reply: This is a problem of nutrition. Nutrition as it is today no longer supplies the strength to human beings that is needed to manifest spirit in matter. A bridge can no longer be built from thinking to will and deed. Edible plants no longer contain the forces they are supposed to give to human beings.

> A problem of nutrition which, if solved, would enable the spirit to become manifest and be realized through human beings! With this remark as a background, one can understand why Rudolf Steiner said that the benefits of the biodynamic compost preparations should be made available as quickly as possible, to the largest possible expanse of land, for healing the earth.

In his *Agriculture*, Rudolf Steiner coins a new spiritual concept of nutrition. We human beings do not merely consume solid and liquid food. We also nourish ourselves more or less consciously by way of our senses and by the thoughts we consume and digest. Rudolf Steiner's concept of nourishment takes this into consideration inasmuch as he speaks of cosmic nourishment (assimilation through the system of nerves and senses) as opposed to earthly/physical nourishment (absorption by way of the metabolic system). The paths that these two kinds of nourishment take in the human organism are polar opposites. The earthly substances we absorb along with food and metabolize by way of the metabolic system create the basis for developing the substance of the nerves-and-senses system. What we assimilate, on the other hand, through the system of nerves and senses condenses to the substance required by the metabolic and limb system.

The opposite applies in regard to the form of the absorbed substance. Mineral, plant, and animal foods have a certain structure and originate from the specific form-processes of these kingdoms of nature. Correspondingly, everything that is assimilated by way of our sense activity and thinking has a particular form or physiognomy. Rudolf Steiner describes how the formative forces of this cosmic nourishment do indeed unite with the forces of physical nutritive matter and maintain the nerves-and-senses system with substance. Conversely, it is the formative forces of physical nutrition in conjunction with the substances of cosmic nourishment that are decisive for the synthetic processes in the metabolic and limb system.

This means that physical diet plays the decisive role in nourishing those organs on which consciousness is based, and with that, the degree of alertness and attention in students. Again, inversely, school offers much in the way of cosmic substance—meaning, when sensory functions and ensuing thought activity are richly nourished, something in turn is required for the development of the metabolic and limb system. Seen from this viewpoint, Rudolf Steiner's statement above that materialism is a problem of nutrition must be considered in a yet more differentiated manner. For this certainly refers not only to physical but likewise to cosmic nourishment. But what is the condition of nourishment by way of the senses in the case of children today? Do they have sufficient opportunity to work with their senses, individually and in combination? Are there enough moments when an adult has the time to observe something in a leisurely way with a child? Isn't our age, all too frequently hurried and alienated from nature, more of a schooling for inattentiveness? Does it not cut us off from experiencing the light, color, sound, and touch of the cosmos? And what about the art of conversation, the receiving of meaningful thoughts, of essence and substance?

On the other hand, due to the difficult economic condition in Germany following World War I at the beginning of the 1920s, many children were undernourished. The concerns of Rudolf Steiner and the school physicians were therefore directed to this aspect of dietary questions. We have a description here, where Rudolf Steiner traces the children's frequent tiredness and lack of interest to problems of nutrition. [*Soul Economy and Waldorf Education*, lecture of January 6, 1922.]

What has to be watched very closely, on the one hand, is the interest that children—not only beings of soul and spirit but beings possessing body, soul, and spirit—show not merely for themselves, but for their environment. One has to develop an instinctive awareness for the child's interest or the lack thereof. This represents one aspect. The other is fatigue in children.

What is the origin of a specific development of interest? It originates from the metabolic and limb system, particularly from the metabolic system. Say that a child loses interest in one or the other direction, let us say in matters involving mental activities—and this is the most obvious case—or he or she shows a lack of interest for outer activities, no longer wishing to take part in games or similar pursuits. Say that he or she even loses interest in tasty foods, the worst sign of all, for children should above all be interested in how foods taste and should, in their own way, differentiate between the various tastes of foods. If a child suffers from a loss of appetite (and a loss of appetite is lack of interest in food), then we must realize: The cause lies in the wrong diet. The diet makes too great a demand on the child's digestive system. I have to find out to what extent a particular child with his or her specific organization is given too many foods of relatively little nutritive value, foods that burden the digestive system too much. Just as I infer the weather from reading the barometer, I deduce from the lack of interest that the diet is wrong. I have to realize that a child's interest or the lack thereof are all-important in regard to the measures that have to be taken in relation to diet.

At present, much more attention is given to questions of diet than was the case in the 1920s. On the other hand, with the onset of modern agricultural chemistry and genetic engineering, which is now increasingly being used, the quality of foods is put into question today as never before. The fact alone that vegetables are not just planted in their natural environment but can be cultivated almost anywhere with the help of fertilizers, pesticides, and hothouses—without any consideration for their original habitat and ecological needs—makes it clear that such plants can no longer assimilate cosmic forces in the same way as the same plants do in their natural location.

In addition, since parents often lack time and money to be concerned about vegetables grown in a healthy manner, the school has the important task of seeing to it that nourishing foods are offered during recess and that, if at all possible, a school kitchen is set up. There are many Waldorf schools where a school kitchen was instituted as a parent initiative. Here the school physician has the important task of making such parental initiatives possible. More work needs to be done to show the importance of a healthy diet for schoolchildren.[21]

Homework: Whom does it serve?

This title is admittedly provocative. It is certainly true that, in many cases, parents and teachers view homework as indispensable. It gives them the reassuring feeling that a child is working and really learning something.

A school physician frequently arrives at a quite different perspective. Often problematic or unwell children in a class are the ones who have difficulty with homework and require a great deal of time for it, time that could be spent on play and physical activity. Furthermore, something that has been explained to them at school in one way is often explained at home or by a remedial teacher in another way. This in turn can cause more difficulties at school. In addition, during visits in school, one can frequently hear from students that it is not until they return home that they write something properly into their notebook, while in school they merely make a rough draft. The reason given is that one can concentrate better at home because it is quieter than in class. But, in school, those children are often the ones who engage in all sorts of foolishness during the lesson, not helping the work proceed in a concentrated, quiet fashion. It would be ideal if the students would truly work in concentrated ways at school, while at home they would have as much time as possible for initiatives of their own: playing, hiking, or other physical, musical, and rhythmic activity.

Rudolf Steiner spoke in a number of faculty meetings about this thorny subject. A few characteristic remarks are quoted here:

A teacher inquires about coping with subjects of instruction and about homework.

Dr. Steiner: Homework should be done on a voluntary, not on a compulsory basis: Whoever wants to do it! [Faculty Meeting of January 1, 1920.]

A teacher: I wanted to ask a question about teaching algebra. It seems to me it would be good to give the students homework. It appears to be especially obvious here that children ought to be doing sums at home.

Dr. Steiner: We must focus on the principles that result from a sound education. A fundamental principle is that we must be certain that the children do their homework, seeing to it that not doing it never happens. Homework should not be assigned unless you know that the children are eager to return the finished work to you. Animated life should enter into doing such work; an activity should be aroused that would not paralyze the children's mental attitude. One way of doing it would be to list certain tasks arising from a subject you have presented to them, and to tell them, Tomorrow I will deal with the following kind of calculations. And then you wait and see whether the children are willing to do the preparatory work. Some will do that, and that will make the others want to do it too. Children should be motivated to do what they ought to do for school because they want to do it. It should come from the children's own willingness to do something from one day to the next.

A teacher: Can't we give them exercises in multiplication, etc., too?

Dr. Steiner: Only in this way. It is the same in other subjects; there too, we have any number of tasks. Then we have the problem of pale children. What we must aim for is to master the instructive material so well that outside of the time spent on it in class we need nothing.

A teacher: I wanted to ask what we could do following the end of the math lesson.

Dr. Steiner: If you notice tiredness at the end, change to easier exercises. There you could do what you expect, what you anticipate, from homework.

A teacher: I have not had the impression that working harder at math tires the children.

Dr. Steiner: All the same, it is not desirable to keep children working with the same intensity for two hours. You can advise the children, you can give them suggestions of doing this or that at home, but not in the form of making the demand of bringing it [to school], not requiring homework as an obligation. [Faculty Meeting of September 11, 1921.]

On the other hand, we must also bear in mind that homework should be done willingly, with pleasure. A need must be felt to achieve this. [Faculty Meeting of December 9, 1921.]

Motivation is decisive for the whole question of homework, or put another way—as Rudolf Steiner said in the faculty meeting of September 11, 1921—the work that is done at home *should be done willingly, with pleasure. A need must be felt to achieve this*." And this, too, is part of a school physician's everyday task to see with what enthusiasm the children show the teacher what they have done at home for school. Even if they have spent considerable time on it and did it with eagerness and joy, one's most favorable impression is when one watches the children proudly show or present what they have attained.

In conclusion, an in-depth study of the subject of homework by Dietrich Wessel[22] shows that the problem of homework has been under discussion as early as the Latin schools of the fifteenth century. In relation to homework, the school physician's position is one of giving advice and protecting the students—of the lower grades, in particular— from too much homework. It is even quite useful—based on medical indications in a particular case—to discontinue homework for a time.

Education between preexistence and post-existence

Less than a year after the founding of the Waldorf School in Stuttgart, Rudolf Steiner spoke in the faculty meeting of July 24, 1920 about the demeanor of the teacher in regard to the children in view of the fact that the children have dwelt in the spiritual world more recently than the teachers and could therefore be the teachers' teacher. This later descent of the students signifies that they bring something like a message out of the spiritual world which the teacher can only experience through them. Rudolf Steiner said that the teachers can say to themselves:

We have descended from the spiritual world into the physical world at a particular time. Those who face us as children descended later. They dwelt in the spiritual world for a little longer period, while we were already here in the physical world. If you see in the child an entity who bears something out of the spiritual world that you yourselves have not experienced in the spiritual world because you are older, this is something that really warms your heart, something that profoundly affects the soul. Besides, this state of being older signifies for us something else. With each child, we receive a message from the spiritual world concerning things we no longer had experienced there.

This awareness of a message that the child brings down is a positive feeling that in complete earnestness can take its place among the teachers of the Waldorf School who are there to fight the downward current of the cultural course of events. Traditional religious confessions do this as well. Sermons are preached from all the pulpits on eternity, postmortem eternity. That is the eternity that people look toward with refined egotism in their souls because they do not wish to perish. The human being does not perish, of course, but the point is how we arrive at the conviction of an eternal soul. The point is whether we come to this conviction out of egotism or out of a vital perception. Here, standing within this kind of view in a living way, we learn to look upon the soul's preexistence. We look upon what the human being has experienced before birth. We look upon the human being here in the physical world and how human life is a continuation of what was previously experienced. . . .

Such considerations become practical when we say: These children have come down out of the spiritual world later than I. Out of what they bring toward me in the way they live, I can surmise what happened in the spiritual world after I myself had left that world. To carry this as a living feeling within us is a fitting meditation for the teacher, a meditation of great and powerful significance. And through such a definite expression of the being of anthroposophy, we truly become what teachers are who work based on the spirit of anthroposophy.

What do children and young people bring today in the way of messages out of the spiritual world? How do we learn to interpret properly their frequently provocative and difficult behavior, so that it gives us insight into what they are looking for and what they are dissatisfied with? As soon as you begin to live with such questions, you look with a different eye upon the increasingly difficult conditions of education. Marianne Altmeier, an anthroposophical art therapist in Germany, tried to approach this challenging behavior through individual therapy, through mutual silence during the artistic work and through speaking at the right moment, and thus managed to arrive at soul processes and questions that lay hidden deeply behind the outer behavior. Anyone who has ever worked in child psychiatry knows of the horrendous case histories that often must be brought up. Regardless of whether destructive rage, aggressiveness, lying, or even depression and hopelessness come to expression in the previous case history, all too often, when you are face to face with such a child or young person, you cannot even detect all the horror in him or her. Instead, he or she may look at you in a questioning or help-seeking manner. Frequently, what happens is that, under these different conditions of life, through the therapist's intensive care, the child's condition changes within a few weeks or months to the degree that much of what disturbed the mind of the child or youth, what caused inner dissatisfaction, was brought to his or her awareness to the extent that a change became possible and a healing process was initiated. One thing is for sure: No difficulty is so great that it could not be overcome if a supportive human relationship comes about through which the child or young person can feel understood and accepted.

Here too, a faculty meeting has the task to consider question upon question. How can one direct the powerful need that many children possess to have an intense connection with technology so that this does not lead to a dependency on technical things? How can the profound longing for self-representation, the experience of identity through artistic expression, be satisfied so that it does not lead to dependency on drugs and/or the modern music scene? How can the inner nature of children and young people receive enough nourishment so that they awaken to [the potential of] their own inner creative forces and do not experience them merely surrogate-like in the multimedia culture?

Or what must happen during the time in school so that, under certain circumstances, all this is put on hold for the rest of the biography, to come fully to development only in the following life on earth? How many Waldorf school students become involved in or seek out circumstances of life in which perhaps nothing can be developed further of the predisposition given them in school. Particularly in a materialistic civilization such as ours, built on egotism, certain perceptions, insights, artistic and religious activities can only be given to the coming generation during the precious years in school as a gift for their life. All too often, they are forgotten or the adolescents distance themselves from them. Still, they are taken along inwardly as an asset of a purely human experience, never to be lost. Rudolf Steiner, for instance, speaks about music and its effect upon life after death as follows [*Balance in Teaching*, lecture of September 16, 1920]:

After death, human beings still wear their astral body for a time. So long as this is the case and until the latter is laid aside completely—you are familiar with this from my book, *Theosophy*—there still exists a sort of recollection, just a sort of memory of earthly music in a human being after death. Thus it comes about that the musical experiences we receive during our life here continue to reecho like a memory of music after death—until about the time the astral body is laid aside. Then the earthly music is transformed in the life after death into the "music of the spheres," and remains as such until some time prior to the new birth.

This matter will be more comprehensible to you if you know that what human beings receive here on earth in the way of music plays an important role in the shaping of their soul-organism after death. It is shaped there during the period of kamaloka. This is the beneficial feature of the time of kamaloka, and we can cause this period—called purgatory by the Roman Catholics—to be easier for human beings if we know that. Of course, we cannot relieve them of their perception there, they must have it, for otherwise they would remain imperfect if they could not observe the imperfect things they have done. But we furnish a possibility that the human entity will be better formed in its next life if, during that time after death when it still has its astral body, it can have many recollections of things musical.

Considerations such as these open up completely new dimensions of preventive medicine. During the school years, children can learn to incarnate themselves, with all that they bring along in the way of karmic burdens and strengths out of previous lives. At the same time, the ground is laid in the child for the possibility to prepare worthily for the great crossing of the other threshold—death. With this as the background, celebrations of the annual festivals in the school, the enormous efforts that are made in practicing for a concert or the preparation of a theater presentation are seen in quite a new light. And particularly now that, due to the five-day-week, there is the danger that there will be cancellations of some instruction and one or the other extras deemed not absolutely necessary, it is the task of the school physician to be solidly understanding of the consequences to the human being. Wherever possible, he or she should speak out of this awareness and support the teachers in their efforts to justify the important subjects to the parents. Much has to be worked out and substantiated anew today in terms of knowledge of the human being in order that it does not literally fall by the wayside due to the pressures of the increasingly difficult conditions of our modern age, reduced financial resources, and simple lack of time.

In conclusion, let us recall the remarks by Rudolf Steiner where he represents love as the primal source of insight for education, and describes the perception of the child that we can attain through love [*Human Values in Education*, lecture of July 17, 1924].

Then, filled with holy awe and reverence, you may ask: What is it that works its way to the surface here? And heart and mind are led back to the soul-spiritual of the human being itself that existed in the soul-spiritual pre-earthly world from which it has descended into the physical world. And you tell yourself: You, child, now that you have entered through birth into earthly existence, you are among human beings, but previously you were among spiritual-divine beings. What once lived among spiritual-divine beings has descended in order to be among human beings! We see the divine made manifest in the child. We feel as though we stand before an altar. But there is one difference. On the altars that are customary in religious communities, human beings make offerings to the gods so that these offerings may ascend to the spiritual world; here we feel ourselves standing as it were before a reversed altar. Here the gods allow their grace to stream down in the form of divine-spiritual beings, so that these beings, acting as messengers of the gods, may unfold what is essentially human on the altar of physical life. We behold in every child the unfolding of cosmic laws of a divine-spiritual nature; we see how God creates in the world. We behold this in the child in its highest, most significant form. Then every single human child becomes for us a sacred riddle, for every child embodies this great question—not, How should we educate it so that, in accordance with the way we have thought it up, it comes close to being a sort of idol? but, How should we foster what the gods have sent down to us into the earthly world? We learn to recognize ourselves as helpers of the divine-spiritual world, and above all we learn to ask: What can happen if we approach instruction and education with this attitude of mind?

CHAPTER 6

Weekly Schedules and Results of Research on Rhythm

Despite the many professional and personal pressures on the teachers, one of the most important tasks of the school physician is to help a hygienic schedule come into being. Particularly in our present time, where there are ever more complaints about disciplinary problems and difficulties of giving any meaningful instruction, we ought to tackle the question of the schedule once again with all the energy and strength at our disposal. The importance of this task becomes evident in the concern and time that Rudolf Steiner applied to his remarks about questions of formulating the schedule from all different aspects. The following characteristic remarks are published in *Human Values in Education* (lecture of July 21, 1924):

> If we wish to educate, we must have plenty of elbow room. But this is not provided in a school run in the customary way according to the dreadful timetable: Religious instruction from 8:00 to 9:00; gymnastics from 9:00 to 10:00; history from 10:00 to 11:00; arithmetic from 11:00 to 12:00. All the later instruction blots out the earlier. One cannot accomplish anything. Teachers are driven to despair if, in spite of this, they have to have results. This is why we have what may be termed teaching periods in the Waldorf School. The child comes to a class. Every day during main lesson, which continues for the best part of the morning, from 8:00 to 10:00 or from 8:00 to 11:00, with short breaks for recreation, the child is taught one subject. This is taught by one teacher, even in the upper grades. The subject is not changed hour by hour. It is continued for as long as is deemed necessary; in arithmetic, for instance, such a period might last four weeks. Every day from 8:00 to 10:00, the subject in question is studied, and what is studied the following day is connected to what was taught the day before. No later lesson blots out the one given earlier; concentration is possible.

When the four weeks are over, and the chapter on arithmetic is thoroughly explored and concluded, a chapter on history may start. Again, depending on the length of time required, this period on history will extend for about four to five weeks.

Here, Rudolf Steiner places emphasis on the four-week rhythm as a minimum in order to achieve a particular effect. This raises the fundamental question concerning the significant role certain rhythms play for learning and development processes in everyday school life. Even though chronological and biological research were only in their infancy in the 1920s, based on his spiritual scientific research Rudolf Steiner could even then give exact indications for a rhythmic formulation of the day, the week, the month, and the year. And in so doing, he anticipated the results of chronological and biological research that have appeared in recent decades.

As early as 1909, Rudolf Steiner gave a lecture in Berlin about the rhythm of each of the components of the human being [*The Being of Man and His Future Evolution*, lectures of December 21, 1908 and January 12, 1909], containing the following remarks:

You remember that certain relations exist between the ego, the astral body, the etheric body, and the physical body of the human being. What we have to say about the fourth member, the ego, becomes more obvious to us when we remember the two alternating conditions of consciousness experienced by the ego in the course of twenty-four hours, of a day. In a certain sense, we take this one day with its twenty-four hours—within which the ego experiences day and night, waking and sleeping—as a unity. If we say: What the ego goes through in one day is subject to the number one, then we must say that the number which in a similar manner corresponds to the rhythm of our astral body is the number seven. Whereas the ego, as it is today, returns to its starting point within twenty-four hours or in one day, the astral body accomplishes the same thing in seven days.

Let us try to understand this with greater precision. Think of waking up in the morning; this consists, as we incorrectly say in ordinary life, in raising ourselves out of the darkness of unconsciousness and seeing the objects of the physically perceptible world around us. You experience this in the morning, and naturally with exceptions, you experience the same thing again after twenty-four hours. That is the ordinary course of things, and we may say that after one day of twenty-four hours our ego returns to its starting point. If, in the same way, we seek the corresponding connections for the astral body, we must say: When the regularity of the human astral body is really present in it, this astral body returns to the same point after seven days. Thus, whereas the ego describes a circle in one day, the astral body moves appreciably more slowly; it makes its revolution in seven days. Now the etheric body goes through its revolution in 4 x 7 days; after 4 x 7 days it returns to the same point. Now I beg you to remember what was said next to the last time. In the case of the physical body, it is not as regular as it is for the astral and etheric bodies. But we can settle on an approximate number: It makes its revolution in about 10 x 28 days, returning then to its starting point… In general, the figures 1:7:(4 x 7):(10 x 7 x 4) are the proportional figures which, as it were, indicate the rotational speeds for the four members of our being. Naturally this is only said figuratively; for it is not a matter of rotation, it concerns the repetitions of conditions, rhythmic numbers.

In the decades since then, the significance of these rhythms for human health—especially the seven-day rhythm and the monthly rhythm—has been described and documented in detail in the textbooks for balneology (science of baths) and medical climatology.[23]

As early as 1978, in his contribution to *Chronobiologische Grundlagen der Prävention und Rehabilitation* [Chronobiological basis for prevention and rehabilitation], Gunther Hildebrandt stated:

Accordingly, from the chronobiological viewpoint, health is an optimal condition of the harmonious time structure of the organism and its integration into the chronological order of the environment. The tasks of prevention and rehabilitation have to be aligned to these measurable criteria of the rhythmic order of functions. On the one hand, these tasks must consist in protecting such a chronobiological order from disturbances. On the other hand, they should consist in strengthening this order by appropriate measures, and if need be, correcting it and making possible its restoration. Depending on the degree of the impediment, various lengths of periods are necessary for complete restoration of the ability to function as indicated by the following table:

Therapeutically Useful Periodic Reactions

	Rhythms within a Day	Rhythms within a Month	Rhythms within a Year
Lengths of Periods	12, 8, 6, 4 Hours	7, 9-10, 14, 21 Days	6, 4, 3, 1½ Months
Function of recuperation	Functional recuperation (elimination of fatigue)	Long-term recuperation (regeneration)	Excess recuperation (increased performance)
Therapeutic significance	Reaction to prophylaxis (toughening)	Healing restitution (normalization)	Compensation for losses (opening up reserves of proficiency)
Adaptive significance	Habituation	Functional adaptation	Trophic-plastic adaptation
Specificity	Decline of non-specific irritability	Positive cross-effects	Specialization
Duration of trophotropic phases	Hours	Days–Weeks	Weeks–Months

In the following, basic elements of a pedagogical chrono-hygiene are outlined:

Nurturing of the daily rhythm, including the night

After greeting one another, each day in the life of a Waldorf school begins with the morning verse. The verse for the fifth through eighth grades is as follows [translated by Arvia MacKaye Ege, published in *Truth Wrought Words*]:

I look into the world
in which the sun is shining,
in which the stars are sparkling,
in which the stones repose;
where living plants are growing,
where sentient beasts are living,
where man, soul-gifted, gives
to spirit a dwelling place.
I look into the soul,
that lives within my being.
The world-creator moves
in sunlight and in soul-light,
in wide world space without,
in soul-depths here within.
To thee, creator- spirit,
I will now turn my heart
to beg that strength and blessing
to learn and work may grow
within my inmost being.

It is not merely beautiful or meaningful to concentrate on a few great thoughts at the beginning of a lesson. Regular repetition of this over a number of years contributes to the development of habits and will. Addressing the ego daily strengthens the personality which, in turn, illumines the activity of the other members of the being in quickening ways. One, the number and rhythm of the ego, is the starting point, the point of reference for all the other time structures in the organism. In the final analysis, everything is connected with the ego rhythm, the twenty-four hour rhythm, and is synchronized into it.

Besides, in this twenty-four hour rhythm, the characteristic high and low points of the sine curve have long been known to represent the daily rhythmic variations in the ego's ability to be active.[24]

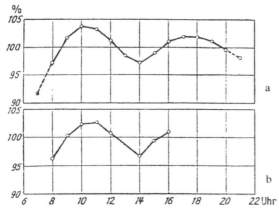

Daily course of arithmetical speed in eleven-year-old children (from Rutenfranz and Hellbrügge, Zschr. Kinderheilk. [Magazine for pediatrics], 80, 1957, 65–82).

a) by Rutenfranz and Hellbrügge, 1957 b) by Baade, 1907.

120

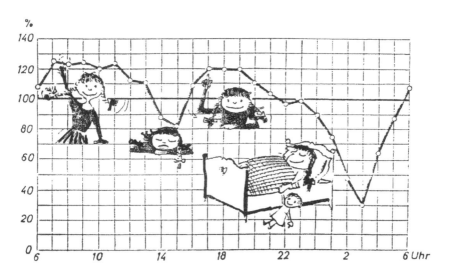

Daily course of physiological performance readiness according to examinations by Bjerner et al, (Bjerner, Holm and Swenson, Br. j. ind. med. 12, [1955], 103-110.]

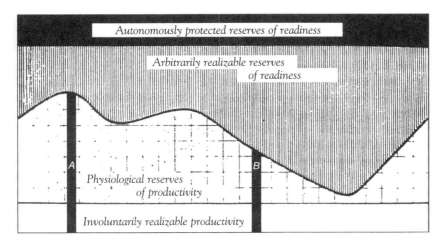

The curve in the above chart which runs from left to right represents: Limit of physiological readiness for productivity

Diagram of regions of productivity and their dependence on the time of day (According to Schmidtke, Ermüdung [Fatigue], Huber, Bern-Stuttgart 1965.)

121

At the end of the above-quoted research, Joseph Rutenfranz remarks:

> Among the types of schools that have emerged in recent years as a result of reforms, the most problematic to me in this connection is the so-called round-the-clock school. Reduction of the school schedule to five days per week and extending class periods into the early afternoon causes the demand for achievement to collide with the lowpoint of physical readiness for productivity. If such forms of schooling are considered desirable in spite of this, then the corresponding organizational forms have to be adjusted to the day's course in accordance with the physiological readiness for work. Generally it can be presumed that the time for special readiness to work is at most between 8:00 and 1:00 for those between the ages of nine and twelve, and that the second peak for mental achievement does not begin until 4:00. In younger children, particularly preschoolers, the peaks move to earlier hours, and the low point at midday is more pronounced. A reasonable school organization should therefore carry out school activities wherever possible during the time between 8:00 and 1:00, or, with younger children between 9:00 and 12:00 During the midday lull after lunch, parents should allow their children time to dream and play—and occupy them with homework (depending on the season of the year) between 4:30 and 6:00.

Rudolf Steiner's indications go far beyond chronobiological recommendations such as these. He describes how the threefold human organism must be taken into consideration particularly in regard to the day's rhythm. On the human organism's inherent rhythms, we first present a chart by Gunther Hildebrandt, and then a basic introduction by Rudolf Steiner.

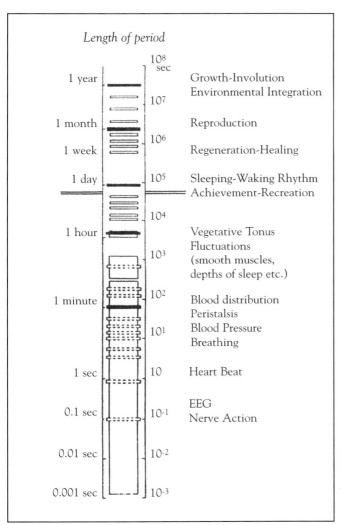

Length of period		
	10^8 sec	
1 year	10^7	Growth-Involution Environmental Integration
1 month	10^6	Reproduction
1 week		Regeneration-Healing
1 day	10^5	Sleeping-Waking Rhythm Achievement-Recreation
	10^4	
1 hour	10^3	Vegetative Tonus Fluctuations (smooth muscles, depths of sleep etc.)
1 minute	10^2	Blood distribution Peristalsis
	10^1	Blood Pressure Breathing
1 sec	10	Heart Beat
0.1 sec	10^{-1}	EEG Nerve Action
0.01 sec	10^{-2}	
0.001 sec	10^{-3}	

Spectrum of human rhythmic function periods (adapted from Hildebrandt 1975)

In regard to this, Hildebrandt comments:

External environmental rhythms have a synchronizing or phase-regulating influence and in this way guarantee the geophysical or cosmically ordered basis for the time-structure of the organism and its proper environmental integration. This is particularly true of the rhythms of the day and of the year, whereas the organism's weekly and monthly rhythms have become almost completely independent. This is apparently due to a generally progressive emancipation from time on the part of civilized humanity.

On the other hand, in the case of shorter rhythmic fluctuations of the spectrum below the daily rhythm, we are dealing with purely endogenous [coming from within] variations of functions that stand in no direct connection to the rhythms of the environment. If the functions of this autonomous realm are investigated more closely, a particular principle of organization becomes evident here. The rhythmical processes of the highest frequency occur in the realm of the nerve system. They serve the interchange of information, that is to say, the reception, the conveyance and absorption of information that is encoded into rhythmic signals. By contrast, the slower rhythms of the autonomous realm serve the metabolism and its realms of functions consisting of absorption and elimination of substance, digestion, secretion, and readying of energy. Whereas the rhythms of information are strictly bound to highly differentiated spatial structures of the nervous system, the metabolic rhythms are involved more or less in all the tissues, and are therefore much less specialized in regard to location. Between these two opposite poles, the center of the rhythmic system affects, as it were, the rhythms of circulation and breathing that swing back and forth between tension and release, expansion and concentration, systole and diastole.[25]

Now, Rudolf Steiner said in a lecture on December 28, 1921 [published in *Soul Economy and Waldorf Education*]:

By acquiring such knowledge of the human being, we not only recognize how human nature is expressed differently in different individuals, but how it comes to expression in diverse ways in childhood, maturity, and old age. For the three members of the human being interact quite differently during the three stages of life, and they have to be adapted to each other.

This becomes crucial, for instance, when we have to consider how to divide the time correctly that we have available for instruction and direction. Obviously we must bring the whole human being into the processes of education and instruction. This means, we have to consider the nature of the head, as well as that of the metabolism and limbs. And since the processes of the other parts likewise take place in each single part, we must make allowances for this fact as well. It goes without saying that metabolic processes likewise occur continually in the head.

When it becomes necessary in the course of instruction for children to sit still in a classroom—more of this later—sit still on their hygienically arranged benches, we deal with them in such a way that no activity works in the limbs and metabolism, but that all the effects have to be brought out of the head. Subsequently, this is balanced out, and rightly so, by relieving the head of its activity. In turn, limbs and metabolism are activated by allowing the children to do gymnastics.

If we are aware of the polar nature of the processes taking place in the head as opposed to the limbs and metabolism, we can well understand the importance of providing the right kind of change in the timetable. Now, having allowed the children to move, jump, and do all sorts of exercises, when we take them back to the classroom to continue our lesson, what happens then?

You must realize that when human beings engage in metabolic and limb activities, those thoughts that are artificially brought into the head between birth and death are outside the head. A child jumps and moves around, bringing the metabolic and limb organization into movement. The thoughts implanted during physical life on earth withdraw. But supersensible wisdom that normally manifests in dreams, now enters the head in an unconscious manner and asserts itself particularly in the head. When, after gymnastics, we take the children back to the classroom, we replace this supersensible wisdom they had earlier during the gymnastic exercises with something that must appear inferior to their subconscious minds. For during gymnastics, not only does the sense-perceptible affect the child in educational ways, but the supersensible as well, since it has particular occasion to do so. This is why the children become inwardly resentful in the following lesson. They may not show unwillingness outwardly so much, but inwardly they do become resentful. By grafting an ordinary lesson upon gymnastic exercises, we ruin the child, we create a basis in the child for tendencies to illness.

This is a fact that has frequently been noted even by people outside anthroposophy—so a physiologist assured me. Here, anthroposophical spiritual research gives you the reasons for it. We can see how we can promote tendencies for good health, if, as teachers and artists of education, we acquire the right knowledge of the human being. Naturally, if we go about it in the wrong way, we produce any number of tendencies toward illness. We must certainly consider this. As you may have noticed, I do not wish to succumb to the glorification of the usual kind of worldly wisdom acquired by human beings. That kind of wisdom would hardly suffice to shape and mold the human organization in the years to come. But if we would not become so inflexible in our organization by the time we reach an older, mature age, so that the outward wisdom that we have impressed into our head through having acquired naturalistic, intellectual concepts, is reflected back correctly in the form of memory pictures, it would eventually stream down into our remaining organism. However paradoxical this may sound, if what under normal conditions should remain in the sphere of the head were to stream down into the limb and metabolic regions, it would cause the human being to become ill. It acts like poison. Intellectual wisdom is indeed like a kind of poison as soon as it enters the wrong sphere, at least as soon as it reaches the metabolic organism. The only way in which we can live with this intellectual wisdom—and I mean this quite concretely, not in any sense as a moral judgment—is by preventing this poison from entering our metabolic and limb system, for there it has a devastating effect.

In the child, however, this inflexibility is not present. If we impress our present-day mature wisdom into the child, the poison [of our concepts] invades the child's metabolic and limb system. You see how important it is to realize from practical experience how much head knowledge we can expect a child to absorb without exposing it to the dangers of becoming poisoned in its metabolic and limb organization.

As a teacher and an artistic educator, your work will promote either health or illness in the children.

On the basis of chronobiological and spiritual scientific results of research, Christoph Lindenberg describes the ideal course of work in the main lesson in the following way:

> Earlier, I mentioned that children already arrive in school in a mentally affected condition. The teacher's task is therefore, first of all, to place the students in a position where they are able to be receptive. The teacher will have to be at the disposal of the students who wish to unload a problem. Prior to the beginning of official instruction, he or she will speak with children who wish to do so. The instruction then

126

begins with the morning verse that is spoken together. This is followed by rhythmic exercises that are intended to harmonize through rhythm. If one knows something about rhythms and how to deal with them, one can work in a calming or in a stimulating way depending on the rhythms, because rhythms influence breathing and pulse in various ways. Then, before starting with a reflection on what has been discussed the previous day, in a few words the teacher can rouse the children's memory in regard to the subject of the day before, so that they are able to focus on it. However, if the teacher begins immediately to call on individual students with pointed questions, the danger easily arises that a thought-block is brought on by such questions in sensitive or weaker students.

The aim of proceeding this way is to bring about calm as well as attentiveness prior to intellectual, perhaps even demanding work that challenges memory and abstract faculties. Through such introductory remarks, as many students as possible should be placed in the condition of being able to participate in this work process. Understood in this way, the teacher is not the one who simply demands achievements. Rather, he or she is the one who initially prepares the basis for such achievements. For the students, on the other hand, it is important to know what awaits them. They can depend on having regular repetitions now. By not constantly being confronted with new situations, they can adjust to something and prepare for it. Since repetition of and work on material by means of thought processes allows for various degrees of difficulty, all the students can participate. The weaker student can simply offer reports on material that has been studied. The stronger students can ask questions, discuss problems, and work out underlying rules or laws. And at the end of this portion of the lesson, the result of the entire process can be written on the blackboard in the form of an overview.

Above, I already mentioned[26] that making demands on memory as well as upon the ability of abstract conceptualizing, something that is practiced in formulating general insights, rules, and laws, appears at first like an intellectual achievement, but it also places demands on musculature and metabolism. Conversation and discussion that usually result here do lessen the relatively strong tension. On the other hand, this tension, this purposeful exercise of memory, must be present too, because students experience their own achievement through it. They realize that they know something and can do something, and this stabilizes their self-confidence. A certain danger is present already in this portion of the work, namely, that, along with repeating and discussing the material, the teacher wanders off into details. Then the students lose their orientation and have the feeling that chaos rules in their heads. This feeling either leads to languor and detachment or to quiet despair. In either case, the actual process of learning has failed, even if for a few students it was most interesting. The teacher can become aware of this the following day by observing that the students do not seem to have retained much that was meaningful. Now this is a dubious symptom because, by structuring and exercising their memory, the students learn to access and exercise their knowledge. Such exercising cannot merely be the result of homework. An exercise is only firmed up through constant nurturing in school. The stabilization of memory thus achieved starts a psychic process which, through the experience of success, the feeling of confidence that one can do something, in the end even has physiological consequences because it reflects back on health and sleep.[27]

In conclusion, the following are a few of the essential statements by Rudolf Steiner concerning the sequence of subjects of instruction on various days whereby special consideration is given to the child's threefold organism.

Music/History, Singing/Eurythmy—the Significance of the Night

In essence, pressing our concepts a little, our instruction divides into two parts, although they continually play into one another. One is that part where we teach children something in which ithey have to participate with their skills, with their whole bodily nature, where we involve children in a sort of self-activity. We need only think of eurythmy, music, gymnastics— even the external functions of writing and arithmetic—in all these, we involve the children in some sort of activity. The other part of instruction is of the contemplative kind, where we direct the children to look at something, where we indicate something to the children.

Now these two parts of instruction fundamentally differ from each other although they constantly interpenetrate during the lesson. As a rule, one has no idea of how much the teacher of a contemplative subject such as history, for example, owes to another teacher who has to work more in the direction of manual skills and ability. If we were to limit instruction of children to subjects of observation and contemplation, their life in older age would be terribly stunted. Children who are merely trained and instructed in contemplative ways will, as adults, become mentally dazed. They will be filled with a certain weariness of the world. Even in the very matter of observation and contemplation, they would become quite superficial in later life. When older, they would no longer be inclined to observe and contemplate much, nor would they willingly take the trouble to give the necessary attention to things of external life, if as children their education had been confined only to subjects such as history, social history, or generally to instruction of a contemplative kind.

In point of fact, when we have to teach a subject of this kind, we owe a great deal to the teacher of needlework, music, or eurythmy. The history teacher is indebted to the teacher of needlework, music, or eurythmy, and conversely the teacher of music or of singing is indebted to what has been taught to the children in the way of history, or other such lessons.

Suppose we want to engage the children's attention to a subject that requires reflection. They sit and have to direct their attention to something we are telling them. We may appeal to their judgment, perhaps even to their moral judgment. But however much we try to spur them on to independent thought, so long as the children sit there listening or thinking, the activity we are calling forth in them is no more than a wakeful sleep-activity—if I may be allowed to use a paradoxical expression. In a certain sense, regarding their soul-spiritual aspects, the children are outside their body, and only continue to share in the activity of their body through the fact that they are not quite outside it, as is the case in ordinary sleep. To a lesser degree, the same phenomenon is produced in their organism during contemplative instruction as is produced in sleep, namely, a certain ascent of organic activity from below to above. When we tell stories to the children, they develop in their organism the same activity that is developed in sleep; the products of metabolism are rising up into the brain. When we ask children to sit, and we occupy them so that they have to think and consider something, it is as though we call up in their organism an activity that belongs to light sleep.

As a rule we imagine that sleep has a strengthening effect on the organism. Every morning we awaken with a headache might of course teach us what the reality is here. We must understand that, as long as we are awake, whatever ails us in our organism is kept back from the higher organs, is not allowed to rise up. But when we go to sleep, and something is amiss in our organism, it decidedly rises up into the higher organs. And so, if we make children study, observe, and consider, then whatever is not quite in order in their organism rises up the whole time. On the other hand, when we teach children eurythmy, getting them to sing or play music, making them do gymnastics or some kind of handwork, or even if we let them write—insofar as they develop activity of their own that way—when we have them do something with their hands, then an activity is present that we have to compare in the same way with an enhanced waking activity.

Through singing or eurythmy, even if that is not intended at all, a hygienic, indeed a therapeutic activity is performed. Such a hygienic, therapeutic activity is perhaps all the more healthy if you do not go about it with amateurish medical intentions, but leave it to your own commonsense healthy feelings and outlook on life. Nevertheless, as teachers, it is good to know how we really work for one another. We should know, for example, that the children owe the beneficial rising of the organic fluids that we need when we give them contemplative instruction—for instance, history lessons—that they owe this beneficial rising to the singing lesson or the eurythmy instruction of the day before. It is good to have such an overall view of the instruction, offered in a school; for if anything appears to be out of order, we shall independently make it a point to work together with other teachers.

On such a basis, it will become possible for us to give each other good advice. The history teacher, for instance, will discuss with the teacher for singing what measure could be taken to help a particular child. If we go about this with the intention of working out programs and elaborate schemes, no good will come of it. We must first have an overview of what is going on. Then this insight will, of itself, give the right impulse for discussion with our colleagues. Thus will cooperation lead to a fruitful result.

You may be quite sure that when a physics teacher notices something amiss in the students, it will under some circumstances occur to her or him to discuss with the singing teacher how matters might be improved by paying special attention to one aspect or another in the singing lesson. A singing teacher in turn will know better than a physics teacher just what is necessary, but he or she will be grateful that attention has been drawn to the problem. Only in this way can living cooperation be achieved throughout the body of teachers. Working thus, we shall be taking the whole human being into consideration, and we shall find that one thing leads to another. [*Education for Adolescents*, lecture of June 12, 1921.]

Looking at the human being in its totality, we find that it possesses an extraordinarily complicated structure that we as teachers have to know how to manage in our educational and teaching efforts. Now, going into more detail, take the children who are doing eurythmy. Their physical bodies are moving, and the movements are transferred to the etheric body. To begin with, astral body and ego put up resistance; in a certain way the ongoing activity of physical and etheric body is impressed on them. Astral body and ego then leave during sleep and connect this impression with quite different spiritual forces. In the morning, they carry it back again into the etheric and physical body. Then there is a remarkable concord between what has been received from the spiritual world during sleep and what was experienced the day before by physical and ether bodies when eurythmy was done. The effect becomes evident that spiritual experiences, undergone between falling asleep and reawakening, harmonize with what was prepared and experienced on the day before. In what is being carried into the human being upon awakening, a special health-giving power latent in eurythmy becomes manifest. I would like to say that a spiritual substance is actually carried down into the human being the next morning, if eurythmy is cultivated in this manner.

It is quite similar in the case of singing. When we practice singing with children, the essential activity that unfolds is an activity of the etheric body. The astral body has to do its best to adapt to the etheric body. At first it resists, then bears all this out into the spiritual world. It returns again, and once more a health-bestowing power comes to expression.

We could say that, in eurythmy, it is more a healing force that actually affects the child's physical condition. In singing, we have an effect that works more on the whole human system of movement and then reflects back on the health of the physical body.

Facts like these can be put to extraordinarily good use in teaching. Supposing, for instance, we could arrange—I speak of it more as an ideal, but such ideals can at least be approached by the body of teachers— supposing we could arrange the schedule so that eurythmy would be done in the afternoon. Then, the eurythmic activity would be allowed to go on working spiritually during the night. On the following day, gymnastics, done in the way I described it yesterday, are scheduled. Then the gymnastic activity would enter the body with health-giving influence. Much could be attained that way by alternating between eurythmy and gymnastics.

131

Again, if conditions allowed it, much could be achieved if children were given singing instructions one day. Then, having carried this experience into the spiritual world during sleep, the next day children would be offered instrumental music, in other words, hearing would be the main thing, not their own participation. Owing to the consolidating effect produced in the human being through listening to music, we shall find that what was acquired by the children the day before (in the singing lesson) is in this way brought to its most healthy expression. You see that if conditions were favorable for meeting all the ideal demands, so that we were able to schedule lessons in the sequence best adapted to the conditions of life, the influence upon the children's health could hardly be over-estimated. Let us go further into detail in these matters. [*Education for Adolescents*, lecture of June 14, 1921.]

Imagining—Judging—Concluding

Take, for instance, lessons in physics. We do an experiment with the children. Now remember what I said yesterday. The human being actually perceives only with the head; it is the rhythmic human being who judges, while it is the metabolic-and-limbs being who draws conclusions (particularly with the hands and feet). Once you call this to mind and, in addition, the nature of the act of perception as such, you will admit that to perceive an act of will performed of our own accord is something deeply connected with the drawing of conclusions, not with mere perception. When I see my own body, my body is itself a conclusion. Perception is present only in the moment of turning my eyes to my body. But by now carrying out a semi-conscious or subconscious process, I gather together through judging all the details that allow me to experience the whole thing, concluding with the sentence: So, therefore, this is a body. Now, this is a perception of a conclusion. The fact is, whenever I perceive, perceive intelligibly, I form nothing but conclusions. Consequently my whole human being is involved in the process.

This is the case when I do scientific experiments, for I am constantly dealing with receiving something through the medium of my whole being. Conclusions continually enter into the process of reception. The judgments are as a rule not perceived at all; they are too deeply hidden within. So we can say that all of human nature is involved when we engage in experimentation.

From the standpoint of education, however, we have not done something very beneficial for the children by experimenting. The children may well be interested in the experimentation, but their human nature as such, their normal organization, is too weak to have demands made on it constantly. That does not work. It is always a little too much if I, the teacher, make demands on the children's whole human nature. When I engage in experiments in front of the children or draw their attention to the external world, their whole being is always too disconcerted. The significant point in instructing and educating is to take the three aspects of the threefold human being into consideration, to allow each to come to its own expression, and moreover, to its corresponding reciprocal relationship.

Now suppose that I first conduct an experiment [with my class]. This means, I make demands on the children's whole being. That is asking a great deal! Then I turn their attention away from the apparatus that is standing in front of them, and go through the whole experiment again, appealing now to their recollection of what they have just experienced. If I recapitulate in this way, letting the children review the experiment in thought without seeing it take place, their rhythmic system is animated. After first having made a demand upon the whole human being, I now make a demand on the children's rhythmic and head system—for I naturally bring the head system into activity as well when I present a recapitulation. So, first I activated the whole of human nature in the children, then primarily their rhythmic system; finally I let them go home. Later on, they go to sleep. While they are asleep and their astral body and ego are away, what I have activated initially in the children's whole being and then in their rhythmic system, lives on in them in their limbs.

Let us now concentrate our attention on the sleeping children in bed. What I managed to achieve with them in the lesson, echoes on in their physical and ether bodies. All the development that the lesson evoked, first in the child as a whole, and then more especially in the rhythmic system, streams up now into the head-nature. Pictures of all that begin to form in the head. And when the children wake up in the morning and go to school, these pictures are encountered in their heads. It is actually so. When the children come to school the next day, they have in their heads, without knowing it, pictures of the experiment I showed them the day before and of which I afterwards gave them a graphic description.

So, now the children arrive with something like photographs in their heads of the experiments I did the day before. Now I can speak in a more reflective way of the experiments and of what I had repeated in a purely narrative form, appealing more to their imagination. Now I go into considerations of what happened earlier. I try to help bring it about that the pictures rise into the children's consciousness. To repeat: I give a physics lesson, I experiment. I restate to the children what has taken place. On the next day I go into considerations that lead the children to become acquainted with the laws that underlie the experiments. I guide the children in the direction of a thought process connected with the latter, but do not force them into a direction where the pictures they bring to me—unconsciously—will lead a meaningless existence. But now consider what would happen if, instead of giving the children nourishment in this way by leading them to reflect on yesterday's experiment, I were simply to go straight ahead next morning with further experiments. Once again I would be taxing their whole being; and the exertion I aroused in them would push its way into every part of their being, bringing a kind of chaos into the pictures and confusion into their heads. Regardless of the circumstances, I must first consolidate what is trying to establish its existence. I must give it nourishment. And in this way, I arrive at the right way of arranging my physics lesson, so that it adapts to the life-processes in the children.

Let's assume that I am giving a history lesson. When I teach history, I am required not to place the facts before the children in a purely external way; all that is in a sense eliminated. I must put forth my skill and ingenuity to adapt the lesson once again to the life-processes in the child, and this time in the following way. On the first day, I tell the facts, the bare facts that occur in space and time. This, in turn, involves the child's whole being, just as does the physics experiment, for the child is obligated to picture it all in space. I must see to it that the children have a picture of what I tell them, they must see it in their mind, see it spread out before them as a continuous whole, and they must likewise picture it in time.

When I have done this, I shall try to add some details concerning the characters or the events. But I do not do this by actually narrating something, but by beginning to characterize. In this way, I direct the children's attention to the facts I first presented, but now I characterize them. Having gone through the same two stages, I have first made demands on the children's whole being, and then, by characterization, have made demands on their rhythmic system. Then the children are dismissed. Next morning they come to me again, bringing with them once more in their head the spiritual photographs of the lesson from the previous day. I shall accommodate them in the right way if I continue yesterday's subject by going into certain considerations. We might, for example, consider together whether Mithridates or Alcibiades could be regarded as decent, respectable human beings or not. On the first day, therefore, I have to present more of an objective characterization; on the following day, more of a discerning reflection. In this way I bring it about that the three members of the threefold human being intertwine with one another in the right manner.

An example of this kind can give you some idea of what can be achieved if you arrange all of your teaching in such a way that it adapts to the children's life-conditions. This, of course, can never be done unless, as is the case with us here, the timetable allows for the same subject to be continued over a considerable period. If, for the first main lesson, the children have physics on one day, and religion on the next, how is the teacher ever to take into consideration what they have retained from the day before? Arranging the whole curriculum on the ideal basis is of course a difficult matter, but we can at any rate see that we approach the ideal whenever possible. And if you study our timetable, you will find that this has been our endeavor throughout. [*Education for Adolescents*, lecture of June 14, 1921.]

Weekly rhythm

In Waldorf schools, careful attention is paid to the weekly rhythm. There are specific verses for the days of the week in the lower grades, or the teacher takes note of the day by one or another remark. Songs and poems are learned in a weekly rhythm, or, as is the case in the Waldorf school in Sekkem, Egypt, on the Holy Friday of the Moslem religion, a weekly festival is held in which something from the week's work of each class is presented to the whole school. [In Waldorf schools in some European countries] children who are not connected to a particular denomination can participate in religious celebrations of Sunday services of the so-called Free Religious Instruction.

Even in Waldorf schools, however, the increasingly debatable introduction of the five-day week in recent years has fundamentally endangered the structure of the week. Here it is important, first of all, to focus on the facts and then to look for the most acceptable compromise. To start with, results of chronobiological research into the five- day week at school should be called to mind. In his article,

"Chronobiologische Aspekte des Kindes- und Jugendalters" [Chronobiological aspects of childhood and youth], Gunther Hildebrandt writes the following concerning the periodicity of sevens and the weekly rhythm:

> The time organization in the human being—aside from its spontaneous rhythm structure, the harmonious structure of which is in the final analysis likewise anchored in the cosmic environment—is capable of developing capacities in the case of disturbances that function in the sense of an "emergency ordering of time" that can intensify the organism's compensating processes. In principle it has long been known that all reactions are regulated in accordance with phases and periods. Such reactive periods (cf.. Hildebrandt 1982) occur in all areas of the spectrum of rhythms. (See graph on next page.)
>
> Here, a structure of an approximately seven-day periodicity has special practical significance because it dominates in many instances in processes of illness and healing. Beyond that, it moreover chronologically arranges physiological adaptation processes.
>
> In childhood diseases, scarlet fever, for example, displays a pronounced periodicity of sevens in regard to the temperature curve which, in case of an uncomplicated course of the disease, unremarkably terminates following only a few periods (second curve from top). On the other hand, multiples of the seven-day periodicity frequently appear along with complications. Even the outbreaks of subsequent illnesses fit into this time-structure. Extensive research projects have meanwhile demonstrated that this time structure of periodicity of sevens is typical of all reactions of spontaneous healing, immunological activities, and adaptive processes of the most varied kind. Obviously, we are dealing here with a quite basal time structure that has furthermore been discovered in the animal kingdom and even in protozoons (Literal translation, see Hildebrandt and Bandt-Reges 1992).

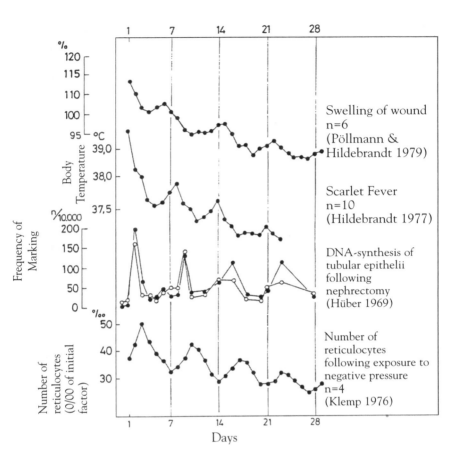

Examples for the structure of periodicity of sevens in various processes of healing, adaptation, and compensation (according to Hildebrandt 1982).

The uppermost curve depicts the course of localized swelling of the wound after an operation to repair a broken jaw which, up until complete remission, periodically increases approximately every seven days. The lowest curve indicates the course of the number of reticulocytes (newly developed red blood cells) in the flowing blood after exposure to a lack of oxygen, hence during an adaptive process, something that can be observed in the same way after blood-letting. The third curve presents the course of the rate of cell division in a

137

compensatory, growing kidney after the other kidney was removed surgically in animal experiments (Hübner 1969). One could cite many other examples, even the therapeutically induced reactions of self-healing, for example, in the course of rehabilitative treatments in a spa, which demonstrate the same dominant time structure(see Hildebrandt 1985). It is certain that, in the case of the periodicity of sevens, we are not dealing with the effects of the normal seven-day week but rather with an endogenous [internally engendered] time structure which the organism can activate at any time for the purpose of time-structured formations of wide-reaching processes of reaction (see Hildebrandt and Bandt-Reges 1992).

In regard to child development, the question naturally arises of what it signifies if childhood diseases that are preponderantly marked by such time structures are today obstructed or completely suppressed by medical intervention in their periodically arranged course. It is evident that the periodicity of sevens represents a factor of the lunar rhythm and therefore is certainly part of the relationship of long-term sequential fluctuations of the time organization. Possibly, the organism heals through resorting to phylogenetically older time structures, similarly to the way that refreshing sleep at night is arranged through the phylogenetically older activity-cycle of ninety-minute periods that likewise stand in simple whole-number relationships to the circadian rhythm (cf. Broughton 1985).

Comparative research has shown that the seven-cycle reaction period predominantly appears in younger people who have at their disposal good self-healing forces, whereas, along with increasing age and tendencies to chronic illnesses, other (longer fluctuating) time structures appear. (Wiemann 1981; Trageser and Weckenmann 1987). Here, surely, is an important starting point from which chronobiological research on childhood and adolescence must be carried further. This applies particularly in regard to the external weekly rhythm which, as a social ordering of the environment, corresponds to the endogenous periodicity of sevens, but in no way needs to synchronize the latter (Hildedebrandt and Geyer, 1984). As a learning, developing being, the growing organism is involved in permanent adaptation that must be dealt with by means of the periodicity of sevens. The shaping and cultivation of the weekly rhythm that today are subject to quite different viewpoints may therefore well be of special significance for health in child and adolescent development.

The introduction of the five-day week and a long weekend into the preschool and school domain is certainly not merely a question of support or disturbance of the reaction processes of the periodicity of sevens. Rather, the question of a more than single day change of the daily rhythmic way of life probably plays a more important role. Experimental research on night shift workers demonstrates that it is not until a two-day change of the ordinary daily course that the circadian rhythm-system reacts with adaptive changes of phases which possess a tendency to continuance. It is a known fact that the extended weekend has not increased the degree of rest, but on the contrary, has increased the difficulties of readapting the circadian system to the workday (so-called idle Monday).

Correspondingly, comparative research of a five- or six-day week at one and the same school has shown that the frequency of absence after a long weekend is significantly higher [with those on a five-day schedule] (see chart below). The frequencies on Saturday are not comparable on account of compensating, intentional absences.[28]

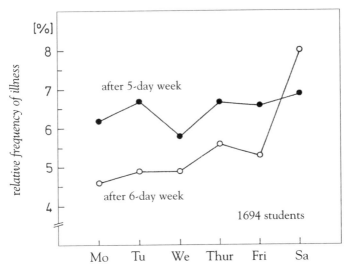

Frequency of absence in the course of a week following a weekend that was preceded by a five-day or a six-day week. Altogether 1694 students of a school that includes first through twelfth grades (according to dates by Klemp, unpublished).

139

If teachers are no longer able to arrange the week as a whole, they are limited in the important possibility of influencing the grounding of the rhythms of the children's astral organization in the physical-etheric constitution through their instruction, and therewith to support the most important time structure of the organism's readiness for reaction.

Innumerable mundane viewpoints oppose this. Modern-day working hours and the increase in part-time work favor free Saturdays for the whole family. Teachers likewise expect more time for preparation and reflection, as well as more time for recuperation from five days of work, than merely having Sundays free. A possible compromise suggestion might be to have a long weekend once a month, perhaps beginning already at noon on Friday to make it really worthwhile. This would create a monthly rhythm within the weekly rhythms without completely destroying the periodicity of sevens. Here too, the school physician has an important task, namely, to awaken among parents, teachers, and above all in talks with the students, an understanding for the negative physiological effect of the five-day week. Adults with their mature organism have a stable endogenous rhythmic system if they had the opportunity of a healthy upbringing. For them, independent association with rhythms and emancipation from predetermined rhythms (for instance through night shift work) is not an insurmountable problem. Besides, in most cases, adults are free to chose whether they will or will not expose themselves to such a way of life that lacks rhythm. And if outer circumstances dictate such a lifestyle, their mature organism is still a certain support for them.

It is a different matter with children and young people who are still growing. There it is important to adjust biological rhythms in a harmonious way to each other, and to allow each of these rhythms in themselves the opportunity to find a healthy, stable expression. Here, the seven-rhythm, which responds to impairment, plays a particularly important role for the maintenance of health during the entire later life. For it is just this rhythm that makes it possible for the organism to deal in a flexible way with disturbances and impairments of all sorts—it is *the healing rhythm*. And it is this very rhythm that will be disturbed in its development by the five-day week. As school physicians, we should work against it. Here it is really important to make every effort. If, at present, it is not possible to succeed in retaining the six-day week in school, nonetheless, on parents' night, one might attempt to organize something privately that would resemble school on Saturday. Children could get up at the same time in the morning, meet in small groups in the homes of various parents, do homework together, and finish what was left undone during the week. Then, reading material suitable to the age group could be offered, and if appropriate, a short excursion or a lunch together could be organized.

When the principle of such a rhythm is comprehended, there are various possibilities of turning the five-day week back into a six-day week where Sunday regains its special position as a day of leisure and rest.

Monthly rhythm

Within four weeks—one month—recovery begins to be complete. The four-week rhythm is the long wave-length rhythm of recovery and convalescence, the rhythm of four times seven days. A few examples from therapeutic medicine can illustrate this. This rhythm strengthens the etheric body, the bearer of the forces of growth, regeneration, and thought. This is why the instructional material in the so-called main lesson is given in four-week periods, so that it is possible in a continuous way to develop a coherence of ideas and meaning relating to a particular subject of instruction. Through all this, the cultivation of memory is promoted in a positive way. (See charts on pages 143–144.)

The regular monthly celebration was part of the original concept of the Waldorf Schools. The intention was to report and present the result of the work of each particular period of instruction. At present, however, the monthly celebrations generally occur three to four times a year.

In addition, the monthly rhythm in many classes is endangered because of the fact that there are more subjects for instruction periods or blocks than four-week units available in the year. Here—particularly in the lower grades from first through eighth grade—one solution can be for the class teacher to take the opportunity of each block, as Steiner recommends, to work out an essential idea, and in so doing, to include various specialized subjects. On the basis of physiological insight, it is, after all, not wise to separate the various specialized subjects from each other in emotionless, dry fashion. Actually, different aspects and a quite different vitality can be experienced in one subject considered in the light of another. A particularly good example for formulating a block is the period about health and diet in the seventh grade. In this regard Rudolf Steiner adds:

In the seventh grade we return to the subject of the human being and attempt to teach what I pointed out to you yesterday, namely, what ought to be taught to people about health and nutrition. The attempt should also be made to apply the concepts the children acquire in the fields of physics and chemistry so as to develop a comprehensive view concerning some specific commercial or industrial processes. All this should be developed out of science, in connection with the instruction in physics, chemistry, and geography. [*Discussions with Teachers*, second lecture on curriculum of September 6, 1919.]

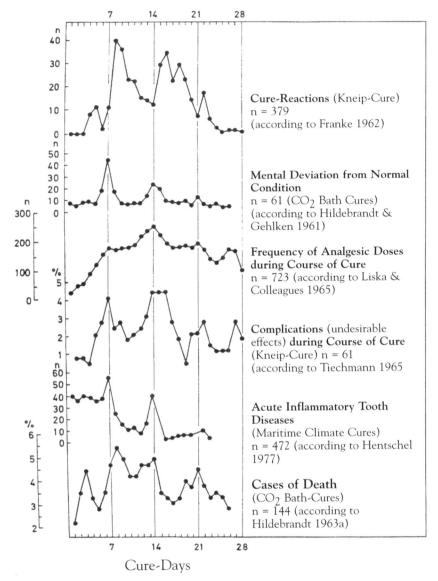

Rate of occurrence of direct and indirect cure-crisis symptoms according to various researchers in cases of differing forms of cures (according to Hildebrandt 1975).

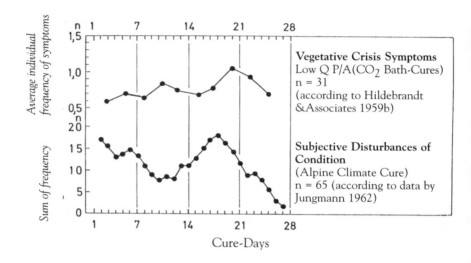

Course of frequency of subjective disturbances of condition in patients with trophotropic states of reaction during CO_2-Cures (above) and in non-selected patients during alpine climate cures (below). The peak of frequency of symptoms is characteristic for the course of the pattern in late reactions.

As was mentioned earlier, the etheric organism works as the bearer of the thought life in four-times-seven-day rhythms. What has been nurtured and worked upon during this period has a chance to be stored in long-term memory in such a way that it is recallable. And this is even more the case when the class teacher in the course of the following block lessons strengthens this monthly rhythm even more by taking up questions of the earlier block lesson from time to time, or arouses the children's curiosity by referring to a future block lesson.

Now, the etheric organism is not only the bearer of the thought life, but also the bearer of the life of habits. This is why it is likewise

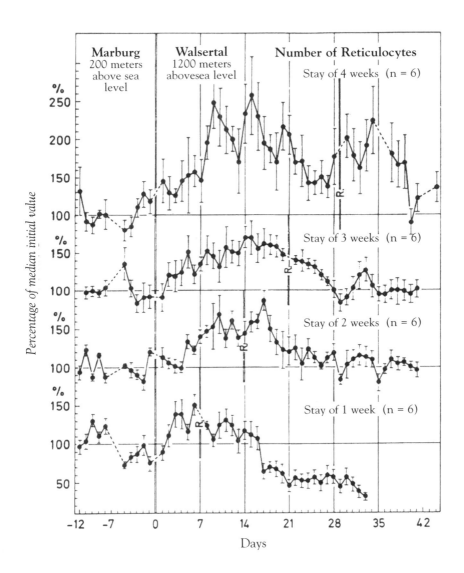

Median course of number of reticulocytes of six healthy test subjects before, during, and after a holiday of winter sports of 1, 2, 3, and 4 weeks at a difference in elevation of 1000 meters (according to Hildebrandt & Nunhöfer 1977).

necessary for manual subjects, and the development of skills that are supposed to become a habit, to cultivate such activities over a period of months until they are really ingrained. It is therefore understandable that foreign language teachers always inquire if it would not be feasible to have blocks for the foreign language lessons. Even teachers of eurythmy and gymnastics wish they could occasionally have periods of more intensive practice. Here, the fact is overlooked that, of all subjects, these that only take place two or three times during the week—to say nothing of choir and orchestra which take place only once a week—are specialized subjects that have the task of nurturing the yearly rhythm. Neither the daily nor the weekly nor the monthly rhythm is relevant here; the annual rhythm is what counts.

Yearly rhythm and care of the physical body

Beside the daily, weekly, and monthly rhythm, the yearly rhythm occupies a central position in the Waldorf schools, for it is the rhythm for nurturing the physical body. After all, the physical body requires nine months for its original development. That is followed by the particularly sensitive period of the first three months after birth —the first trimester. It takes a year until the physical body has acquired its basic stability, and it reestablishes this stability year after year.

The graphs on pages 147–148 depict a few typical annual rhythmic changes of various functional rates and reactive characteristics.

The significance of the yearly rhythm starts with the beginning of school. Not only do first graders experience it as a special celebration, but so does the whole school. This is continued as every class is addressed and given special attention within the school community at

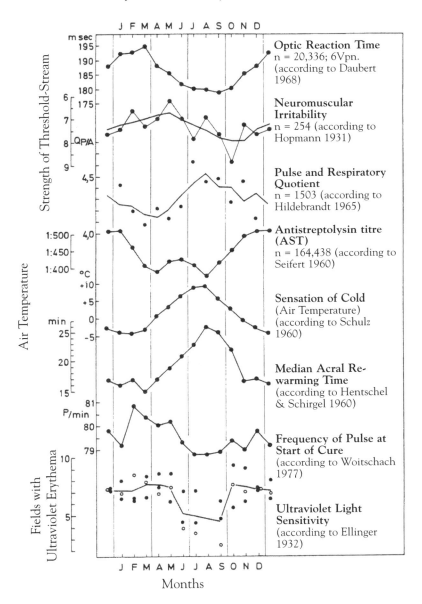

Annual rhythmic patterns of several human functions and reactions (combined from results by various researchers).

147

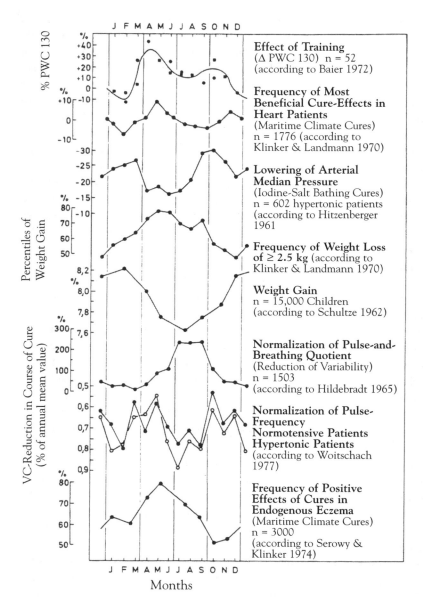

Annual effect patterns of various cures and patient groups, according to results from different researchers (Hildebrandt 1980).

the beginning as well as at the close of each school year. In this way, the school year's beginning and end are powerfully impressed upon the consciousness.

In addition, there is the cycle of the annual Christian festivals. Through them, central motifs of human development receive confirmation and new impulses. It begins with Christmas, the celebration of being a child, of joy and rejuvenation, of the birth of the ego on earth—the festival of evolving, of developing.

In the Waldorf school, this festival not only receives special emphasis at the beginning of the main lesson during the preparatory time of Advent, but likewise through the presentation of the Oberufer Christmas Plays, which can lead to deep pictorial impressions that accompany one's entire later life. Since, for various reasons, these plays can no longer carry out their intended function in many Waldorf schools, this function is urged upon school physicians' thoughtful concern. What counts in the case of these plays is that the images of the creation of the human being, the birth of Christ, and the confrontation with evil, from which the ego emerges victoriously, should be presented as impressively, simply, and honestly, but also as beautifully as possible. It does not matter either whether as many different people as possible, teachers or parents, play these roles year after year and, along with it, change the scenes depending on their intentions in the most individual manner, even including the costumes and the staging. Rather, these images are comparable to a meditative exercise. What matters here is inwardly to move a word, a thought, an image in such a way that it can *live* and always depict new aspects. The clearer and more truthfully the images of the Christmas plays are presented and conceived, based on good brief directions by the producer, the better they can "mature" and be deepened. And through the intensity of presentation and expression, they can be impressed into the audience's consciousness. Not only do the teachers have an opportunity to show the students how they, as a group, experience themselves as seekers and servants of Christ, the students also have the opportunity to see their teachers in certain roles as they mature and grow individually year after year. This reaches the point where certain identifications occur regarding angels, God the Father, a shepherd or a king. In our present time, marked as it is by "action," sensations, and quick alternation of information and gags, it is really like a remedy if nothing but the same thing occurs each Christmas— only changed, more profound, with more presence of mind, more true. When we present the plays, or watch them, this curative impulse links the entire school community to the "Teacher of Human Love."

In the new year follows the time of Mardi Gras, then the period of pre-Easter and the Easter festival. The latter is celebrated more individually in the classroom in many schools and does not emerge as a general school festival. Within the course of human development, the Easter festival corresponds to the age of puberty, when for the first time, the possibility of dying, the necessity of dying are sensed existentially, along with all the frightening experiences, but likewise longings, connected with death. Moreover, in the emotional ups and downs of exultation and deep depression so typical of young people, the ego experiences itself as being subjugated to the laws of the soul's elements; it dimly senses that it has to learn to pass through deaths, births, and transformations.

The Whitsun festival corresponds to adulthood, the actual birth of the ego in the course of individual development. Inasmuch as the ego gains control, it learns the language that every human being on earth understands—namely, humanness, brotherhood, understanding one another in spirit. Along with this ego experiencing, a new possibility of community-building awakens. The more independent human beings become, the freer they become to join with others in particular tasks.

Thereafter, the St. John's festival [June 24] and Michaelmas [Sept. 29] are the great direction-giving festivals in adult life, meaning: constant working on oneself, sharpening one's conscience and sense of responsibility, the burning away (St. John's fire) of all hindrances so that spiritual goals and tasks can light up. In the fall there is a renewed determination to work on one's own self. It is furthermore a matter of daily confrontations that must be weathered in the social realm, in one's profession, and in the various connections of life, in which the evil in the world and in one's own soul can rise ever more into consciousness and can show its dragon nature. Here, Michael's victorious battle with the dragon stands before us as a perceptual challenge, as a test of courage for the heart—for instance, when it is important to have the courage to speak the truth—but likewise for liberated action. Organizing these festivals in the class unit together with the students, and, if possible, within the entire context of the school (for example, as summer and autumn festivals), will generate decisive highlights in the young person's experience of the year's course. The cycle of the year and the changes of the seasons support the young person's physical and mental maturing process with their accompanying dynamism.

Furthermore, the course of the year is the domain for all of those subjects, which, like a red thread, pass through the entire year and can retain continuity through the weeks and months: speech, eurythmy, religious instruction, music, and gymnastics. If these subjects are inspired seasonally, they gain constructive, impressive force by strengthening the physical body. In a different way, they then appear no less important than do the often envied subjects of instruction that are offered in blocks. This yearlong activity of instructional subjects in the upper classes makes it possible to build up closer contact to the students than is possible through the round of block lessons occurring merely once a year.

In his early work, *Education of the Child*, Rudolf Steiner adds another decisive point for nurturing the physical body:

Joy and pleasure are the forces that entice the physical forms of the organs to emerge in the right way. In this regard one can sin badly, for sure, in that one does not properly set the children into the corresponding physical relationship to their environment. Joy with and through the environment thus belongs to the forces that work in a formative way on the physical organs. The joyous mood of the teacher and, above all, honest—not strained—love are vital. Such love that streams warmly, as it were, through the physical surroundings, hatches the forms of the physical organs in the true sense of the word. If imitation of sound prototypes is possible in such an atmosphere of love, then the children are in their proper element.

"Laughing is healthy," is a folk saying—but how can one create a joyous atmosphere in the classroom, particularly during the first school years? It was said of Eugen Kolisko that he radiated a most amiable, cheerful, and good-natured attitude. Cheerfulness can certainly not be preached—one can only radiate it and thus affect others in contagious manner. Particularly school physicians should always keep in mind that joy and health are more contagious than any illness.[29]

CHAPTER 7

Physiological Effects of Education

To understand the physiological effect of instructional subjects and of the method by which they are taught, one must understand the law of the metamorphosis of growth forces into the body-free soul-spiritual activity in thinking, feeling, and willing (cf. chapter 4). The following is a development of principles introduced in chapter 1. It is one of the most important tasks for cooperation between physicians and teachers to work together on a comprehensive "physiological curriculum." Though daily practice in the school plainly shows the correctness of Waldorf education, nonetheless, there has been little documentation of the effects and experiences achieved so far. To work on methods of suitable documentation is an urgent task for the new millennium.

Medical and pedagogical questions in the preschool and nursery years

In early childhood, the components of the human being work entirely on building up the body and its function. Everything that affects children at this age is imprinted directly into their constitution. It is therefore a particularly important task for the school physician to look after the kindergarten and, if applicable, the day-nursery connected with it.[30]

Following retirement from his Waldorf teaching activity, Helmut von Kügelgen devoted himself from age 63 to 82 exclusively to the care and development of the International Association of Waldorf Kindergartens. His concern was directed especially to the training of men and women as kindergarten teachers and to making them aware of their responsibility for the decisive effects of their educational activity upon the children's entire life. This gave rise to a wealth of study material. Two short contributions follow:

On Elementary Eurythmy in the First Seven Years
Helmut von Kügelgen

Eurythmy can start when, at age three, the most intimate connection with the mother is loosened, and the first threefold step of becoming a human being has been completed: learning to walk, learning to speak, and—in saying I—developing the beginnings of thought-imbued consciousness out of speech. Thus, the first segment of pedagogical eurythmy of which we shall speak here, the so-called preschool eurythmy, extends from the third year up to school age.

Nora von Baditz describes how an indication by Rudolf Steiner gave her the decisive impulse for this work: When one does elementary eurythmy with small children, they can gain an ego force that neither school education nor the interventions of destiny are able to bring about. How are we to understand such an enigmatically profound statement?

On the one side, the infant is wholly gesture and movement; on the other, it is a sense organ with all its senses and its whole body. It tastes right down to its big toe. It is frightened in a way that takes hold of its entire being, such as adults can only experience and feel when in shock. This is how intensely the child perceives with its entire being and fits these perceptions into the configuration of its body. In its potential of standing erect, in its first movements, however, the will that slumbers within it becomes effective as movement, walking, hopping, dancing, and motion of the hands. In the child's games and gestures, the entire drama of its destiny-imprinting will is heralded. Meaningful, good, beautiful movements heal and strengthen the will forces that are built and developed out of the bodily health of the first seven-year period, and the soul-health in the second seven-year period, and that then can rise up into full consciousness and independent use of the will in the third seven-year period. Throughout life, the ego force, out of which human beings create their own biography from the assets of their education, from their social particulars and destiny components, will manifest by means of initiative, steadfastness, mobility, and the ability to take things in hand. Artistically formed eurythmy movement does the preliminary work of uniting the ego with the will and incarnating it into the healthily sculptured organs of the body. This is why elementary eurythmy in early childhood can pass on such an essential life-bequest.

We must realize, however, that perception (the entire child is a sense organ) and "will in the gesture" are not joined together in the child by means of consciousness, but rather through imitation. Imitation is the magic word for education in the first seven-year period. It is the elementary stage of freedom for the human being, freedom's true basis, for it chooses and works out of the hidden sanctuary of the ego. In it work the child's forces of trust and the incarnation forces with a power of love and devotion only comparable to the religious ardor of union. Right into the disposition of health, the manner of speaking, the gestures, the temperament, the basic soul mentality, the child becomes what he or she incorporates through imitation from the social environment.

This is the one side. Imitation is rooted in the sphere of the ego's being and does not simply imitate everything without choice. Siblings, children in the same eurythmy group, who experience the same adult, embrace what has been presented and acted out before them with astounding variations. For example, in a eurythmy lesson, one child enters into the gestures of the adult with every fiber of its body; another child merely follows them with its eyes or with gentle movements of the hand. One child awaits the prancing of the little ponies, another the ringing of the dwarf's silver bell or the stomping of the giants. Adults may not interfere in authoritative ways in this flowing of will and decision, demanding some sort of learning results; if they do, they thwart the secret ego activity training itself in imitation as ability of choice and decision-making in an unconscious, yet powerful existential way.

The adult therefore only offers what is his or hers to give, namely elementary eurythmy, but he or she does not interfere in the child's course of movements, in the flow of its will with praise or blame, demands or corrections. Still, adults can infinitely increase their liberating and far-reaching influence on the imitating child when they radiate cheerfulness and joy of life. In the light of gladness—not to be confused with abandon and romping around—joy of life and lightness come about. Joy arises that soars beyond all moodiness and emotional depression, the elevated joy in which the child moves about freely, thus incarnating his or her soul-spiritual being in a healthy manner into the body provided by heredity. Indeed, the capacity of imitation that was weakened by too many sense impressions or a lack of proper movement becomes invigorated again. Heaviness and tiredness are overcome, nervous restlessness is harmonized. Difficulties in finding a connection to eurythmy actually turn up only where the basic principle of working with small children is harmed, that is, the principle of imitation itself.

Now, what is "elementary eurythmy" and what demands does it place on the adults? Since the forming, invigorating forces that proceed from eurythmy movements merge through imitation so intimately with the life processes of the child, every single gesture demands a particular responsibility. It is not a matter of diverse variety; rather, everything depends on first-rate quality. During preparation, it is important for the eurythmist to refer back to the source, to the pure original sound-gesture that gains substance from the motions of the planets and the zodiac. "Elementary" does not mean simplified or playful eurythmy, but eurythmy concentrated on its original source. If I search out the germinal, the original, I myself am once more active in research and formulation. This, in turn, has an effect on the child's development that is urgently moving toward the future. It is therefore not a matter of reducing the great diversity of artistic eurythmy to where it acquires a simple "child-befitting" form. Rather, it is an ever renewed exercising of the fruitful basic elements.

Children should likewise prepare for the eurythmy lesson— through expectation and the joy of looking forward to it. Rudolf Steiner originally wanted to have no more than one hour a week, so that this joyous expectation could live in the children and they would not be "overfed," so to speak. If the eurythmist then weaves the sounds without naming them into the events of the lesson, the children slip into the movements that are beneficial and familiar to them. Above all, the activities of the little ones are motivated out of work-games, out of the whole relationship of nature with its annual rhythms and festivals, animals and plants, its winds and clouds, brooks and stones, elemental beings and stars, and likewise out of the realm of fairy tales. Fairy tales and little stories should be condensed into brief, rhythmical, free verses.

Alongside this, in the musical domain, the teacher guides the children mainly to the experience of the fifth and its mood. Following the stimulus by Nora von Baditz, the beautifully rounded movement of the fifth was called "the golden door." To grasp the essence of the fifth is to experience the human being still within the divine harmony of the spheres. One sees this in the golden doors into which the children transform themselves in the gesture of the fifth: They themselves stand at the threshold of earthly competence.

We are Participants in the Creation of the Human Being
Helmut von Kügelgen

We adults are never so near the world-creator-forces as when we experience, accompany, and share responsibility at the threshold of birth and the first breath of a child, its first smile, its first saying "I" in the course of the third year of life—as mother who gives birth to and nurses the child, as father who extends love, patience, and concern. We can also do that when some destiny places us in the position where we perceive incarnation from this proximity, whether alone or in the place of the naturally closest person. Oh, how near we are to the world-creator-forces of the soul-spiritual element! From day to day, from week to week, through the months of this so very brief time, the individuality is ever more clearly inscribed "into the flesh" of the child. We directly participate in this process between inherited corporeality and individuality. When breath and heartbeat, sense activity and digestive activity, the doings of the limbs and movement of the instruments of crying and speech—all the inner organs—when all of this stirs and moves, when the organs form through use and awaken increasing life from the active and mobile forces of will, then we may have an inkling of the decisions now being made for the entire life. They are decisions made most likely by the being who has appeared among us, decisions it wills to make and wants to make! Yet, certain conditions are laid upon it: hereditary substance, our behavior, the surrounding world and its impressions. For the individuality, they are partly helpful, as well as seriously impeding, conditions. Which decisions will the individuality make? Well, in experience, perception, and imitation, organs are formed and perfected, muscles are developed, rhythms and the activities of the glands are practiced. The arch of the little flat foot is raised at the moment when the leg is needed for standing and walking. The bones of the upper leg and all the parts and organs of the body form so as to develop the constitution for this active, tiny, will-imbued person. We cannot change hereditary substance; we can only help it to become individualized, become an instrument of the ego, when the uttering of the word "I," the rebellious age, and childhood illnesses work on the body, penetrate and transform it.

Initially, however, the ego, incarnating as it is into its destiny, lives as yet wholly in the urge toward activity, in the life forces. The next steps become evident in that the senses not only arouse greed, but can also lead to soul experiences and deliberate desire. Scream and sensation learn to find expression in speech, in a given language that can hold meaning and thoughts. We could say that we owe the fact that this is so to our state of being God's children—for as human beings we have been made so that truth satisfies us, beauty delights us, and benevolence arouses in us the voice of conscience. We owe it to the creative power of love for which we struggle, love that accompanies us and has made us. It transforms and redeems the powers of evil, the dissolving and the hardening powers. To whom do we owe this? It cannot be put into words more simply and more grandly than in the way it is inscribed in the ancient scriptures: Out of divine creation, image of a spiritual entity—that is how we are born! Through transformation, through the impulse of dying and becoming, we will to discover and realize ourselves as we develop to adulthood. The divine voice of conscience in our ego is the representative of humanness, whom the Gospel of John calls Logos, the creative Word of Worlds, without which nothing comes into being, without which we do not come into being and cannot rise up to our state of human dignity. Very simply and comprehensibly, we can even call this impulse, this innermost voice of conscience in human beings, the child of God in earthly man, the true love. And that is why this love liberates and redeems, or unites and gives firm support—it makes whole and heals—out of creative thought; it takes hold of the sensitive heart and reaches all the way into realization in the visibility of the world of body and matter. Without this love we can do nothing. And the consequence of lovelessness culminates in the destruction of the body, in life in hospitalization, in idle and disorderly indigence, and in criminality.

The question must be directed to the highest level. When we think about healthy, healing measures or arrangements befitting the dignity of the human being in regard to children in the first three years, how do we fill the child's environment with real love? Secondary to this question, however, arise the legion of problems in ordinary life. If care of the child's development is taken up as a profession, or a part-time vocation, it must be paid for and requires its laws that are based in the social realm. Neither through money nor through rigid demands of duty can "true love" be produced. Even what is called "fondness of children" is insufficient. If we do not penetrate to that sphere where, beyond professional engagement and sympathetic inclination, we enter the deeper levels of spiritual knowledge of the human being and the will force that is ready for sacrifice, we do not reach the level of "true love." For only there, insight and force of will join together in that light-filled warmth, through the rays of which children grow up in a healthy way.

Treating children according to their temperaments

Here, in Rudolf Steiner's own words, are a few basics for the treatment of the human temperament. They make clear how essential it is for teachers to develop all four one-sided temperaments in themselves to a certain degree. Teachers will be able to understand their children all the better, the more they can find these characteristics in the beginning within themselves. (See also "Rudolf Steiner über die Temperamente," [Rudolf Steiner on the temperaments] compiled by Detlef Sixel.)

Children come to school and display the four temperaments—the melancholic, the phlegmatic, the sanguine, and the choleric—always, of course, in all possible variations and combinations. In Waldorf education, great value is placed on discerning the child's temperaments accordingly. The actual seating of the children in the classroom is arranged on this basis.

We try, for instance, to discover those who are choleric; we place them together so that it is possible for the teacher to know: There, in that corner, I have the children who tend to be choleric. In another corner, the phlegmatic children are seated; somewhere in the middle are the sanguine ones; again, somewhere else, the melancholic children are seated together. This method of grouping has great advantages. Experience shows that phlegmatic children when seated together become so bored with themselves and each other that, wishing to drive out this boredom, they begin to rub off on one another. Choleric children, in turn, pummel each other so much that in time this becomes very much better. It is the same with the sanguine children and their fidgety ways. Again, melancholic children see what melancholy is like in those around them. Thus, dealing with the children in such a way that one sees how "like reacts favorably on like" is very good even from the external point of view, quite apart from the fact that by doing so the teacher has the possibility of surveying the whole class, for this is much easier when children of similar temperament are seated together.

Now, the essential point is to discern human nature so well that a teacher is able to deal in a truly practical way with the choleric, the sanguine, or the melancholic temperament. Naturally, there will be cases where it becomes necessary to build the bridge that I referred to earlier, the bridge between school and home, and this must be done in a friendly and tactful way. Suppose, for instance, that I have a melancholic child in the class with whom I can scarcely do anything. I cannot quite figure it out. The child broods and is withdrawn, she is preoccupied with herself and pays no heed to what is going on in the class. An education that is not based on insights into the human being gives rise to the opinion that everything possible should be done to attract the child's attention in order to draw her out of herself. As a rule, however, this will make things worse, and the child broods more than ever. These means of effecting a cure, thought out in an amateurish way, help but little. At most, the spontaneous love a teacher feels for the child will be more helpful. The child knows that the teacher has sympathy for her, and this stirs and moves her more subconscious nature. Anything in the way of exhortation is not only wasted effort, but is actually harmful, because the child becomes more melancholic than before. But in class it helps greatly if you try to enter into the child's melancholy and try to discover the direction in which her conceptions tend. Then you show interest in the child's ideas, and through what you yourself do, you become, as it were, melancholic with the melancholic child. As a teacher, you must bear within yourself all four temperaments in harmonious activity. The way you behave toward the child is then in direct contradiction to the child's melancholy, and if you always continue this, the child perceives what you are, and she bears this insight into what you say. In this way, the loving reaction to the child that is behind the mask of melancholy you assume, gradually seeps into the child. This can be of great help in the class.

But now we go on and arrive at the realization that every manifestation of melancholy in a human being is connected with some irregularity in the function of the liver, unlikely as this may seem to modern physiologists. It is a fact that every kind of melancholy, especially if it goes so far in a child as to become pathological, is due to some irregularity of this kind. In such a case, I must turn to the parents of the child and say: You have to add more sugar to its food than you usually do, for sugar affects the normalization of the liver function. And by giving the mother the advice to let the child have more sugar, I shall make it possible for school and home environment to work together so as to reverse the trend to pathological melancholy, and to create the possibility for the child to find the right treatment.

Again, I may have a sanguine child, one who moves from one impression to another, who always wants the next thing when it has just taken hold of the preceding one, who strongly begins to have an interest in most anything, only to lose interest equally soon. A child with these characteristics is as a rule not dark-haired, but blond. I have to find ways of dealing with such children at school. In everything I do I shall try to be more sanguine than they are. Very quickly, I shall change the impressions I make on them, so that they are not left to their own devices of hurrying from one impression to another, but must keep pace with me. They become sick of that and finally give up. But between what I do in this way over and over in a sanguine manner when I wish to teach them, and what they want to do in accordance with their temperament by hurrying from one thing to another, there develops a kind of harmony in them as a reaction. I can thus deal with the sanguine children by presenting them with rapidly changing impressions, always thinking up something new so that they see black one moment, white the next, and must continually hurry from one thing to another. Now I get in touch with the mother. Assuredly I will hear from her that the child craves carbohydrates or sweets of some kind. Perhaps he or she is given a lot of candies or secretly nibbles on them, and maybe dishes are sweetened inordinately at home. Even if this is not the case, it is possible that the mother's milk was too sweet and contained too many carbohydrates. I then advise the mother to put the child on a diet for a time that contains less sugar. In this way, co-operation is brought about between home and school. [From Rudolf Steiner, *Human Values in Education*, lecture of July 23, 1924.]

Proper breathing

For those who become newly acquainted with Waldorf education, it is surprising that in the first lecture on *Foundations of Human Experience*, reference is made to two fundamental tasks the educator must consider in regard to human experience: learning to breathe and learning to sleep. Rudolf Steiner remarks in regard to learning to breathe properly:

Of all the relationships human beingss have to the physical world, the most important is breathing. Breathing begins the moment we enter the physical world. Breathing in the mother's womb is still a preparatory breathing, in a manner of speaking, it does not place the human being into a perfect relationship with the physical world. What should properly be called breathing begins only when the human being leaves the mother's womb. Breathing is extremely important for the human entity, since the entire threefold system of the physical human being is contained in this breathing.

We include the metabolic system as one of the members of this threefold physical human being. On the one side, metabolism is intimately connected with breathing; on the other, the breathing process is connected metabolically with the blood circulation. The blood circulation absorbs the substances of the external world, introduced by other means, into the human body, so that, in a sense, breathing is connected with the whole metabolism. This means that breathing has its own functions, but in this way it is also connected with the metabolic system.

On the other side, breathing is also connected with the life of nerves and senses in the human being. When we inhale, a congestion in the runoff of brain fluid occurs through the compression of the veins. This causes a slight lifting of the brain from its position in the fluid. When we exhale, a slight counter-movement occurs, that is, a sinking. In this way, the breathing rhythm affects the brain.

Even as breathing is connected to the metabolism through the supply of oxygen, it is related on the other side to the life of the nerves and senses. We can say that breathing is the most important connection between the human being who enters the physical world and the outer environment. Moreover, we must be aware that, when the human being enters physical existence, breathing does not yet fully function so as to support physical human life; the proper harmony, the correct relationship between the breathing process and the process of nerves and senses has not yet come about.

In observing children, we must say in regard to their nature that they have not yet learned to breathe so that their breathing properly supports the nerves-and-senses process. . . . In a higher sense, children must learn to receive into their spirit what they can be given by being born to be breathers. You see that this aspect of education tends toward the soul-spiritual. By bringing the breathing into harmony with the nerves-and-senses process, we draw the soul-spiritual into the child's physical life. [*Foundations of Human Experience*, lecture of August 21, 1919.]

Now, what possibilities does the teacher have for influencing the rhythmic system, particularly the breathing? Here, the nurturing of the emotional life itself certainly takes first place, for feelings stimulate the rhythmic system and are borne by it, whereas thought stands in a direct relationship to the nerves-and-senses system, as does willing to the metabolic-and-limb system. Feelings motivate and open the children up, or cause them to back away. With joyous interest, children can attentively turn to their surroundings, thereby activating the functions of their nerves and senses in a healthy way, and bring them into a relation with the breathing process. In pain, in listlessness, in boredom, children withdraw into themselves and cannot carry out this work. Rudolf Steiner speaks about the cultivation of the proper mood of feeling as a precondition for every learning process [*Education for Adolescents*, lecture of June 15, 1921]:

The transition from conceptual thinking, or the emotional grasp of a content, to learning by heart will never come about in the right way unless the content has first made a powerful appeal to the child's feelings. We should never allow anything to be memorized until we have seen to it that the children have acquired a clear and sharp feeling for all the details of the content, a sense, above all, that enables them properly to form their own relationship to it.

Let us look at an extreme case. Take prayer: Children should be admonished to enter into a mood of reverence when they are supposed to learn a prayer. We have to see to it that the children first acquire this reverent mood. We ought to be horrified at the very idea of giving children a prayer without having first brought them into the right mood for it. Never should a child be allowed to recite a prayer without having an attitude of reverence.

Again, we should not ask a child to recite a charming little poem without first evoking a little smile, a sense of joy and delight in that child.

Now all this has a decidedly physical and bodily significance. Every time we teach children something that has a tragic or noble quality, we essentially exert an influence on their metabolism. In turn, if we teach children something that has a pretty, graceful quality, we affect the children's heads, their system of nerves and senses. In this regard we can proceed in a hygienic manner. Suppose we have a child who is quite superficial and always looks for new sensations. Having first brought such a child into the right preparatory mood, we give him or her some sublime or tragic bit of literature to learn by heart. That can be of real help. We must certainly take such matters under consideration during instruction.

Just as breathing has to mediate between the nerves-and-senses system and the metabolic system, the feeling soul of the child is easily brought into close connection with the appearances of the surrounding world through joyousness, gaiety, and amiability. By contrast, sadness, pain, greatness, and splendor awaken feelings that enable children to experience themselves powerfully within themselves, right up to the phenomenon of withdrawal into their own body in pain and sorrow.

A second possibility to contribute to learning to breathe properly is the rhythmic formulation of the instruction itself. In the main lesson, this begins with its rhythmic portion, that is to say, with turning to the child's rhythmic system. Proceeding from here, the actual content of instruction begins in accordance with the subject matter. At the end of the main lesson, the point is to lead the subject of what has been learned into the children's own activity. This means to join it to their will, which, depending on circumstances may also be led over into an appropriate assignment of tasks to be done at home.

The third fundamental way to affect breathing is the cultivation of "right speech." For no other subject matter did Rudolf Steiner give as many indications in the curriculum as for the nurturing of speech. Already in first grade, speech exercises, age-appropriate poems, listening, and storytelling should be practiced. In regard to this, Rudolf Steiner comments that it is this careful cultivation of speech that is the decisive help for regulating the breathing and positively stimulating the growth of the lungs. In the twelfth lecture of the teacher training course in Basel [*The Renewal of Education*, lecture of May 7, 1920], Rudolf Steiner stated:

Particularly during childhood, the effect of properly treated soul experiences on the physical organism is of immense importance. It is therefore essential to try to induce the child again and again to learn to speak clearly and resonantly, to "round off" each syllable and sentence and to speak with a full voice, as perfectly as possible. In the human being, healthy breathing depends on sound speaking. And, indirectly, the proper development of the human chest organs depends on proper speech. It would be interesting from this point of view to gather statistics of the chest illnesses so rampant at present. One should ask: To what extent is tuberculosis caused by too little care having been taken at school with regard to appropriate speaking and pronunciation of syllables, above all, by much too little attention having been paid to how fully a child breathes while speaking? Speech must not proceed from breathing, rather, breathing must proceed from speech. A proper way of speaking, a right feeling for speech, and for the length and shortness of syllables and words, must be developed; then breathing will adjust itself. It is nonsense to believe that breathing should be trained in order that right speaking can be achieved. Proper breathing must be a result of rightly experienced ways of speaking. Then that reflects back on breathing. Generally, we should focus in this manner more thoroughly on the connection between the physical and soul-spiritual elements of the human being.

Proper sleeping[31]

From adult life, we are familiar with the rhythmic change of sleeping and waking, two distinctly separate conditions of consciousness and life-condition. In sleep, the body is regenerated, in particular the nervous system, and the events of the previous day are absorbed so that one wakes up the following morning with new viewpoints and likewise with capacities that have been acquired during the night. Everyone who, for instance, exercises daily, be it with a musical instrument or a meditative exercise, notices that taking this effort of the previous day through the night firms it up and produces a capacity-basis for continuing the exercise the following day. In a manner of speaking, the effort leaves an impression on the body and slowly becomes a habit, even a substantial one eventually, one with which we concern and connect ourselves intensely during the day. In the child, this clear boundary between sleeping and waking is still in the process of developing. Aside from this, it is a fact that infants literally sleep into life and that phases of waking only gradually grow longer in the transition from infancy to the age of kindergarten, until finally the midday nap is eliminated and children remain awake throughout the day and sleep during the night. Nonetheless, the child's wakeful consciousness, in the sense of the modern objective day-consciousness, matures only gradually. At preschool age, the surroundings are still physiognomically perceived by the child, that is to say, perceived as ensouled and expressive—not yet in an abstract, objective manner as merely "something external." Sleep likewise does not yet cause such a clear separation of astral body and ego from the nervous system, bearing them into the realm of nature's elemental beings and the beings of the higher hierarchies. This clear separation of astral body and ego from the physical and etheric constitution during the night for communication with the spiritual world only begins around the ninth or tenth year.

This signifies, however, that in the first years of school, children are still a little bit asleep during the so-called waking hours. They are much more strongly given up to sense impressions, in the way an adult behaves during sleep in regard to the spiritual world. Impressions during the day can therefore also work deeply into the body in children, and produce a healthy or an ill effect. For this reason, every word, thought, and act that the teacher lets happen in front of the children must be "worthy of the night." That is to say, it must be spirit-permeated, spirit-connected, or at the very least contain longing for the spirit. What is brought forward in instruction needs to be imbedded in the creative process, which is always simultaneously a spiritual-material process. Only then can we actualize what Rudolf Steiner says in the following statement from *Foundations of Human Experience*: All we can do is to use the time spent by human beings on the physical plane in such a way that the very thing we do with them *can gradually be taken by them into the spiritual world.*

Only in sleep, when the astral body and ego are truly released from the physical body and etheric body, can everything be completely borne across into the spiritual world. Earlier, spiritual and physical world were still more closely connected with one another in wakefulness as well as in sleep. Concerning this, Rudolf Steiner explains:

Another thing small children cannot yet properly do is something we must focus on so that accord can be created between their two components, between physical body and spirit-soul. What small children cannot yet do properly at the beginning of their earthly existence—you will notice that, normally, what we must spiritually emphasize appears to contradict the external world order—is to carry out the alternation between sleeping and waking in a way appropriate to the human being. Viewed from the outside, we can, of course, say that children sleep quite well. They sleep much more than older people do. They even sleep into life. But children are not yet capable of the very thing that constitutes the inner basis of sleeping and waking. They experience all kinds of things on the physical plane. They use their limbs; they eat, drink, and breathe. But engaging in all sorts of things in the physical realm while alternating between sleeping and waking, they cannot take what they experience in the physical plane— what they see and hear, and what they do with their little arms and legs— and carry it into the spiritual world, work on it there, and bring the results back to the physical world. We can characterize children's sleep by saying that it differs from the sleep of an adult. Normally, adults process their waking experiences during sleep. Children cannot yet carry their waking experiences into sleep. Thus, in sleep, they settle into the general cosmic order without taking their physical experiences into the cosmic order. Through proper education, human beings must be brought to the point where they can carry their experience in the physical plane into what the soul-spirit or the spirit-soul does during sleep. As teachers and educators, we cannot teach children anything at all from the higher worlds. What human beings receive from the higher worlds comes to them during sleep. All we can do is to use the time spent by human beings on the physical plane in such a way that the very thing we do with them can gradually be taken by them into the spiritual world. Then, what they have taken with them can flow back into the physical world as strength, strength they can bring from the spiritual world to become real human beings in physical existence.[32] [*Foundations of Human Experience*, lecture of August 21, 1919.]

As an illustration of this fact, a child's drawing is reproduced here that Caroline von Heidebrand published in *Erziehungskunst* [The Art of Education] in 1934.

A three-year-old boy draws himself sleeping in bed. Streams move out of him that unite with a blossom that has twelve petals.

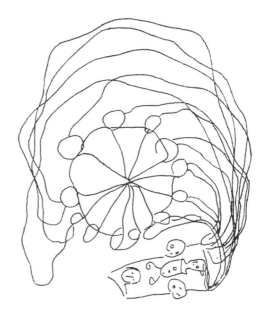

In regard to this Rudolf Steiner says:

As small children, we are more or less in a state of sleep. This is also why . . . as small children, we are much more exposed to the extraterrestrial influences than later on. Only gradually, we work our way further and further into earthly conditions. But as children, even what is within the skin is still pliable and can be formed more than later on. [*Man: Hieroglyph of the Universe*, lecture of April 17, 1920.]

For teachers to be in a position to carry out this healing work that helps build up the body of the child during their instruction, they themselves must convey something of their night experience into their day experience, especially their connection with the nature of the Third Hierarchy: the angels, archangels, and the time spirits. The teachers themselves are linked through their thinking with the world of the angels, through their feeling with the world of the archangels, and through their will with the world of the archai. [See Rudolf Steiner's *Man's Connection to Spiritual Beings*, lecture of April 28, 1923.] Everything in the teachers' thinking, feeling, and will that has a connection to the reality of spirit and does not merely tend toward the superficial side of life, brings them—and the students to whom they convey it—into a relationship with the world of the angels, a relationship that invigorates both teachers and students.[33]

CHAPTER 8

Rudolf Steiner's Comments
on Subject Areas

One of the most inspiring aspects of a school physician's studies must surely be to follow up on Rudolf Steiner's indications concerning the effects on the human being of studying various subjects. This leads to the realization that all the scientific, artistic, and religious contents that can be offered to children and teenagers are tools to develop the subtle differentiations of their body, soul, and spirit. As this development proceeds, it becomes clear that everything in this education depends on the acquisition of faculties—not at all on introducing the students to traditions of knowledge in the most reliable way possible, or adapting them to outer life in the fastest possible way. Rather, subjects are arranged so that students can put their soul-spiritual capacities to the test, in order—by means of the world around them—to awaken to their own selves. It is hoped that the examples of the physiological effect of instructional content given here will be a stimulus to study them in the context of Steiner's lectures, and to work with teachers on an understanding of these suggestions. An importrant resource is the comprehensive collection of curricular indications gathered by A. E. Karl Stockmeyer.[34]

Forming mental images

First and foremost, the forming of mental images makes use of the etheric organism, as this organism is at the free disposal of the soul-spiritual activity by way of the nerve-sense organization.

We ought to be fully aware of the fact that while the forming of perceptions is a function of the head, judging and drawing conclusions is not.

You may conclude that the head will gradually be put out of use altogether through spiritual science. In a deeper sense, this would in fact correspond to reality. As human beings in our life between birth and death, we do not gain a great deal from our head. Outwardly, in physical form, the head is certainly the most perfect part of us; that is because it is a replica, an image of our spiritual organization we possess between death and a new birth. Our head is like an impress of what we were before birth, before our conception. All that is soul-spiritual in us has left its mark there; we have therefore in our head an image of our pre-earthly life.

Aside from the physical body, it is only the ether body that comes to full activity in the head. The other components of our being, astral body and ego, do indeed fill the head, but we find there merely a reflection of their activity; they are active on their own, and the head merely mirrors their activity.

From the outside, our head represents a picture of the supersensible world. I spoke of this in the lecture I gave you last year, showing how we carry our head as an entity apart and different from the rest of our organism. We might think of the rest as a kind of carriage, and the head as the person who sits in it; or, if we take the rest of our organism to be a horse, then the head is its rider. The head is really set apart from this connection with the external world. It sits upon the body like a parasite, and behaves like a parasite too. We must dismiss from our minds the materialistic notion that, for this life on earth, our head means such a great deal. A mirroring apparatus, that is its use for us, affording us a picture of our life of soul and spirit before birth. [*Education for Adolescents,* lecture of June 13, 1921.]

History, geography, geology: finding oneself through experiencing the world

When do history, geography, and geology promote development, and more importantly, how?

To want to teach history to a child before the 9th or 10th year is a quite futile endeavor, for the course of history is a closed book to the child before this age. It is only with the 9th or 10th year—you can observe this for yourselves—that children begin to be interested in individual human beings. If you portray Caesar, or Achilles, Hector, Agamemnon, or Alcibiades simply as comprehensive, integrated personalities, allowing the remaining historical details to appear only as a background, if you paint the whole picture in this way, the child will show the greatest interest in it. It will even be evident that he or she is eager to know more and more about this sort of thing. The child will feel the urge to enter further into the lives of these historical personalities if you describe them in this way. Comprehensive pictures of personalities complete in themselves; comprehensive pictures of what meal-time was like in one or some other century; sculptural descriptions of how people used to eat before forks were invented; pictorial descriptions of how one dined in ancient Rome; how a Greek walked, conscious of each step, aware of the form of his leg, feeling this form; descriptions of how the people of the Old Testament, the Hebrew people, walked, who had no feeling at all for form, and let their arms hang loose and legs trail; evoking feelings for these details that can be expressed in pictures—this is the way to teach history between the ages of 10 and 12.

Thereafter, we can proceed to historical relationships, for it is only now that children become receptive to concepts such as cause and effect. Only now can interrelated history be presented. Everything that lives in history must be worked out so as to show development. Call up before you the following picture. We are now living in the year 1924 [the date of the lecture]. Charlemagne lived from 760 until 814. If the year 800 is taken as the approximate date, we find he lived 1120 years before us. If we imagine ourselves now living in the world as a child growing up, we can reckon that in the course of a century we can have a son or daughter, father or mother, grandfather or perhaps even a great-grandfather, that is to say, three or four generations following one after the other in the course of a hundred years. We can picture these three or four generations by picturing that the son or daughter stands in the foreground. The father or mother will stand behind, resting their hands on the shoulders of the one in front; the grandfather in turn places his hands on the shoulders of the father, and the great-grandfather puts his hands on the shoulders of the grandfather. Now you have gone back one whole century. If you imagine placing son, father, and grandfather one behind the other in this way as people belonging to the present age, and behind them the course of the generations in a further ten centuries, you will get all told eleven times three or four generations, let us say forty-four generations. If, therefore, you were to place forty-four people one behind the other, each with his hands on the shoulders of the one in front, the first can be a person of the present day and the last can be Charlemagne. In this way, by placing one person behind the other, you can acquire an idea of how long ago this is, and say: This goes through eleven centuries. In this way you can change the time relationships in history, which are so difficult to realize, into relationships that are purely spatial. You can picture it also in this way: Here you have one man who is speaking to another; the latter turns round and speaks to the one behind, who in turn does the same thing, and so it goes on until you come right back to the time when Peter spoke to Christ. In doing this you get the whole development of the Christian Church in the conversation between the people standing one behind the other. The whole apostolic succession is placed visually before you. [*Human Values in Education*, lecture of July 24, 1924.]

Another important phase in the child's development lies between his or her twelfth and thirteenth year. During this period, the spirit and soul elements in the human being are reinforced and strengthened, that is to say, those spirit and soul elements that are less dependent on the ego. What we are accustomed to call astral body in spiritual science permeates the etheric body and unites with it. Of course, the astral body as an independent being is not born until puberty, but it manifests in a particular manner through the etheric body by permeating and invigorating it between the ages of twelve and thirteen. Here then lies another important milestone in the young person's development. If we deal correctly with what is inherent in him or her, this milestone is expressed in the way the youngsters begin to develop an understanding for the impulses working in the external world that resemble impulses of spirit and soul, such as those, for example, at work in the external world as forces of history. I have given you an example of how the working of these historical forces can be brought within the scope of teaching at the elementary school level. But, although you will have to transpose what I said to you into childlike language, you can be as childlike as you will in your expressions and you will achieve nothing in the way of awakening in the children a proper understanding of historical impulses if you approach them with historical observations before they have completed their twelfth year. Prior to this, you can tell them about history in the form of stories—biographies, for instance. This they would be able to grasp. But they will be unable to grasp historical connections before they complete their twelfth year. Therefore you will do damage if you fail to observe this turning point. The children now begin to develop a yearning to have explained to them as history what they have earlier taken in as stories. So if you have told the children stories, for instance about one or

174

other of the Crusaders or other historical figures, you must now endeavor to transform this material in a way that will allow them to perceive the historical impulses and historical links involved.

When you observe something like this and notice unmistakably that, if you do things properly, the children understand you from their twelfth year onwards, you will say to yourselves: Up to the children's ninth year I shall in the main restrict myself to what we have discussed as the artistic element and out of this bring writing and reading, and later arithmetic as well. I shall not make the transition to natural history until after the point is reached that we discussed yesterday; and I shall wait with history, except in the form of stories, until the children have reached their twelfth year. At this point, they begin inwardly to take an interest in great historical relationships. This will be especially important for the future, for it will become more and more necessary to educate people in an understanding of historical coherence, for hitherto they have never really achieved a proper view of history. So far they have first and foremost been members of the economic and national life in which they were integrated and participated mechanically, coping quite adequately with the requirements and interests of this economic and national life by knowing a few anecdotes about rulers and wars, which is not history, and a few dates when rulers and a few famous people lived, and when wars took place.

In the future, instruction in school will have to be particularly concerned with the way in which the cultural life of humankind has developed. It will have to contain proper teaching on the impulses of history. These impulses will have to be included in the curriculum at the right moment in time. [*Practical Advice to Teachers*, lecture of August 29, 1919.]

It is important for us to gather together all of our own temperamental tendencies and teach history lessons with strong personal interest. The children will have time enough in later life for objectivity. To make our teaching entirely objective when we tell the children about Brutus and Julius Caesar, for instance, to refrain from showing any emotion in the picture we give of these two contrasting characters, is to teach history badly. We must be emotionally involved. We need not become wildly excited and rave, but in a subtle way openly show sympathy or antipathy in regard to Caesar and Brutus when we depict the situation. The children must be stimulated to empathize with what we thus present to them. Above all, subjects of this kind—history, geography, geology—should be presented by us with real feeling. Geology, for instance, becomes particularly fascinating when the teacher has a profound, sympathetic understanding for the geological formations under the earth's surface. . . .

If we develop empathy first of all in ourselves, we reach the point of allowing children to share in these matters. Such a method will naturally make things more difficult for us. We shall certainly have to work hard. But it is the only way to bring life into our teaching. And what we impart with feeling fosters the growth of the children's own inner life, while what we give them in mere perceptions is dead and remains so for them. . . . We reach what is inherently found in the blood and has significance here and now on earth by imbuing our perceptions with true feeling and then teaching them to the children. [*Education for Adolescents*, lecture of June 13, 1921.]

When we consider human beings who draw conclusions, who are active in this way, and we see how they stand within the whole world—not becoming disengaged from the world through the head—when we call such a person to mind, we see at once that he or she is unthinkable without space. Insofar as I am a being of legs and feet, I am a part of the world of space. When we consider this in its spatial aspect, it has the effect of placing our astral body firmly on its legs, so to speak, when we teach geography to children. The astral body actually becomes denser and more powerful below. When we deal with what is spatial, we solidify the human being's soul and spirit in the direction of the ground below. In other words, we bring about a certain solidification within the human being by teaching geography in a vivid, descriptive way. But it must be done in such a way that we always call forth the awareness that the Niagara is not located near the River Elbe. We must always evoke the consciousness of the vast distance of space between the Elbe and the Niagara.

When we become truly involved in doing this in a descriptive way, we place the human being into space. In particular, we develop in children something that will teach them world interest, and we shall see the effects of this in many directions. A child with whom we study geography in an intelligent manner will have a more loving relationship to his or her fellow human being than one who does not learn what it means to be side by side with others. The children will learn to feel that they live alongside other human beings and will be considerate of others.

Such things play no small part in the moral training of children, and the lack of attention to geography is partly responsible for the terrible decline in recent years of the brotherly love that should prevail among human beings. A connection of this kind may escape observation altogether, but it is there, and plays its part. For a certain subconscious intelligence or lack thereof always prevails in the phenomena of civilized life.

History instruction that deals with time has a quite different effect. We can only teach it properly if we give due consideration to the time element in it. We shall be failing to do this if our lessons offer only pictures. Suppose I were to tell a child about Charlemagne as though he might be the child's uncle who is still alive. I should be leading that child astray. If I speak to children of Charlemagne, I must see that they realize how far removed Charlemagne is from us in time. I must bring it home to them, for example, by saying: Imagine you are a little child standing here, and you take hold of your father's hand. The children can picture that. Then I make sure that they understand that the father is much older than they are. And now I tell them: Imagine that your father is holding the hand of his father, and he the hand of your father's grandfather. I shall then have led the children back about sixty years. And now I can go still further back from the grandfather and say to them: Imagine thirty ancestors, one behind the other. I have made them picture a whole long row and explain that the thirtieth might have been Charlemagne. In this way children acquire a sense of distance in time. We should never present isolated facts to them; the history lesson should always create a sense of distance in time. This is important.

In treating different epochs, we must point to the characteristic features of each and, in this way, give children an idea of how the various epochs differ from one another. Our aim must be through it all to let history live chiefly in time concepts, so that the children see it all from the aspect of time. This will work powerfully upon their inner being and stimulate it.

It is quite possible to teach history in such a way that it fails to assume the right position. History lessons may, for instance, take hold of the children's mentality in a form of a strong bias in favor of certain interests. Suppose we perpetually teach them the history of their own country, and pay little attention to more distant events. We then put history in the wrong light, encouraging false patriotism and so forth in children. I don't think you will have far to look for examples of this. This way of teaching will tend to make the child's state of mind stubborn and moody. This will be a side effect. Above all, it will cause a person to be disinclined to objectivity in regard to the world's phenomena. And lack of objectivity is the outstanding evil of our age. Insufficient study of geography, and a false method of teaching history throughout this age have contributed considerably to the grievous troubles of our time. Probably you yourselves can look back and recall what you were subjected to in your history lessons. It will help you understand why you find it difficult to see various events in their true perspective.

These are examples that indicate the direction education and lessons must take if we are to connect them in a healthy manner with the conditions and impulses of life. We simply cannot teach with the object of seeing how quickly we can be finished with some subject matter. Rather, the life conditions of the children in regard to body, soul, and spirit must take first place in our thought. We must always keep in mind the human element, seeing the children in their totality, insofar as they are beings who continue to work and participate even when they are asleep. For if we do not take into consideration the fact that children also sleep—and modern education without exception takes no interest at all in the fact that a child sleeps, or at most only from the point of view of hygiene—this has a quite definite effect. By leaving out of consideration the fact that what we have taught children during the lessons continues to work on during the night in some form, when a part of their being is outside their body, we turn them into automatons.

Truth to tell, in many respects, education and training in schools today cannot be said to educate and train children to be human beings, but tends rather to produce the most noticeable type of human automaton—such as the types found any day among bureaucrats. Education is directed to the end that human beings shall no longer be human, but a finished product of education, having passed first and secondary examinations, leading a well-defined, circumscribed existence. You encounter such a person, and it matters not whether one is A, the other B, if one is an assessor, the other an attorney. This is the result of an education that has only taken account of the waking human being. It implies a denial of humanity's spiritual part and is accordingly blind to all that takes place during sleep.

In recent philosophy, this point of view became shockingly evident in Descartes and in Bergson. These philosophers asserted that the continuous and permanent element in the human being is the I; they said that we must look always to the I in a person, for there we take hold of reality. I would seriously like to point out that if this is true, these philosophers cease to exist as soon as they fall asleep, and begin to exist again when they wake up. For the I is absent during the intervening period; it recedes from our grasp. It withdraws, and the formula of existence propounded by Descartes and Bergson should not be "I think, therefore I am," but should go thus: On the 2nd of June, 1867, from 6 a.m. to 8 p.m., I *thought,* therefore I *was.* On the following day I again *thought* from 6 a.m. to 8 p.m., and again I *was.* Existence becomes rather a complicated matter with such a philosophy. The intervals would have to be omitted. But people do not think of that. In all seriousness, they wish to be concerned only with all manner of abstract ideas, not with realities that lie at the basis of the human being.

In instruction, however, we have to deal with realities if we want to educate our children to become adult human beings. We need not trouble ourselves so much that the right conditions will come about. If people are educated to be true human beings, they will themselves create the right conditions.

This brings home to us a deep understanding for why the cultural life must be free and independent. Children can only be educated to become true human beings if we direct our work with them solely to that end, knowing as we do that social and political conditions are not products of the state, but consequences of this education toward true humanness that men and women received as children. This is why the cultural life cannot be an appendage of the state or the economy, but must develop independently on its own. [*Education for Adolescents*, lecture of June 14, 1921.]

Artistic instruction and developing the faculty of judgment

Every artistic activity challenges artistic judgment. This judgment is carried above all by the astral body, which has its support in the rhythmic system, including the arms and hands.

Now, ideation and mental picturing are connected with the head, but not judgment. Judgment is connected with the middle organism, particularly with the arms and hands. In reality, we really judge with our arms and hands. We think and form mental pictures with our head. If we therefore picture the content of a judgment, the judging itself takes place in the mechanism of arms and hands; only the mental mirror image occurs in the head.

You will be able to grasp this in your mind and will comprehend this important educational truth. You can say: Our rhythmic (middle) organism exists in order to mediate the world of feeling; the rhythmic system is the seat of feelings in human beings. Now, judgment has a deep relationship to feeling. This is true even of the most abstract judgments. We assert, for example, that Charlie is a good little boy. That is a judgment; as we make it, we have a feeling of affirmation. Feelings of affirmation, and likewise of denial, play a large part in judgment, and so altogether does the feeling that is expressed in the objective, in relation to the subjective. And only because feeling belongs so much to the semiconscious, we do not notice the extent to which feeling participates in judging.

Since we human beings are destined to be preeminently judging beings, our arm organism is brought into harmony with the rhythmic organism, while at the same time it is liberated from the continuity of that rhythmic organism. Thus, in the physical connection between the rhythmic organism and the liberated organism of the arms, we have a physical-sensory expression for the connection of feeling with judgment.

In turn, the drawing of conclusions is connected with legs and feet. Naturally, you would be laughed at, if you were to tell a psychologist today that you draw conclusions, not with your head but with your feet, yet it is true, nevertheless! If, as human beings, we were not organized to depend on legs and feet, we should not be able to draw conclusions. This is how it works: We form percepts with our etheric body, and that has its support in our head organization. But we judge—judge meant in its original, elementary sense—with the astral body; and that has its support in arms and hands. Concluding is accomplished with legs and feet; for the ego — it is with the ego, of course, that we draw conclusions—has its support in legs and feet.

You see from this, the whole human being participates in logic. It is most important that we should find our way into seeing this, picturing how the whole person participates in logic. Modern knowledge knows very little about the human being, for it does not know how our whole being participates in logic. It believes that matters are always managed by our head.

Now, to the extent that we are beings of legs and feet, we fit in a quite different way into the physical world than we do as head-beings. We can illustrate this by making a drawing (see drawing on p. 181). Picture a human being, drawn diagrammatically, and form the following concept: Assume the man lifts a weight (A) with his hand—say, a kilogram. Now, think the man away who lifts the weight with his hand; attach a rope (making the sketch to the right of the man's figure) (R) here to the weight, carry it over a pulley (P), and hang another kilogram of weight at the other end of the rope—or perhaps a slightly heavier weight (B). The heavier weight will draw the first weight upward. Now we have a mechanical contrivance that does the same thing as I do when I lift the weight with my arm. When I use my arm to lift the weight, I perform the same action as is performed by attaching a heavier weight and letting it pull up the lighter one. I unfold my will, and thereby accomplish something that can also quite well be accomplished with a purely mechanical contrivance. The

180

picture of the action is the same in each case. This drawing up of the kilogram weight which we can observe is a perfectly objective event. And if my will intervenes, the outer picture does not change. [*Education for Adolescents*, lecture of June 13, 1921.]

Love reaches out to include all things. It is the innermost motivation for all actions. We ought to do what we love to do. Duty should grow to be one with love; we ought to love doing what we ought to do. For this to

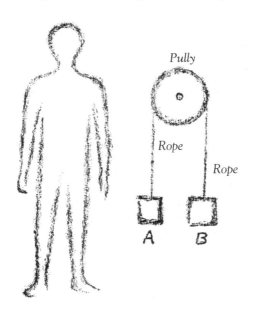

develop in the right way, we must be by the side of our children in the right way. Throughout the whole period of elementary school, we have to take pains to develop the children's sense of beauty. [*Education for Adolescents*, lecture of June 19. 1921.]

Lifting unconscious questions into consciousness

Even if a student is unable to formulate what he or she experiences inwardly as a question, the teacher must be in a position to do so and ensure that the question is indeed formulated. Moreover, the teacher must be able to satisfy the feeling that arises within the student on the occasion of this question. For if a teacher does not, what happens above all is that the experience accompanies the young person into the world of sleep, into the condition of sleep; and in sleep, such unformed questions give rise to a whole host of deleterious substances that develop only at night, the time when poisonous substances should really be rendered harmless and absorbed rather than newly produced. Poisonous substances are produced that gradually build up dreadfully in the young person's brain when he or she returns to class.

This must and can be avoided. It can only be avoided, however, if the students do not have the feeling: Once again the teacher has failed to give us the right answer; he hasn't answered the question appropriately. We cannot receive the proper answer from him. Here we have the latent weaknesses that are often not referred to openly, when students have the feeling that the teacher is not up to giving them the answers they need. Moreover, this inadequacy is not merely determined by the teacher's personal ability or inability, but in particular by the method of teaching.

If we therefore devote too much time inundating youngsters at this age with a large amount of information, or otherwise teach in such a way that their doubts and problems are left unresolved, then the situation arises even though it lies on a more objective level where the teacher's latent weaknesses are exposed, weaknesses that are not directly expressed. This is something that must be of primary concern in dealing with this age group. The young person really must be able to feel that the teacher knows what he or she is doing in every respect. Earlier, the natural feeling for authority is present, and I might say that many a teacher not overendowed with competence is looked up to in every way as an authority by the students in the lower classes. Other factors are of importance there. But from the ages of fourteen or fifteen onward, the students' subconscious minds—more even than their conscious minds—keep track of any remaining questions that have arisen in their souls and that the teacher has failed to answer. This, above all else, is what we must especially aim for in our teaching, namely, that we always try to make our presentations transparent, so that, as it were, things do not get in the way of each other in the students' minds, thereby preventing them from arriving at a clear judgment.

There will be no need to work out a particular methodology for one or the other subject in regard to this age-group. Teachers who can simply place themselves into the right relationship to students of this age should be able to introduce the most diverse methods; indeed, it would be good to do so. The essential thing is to share a certain common ground of interest with the students from beginning to end of the lesson. The teacher must be interested in the subject, and if that is the case, he or she will actually be able instinctively to hit on the right approach for this age. Hence it is especially important when working with this age group—in some respects even more so than previously—to emphasize the value of thorough preparation. And, if I may say so, the prize goes to the teachers who, in preparing the content of a lesson, whatever it may be, discover one new, just one single problem with regard to how the subject is to be treated, thus constantly re-awakening their interest in it. There should not be a single one among the teachers who would counter this by objecting that it is impossible to rekindle interest anew each time one has to prepare some aspect of chemistry, mathematics, history, or literature, especially when one has given the same lesson so many times, nor that one cannot approach the material as if coming across it for the first time. It is perfectly possible to rekindle interest in what one has to teach, even if it is the multiplication tables. But as difficult as it is in the case of the multiplication tables, it is far easier in respect of what one has to present to the upper classes. [*Balance in Teaching*, lecture of June 21, 1922.]

The effect of instruction on the ego

When the teacher fails to bring about the right sort of link between the ego and the physical organization, it is possible that the ego remains too much outside. The result is that the person turns into a dreamer or visionary, or generally becomes useless in the world, because he or she is caught up in fantastic conceptions. This is the other extreme: the mistake of not letting the ego submerge sufficiently in the organization. Even people who as children have a predisposition for dreaming, for spurious romance, for spiritual pursuits in the wrong sense, can be protected from these leanings as adults, if the educator sees to it that the ego is not unduly excluded from the remaining organization, but permeates it in the right way. . . . But how do we go about doing this?

We can accomplish something in these directions by acquainting ourselves with the means by which we can cope with such conditions, and they are as follows: Everything that necessitates forming representations of figures and space, like geometry and arithmetic, contributes in instruction and education to the result that the ego settles properly into the organization when children form such representations and digest them. Furthermore, those elements of speech that lean toward music, rhythm, recitation and the like, add to the ego's correctly fitting into the organism.

Music, especially training of memory of tone, has a beneficent effect upon a child with a tendency to fanciful imaginings.

These are the means with which we must work in the case of children in whom we note that their ego does not seem to want to enter the organization properly, and who therefore might easily remain too fanciful. When, on the other hand, we notice that children are becoming too closely bound to the physical, that the ego is becoming overly dependent on the body, we only need to let them draw those geometrical forms that are ordinarily taken hold of by thought. When we ask the children to draw the geometric forms, we create the counterbalance to an excessive absorption of the ego. Thus you see that it is possible to educate in the right way, provided the subjects of instruction are properly employed.

If children—due to their talent or because of other circumstances—need instruction in music, and if we notice further that they are becoming too dependent on their physical organism, that a heavy element is entering into their singing, then we must try to lead them right away to listening, rather than to tone memory. We can always attempt to regulate their tendencies, in one direction by encouraging the absorption of the ego in the way I have described, and in the other by preventing too great an absorption of it. One of these conditions is certain to arise if we fail to maintain the proper balance.

In speech instruction, it is particularly beneficial to work in a regulating way, for the element of music in speech contributes to the ego's absorption. If I notice that this is taking place to an excessive degree, I take up something with the child that deals more with the meaning, the content, of speech. In this case I interest the child in matters in which meaning is the important feature. But if I notice that the children are becoming too fanciful, I try to place them in a position where they have to learn more of the recitative, rhythmic element, the beat of speech. Teachers must acquire these skills artistically, and in so doing they can achieve a certain dynamism.

There are subjects of instruction by means of which one can effectively avoid the ego's over-absorption by the remaining organization. These are, in particular, geography, history, and everything relating to drawing and to whatever is pictorial. This is preeminently the case when one develops a segment of history in a narrative style, and vivid emotions for a personality are engendered in the child, veneration, love, (or hate, if you like, provided the personality under discussion is contemptible). This emotional participation is the important thing, and by means of it, especially in teaching history, one can do a great deal toward preventing the child from

184

becoming too closely bound to the physical. But if we notice by means of the necessary insight into the children's development that, through a little too much of this sort of instruction in history, they begin to show signs of being too fanciful, we must try something else, as has been described. All this must then be harmonized with the curriculum. It must be started at the right age for the children, and it is therefore advisable to keep observing them for years. If a child becomes too fanciful through the narrative presentations of history, then, when the right time arrives, one must permeate the subject with ideas, with the great interrelationships in history. To sum up: Individual treatment of events and personalities in history prevents the ego from being absorbed too much by the bodily organization; illuminating history with ideas that cover whole epochs stimulates the ego's entrance into the physical organization.

Again, through much drawing and working with pictures, the ego can easily be lifted out of the organization, and this too can make a child fanciful. But then one can immediately resort to the counter-measure, for if children show signs of instability as a result of such work, or perhaps even through writing, the remedy is to have them interpret the meaning of what they have drawn. Have them think, for instance, of something in connection with the rosette they have drawn, or admire the forms of the letters of the alphabet, and then project them into their consciousness. While mere writing and drawing lift the children out of themselves, the observation of what they have drawn and written immerses them in themselves again.

Such things show us how we can employ these details of education and instruction in the right way, provided we raise them to the level of art. It is of quite special importance that we should really occupy ourselves with such things. Consider, for instance, the instruction in geography. In the main this tends to prevent undue absorption of the ego, so we can employ it with good effect in the case of children who threaten to become too bound to the body. On the other hand, if children tend to become excessively fanciful through instruction in geography, this can be counteracted by insisting that they should grasp concepts such as differences in layers and strata, or by interspersing geography instruction with a topic that requires thinking in more geometrical terms. This will bring the ego back again into the organization. [*Balance in Teaching*, lecture of September 22, 1920.]

Stimulation of intelligence

Let us assume, as a starting point, that we are engaged in the perception of a picture, that is, in an experience that is transmitted primarily through the organ of sight—a drawing, some shape in our surroundings—in short, in anything that becomes a property of our soul by virtue of our eyes. Here we must distinguish between three sharply differentiated inner activities.

First we have perception as such; it actually takes place in the organ of sight. From this, we must distinguish comprehension; and in this connection we must know that all comprehension is transmitted through our rhythmic system, not through the nerve-sense system. Through the latter, only perception is transmitted; and we comprehend a pictorial process, for instance, merely because the rhythmic process, which, regulated as it is by the activities of heart and lungs, is carried by the spinal fluid up to the brain. In reality, comprehension is transmitted physically by the vibrations that occur in the brain and have their origin in our rhythmic system. It is through breathing that we are able to comprehend.

You see how erroneously these things are generally considered by physiology today. It is believed that comprehension has something to do with the human nervous system. In reality, it is based on the fact that the rhythmic system receives our observations and mental images and works on them further. But because the rhythmic system is linked with our comprehension, it comes into close relation with our feeling. Anyone who practices intimate self-observation will notice what connections exist between comprehension and actual feeling. In essence, we must really feel the truth of something we have comprehended if we are to subscribe to it. An encounter occurs within us between the fruits of understanding perception and the soul element of feeling through the rhythmic system.

Then there is a third aspect, namely, to receive all this in such a way that memory can retain it. In every such process, we have to distinguish between perception, comprehension, and an inner digesting of the latter to the extent that memory can retain it. This digesting or processing is linked with the metabolic system. Those most delicate inner metabolic processes occurring in the organism, which we as educators must heed well, are linked with memory, with the capacity for remembering. Just observe the difference between memories of pale children and those with healthy, pink complexions; or study how different the various human races are in regard to their power of recollection. These are matters based on the most delicate metabolic arrangements and processes. If, for instance, as educators we are in a position to come to the aid of pale children by bringing about a bit of healthy sleep for them, engendering a livelier inner stimulation of the finer processes of metabolism, we can greatly benefit their memory. But we can also help their memory by taking pains, as teachers, to maintain the proper balance between mere listening and active work on the part of the children. Assume that you let the children listen too much; they will arrive at perceptions, to be sure, and after a fashion at comprehension as well, for through their constant breathing the spinal fluid is kept in a state of activity; but the children's will is not engaged sufficiently. As you know, the will is connected with metabolism. Since mental digestion is also connected with the will as well as with the metabolism, you will not be able to teach and educate well if you accustom the children too much to watching and listening, and do not have them do enough constructive work of their own, because the will is thereby insufficiently active. You must therefore find the right balance between listening and watching on the one hand, and active work on the part of the children on the other. For nothing is well retained that is not processed in a person in such a way that the will works into the metabolism, thus enkindling the capacity for memory. These are very delicate considerations in physiology that must gradually be accurately grasped by means of spiritual science. [*Balance in Teaching,* lecture of September 21, 1920.]

Speech instruction

Attention has already been drawn to the significance of speaking and cultivation of speech along with the development of healthy breathing (see p. 163). Here, one more important thought should be considered, a thought that is trailblazing in any dealings with speech:

The fact that a child learns to speak before coming to school makes it evident that the sense of truth is in some way brought along from birth. Now, in speech we have a sort of embodiment of truth, an embodiment of the process of cognition. Are we not obliged to have recourse to speech when we want to get at the truth about the world? [*Education for Adolescents,* lecture of June 19, 1921.]

Thus, to live with the question of truth—that it is to be found in the word itself and not merely to be attained through contemplation—is profoundly calming and benefits health. With this, the ego feeling has a direct support. Rudolf Steiner points in this connection to the working out of a completely personal relationship to language.

But whoever has become aware of the relationship between the soul-spiritual and the physical nature up to the change of teeth, will recognize something of extraordinary importance for the period which follows. You see, a certain time, though it is comparatively short, is needed for human beings to grow their milk-teeth as infants. Then a longer period elapses before the milk-teeth are exchanged for the second teeth. We shall learn in due course that the second teeth are far more intimately connected with the individuality than the first teeth, which are more the result of heredity. But it is not only the teeth that we have to acquire for a second time—this time more out of our own resources, whereas the first teeth were received through heredity.

It is similar in the case of human speech. And here I wish to allude to something that will be dealt with in greater detail during the following lectures, for the secret of the development of human speech is mainly hidden from those who take the natural-scientific approach of today. It is not known that, in a similar way in which the first teeth are received through a kind of inheritance from the parents, speech is first received by means of imitation of external influences emanating from the environment. But, later on, the development of language becomes a more individual and inner organic principle.

During the first years of life we learn speech from our surroundings. But the speech that is learned and spoken up to the fifth or sixth year is related to the whole human being in a similar way as are the milk-teeth to the second teeth. For what is activated in the adolescent after approximately the age of fourteen or fifteen when he or she speaks, is likewise acquired a second time, as were the second teeth. The outer physical symptom of this phase is the change of voice in the case of the male. In the female's development this particular change remains more inwardly hidden, but it is nevertheless present. Because these forces work differently in the larynx of the male, they are manifested outwardly. This is the outer manifestation of what is happening within the totality of the human being during these important school years, not merely in the physical body and in the soul, but in the entire soul-body organism. It is continually developing, from year to year and from month to month, linking itself to what has already been acquired in the form of speech that was imparted through environmental influences. Anyone who knows how soul and spirit work in the human being up to age fourteen or fifteen, anybody who observes this in the students through instinctive intuition, will transform these observations into immediate, living reality. We will notice how one student produces guttural sounds [sounds articulated in the back of the mouth which do not occur in English] in this way, labials [sounds made with the lips: b, p, v] in that way, and palatal sounds [sounds made by the front of the toungue behind the tip near or touching the hard palate: ch in German ich, y in English yeast] in still another way; how another produces palatals more easily, while a third pupil has a natural affinity to labials, and so on. Such perceptions can develop into quite an extensive science that indicates in all details what is developing in a child's organism as soul-body and body-soul elements.

Now, if one has achieved a sense of observation for the transformations of speech that take place in young people between the ages of seven and fifteen—something to which ordinarily no attention is paid at all—one will recognize how soul-forces work through language in a sublime way. But these relationships escape one's notice, if powers of observation are trained without the aid of spiritual science, which enables us to discover the following facts: In the first years, up to the second dentition, we see how the forces of ideation are bypassed, as it were, in the change of teeth, so that after this has taken place, ideation can subsequently develop. Ideation now withdraws from the physical organization, so to speak, and turns into independent soul elements. Later, mainly between the change of teeth and puberty, the will likewise withdraws from the overall bodily organism of the youngster—although frequently the onset of this process makes itself felt earlier—becoming localized in the larynx and the speech organs. Just as the faculty of ideation draws inward to become an independent soul force, so at the age of fourteen or fifteen—sometimes earlier—the will-element becomes localized in what develops out of speech and its organs. The organic changes in the boy's larynx are a visible sign for this culmination of the will forces. We shall have to speak later about the corresponding changes in a girl's development.

If we look at these processes through the eyes of spiritual science, concepts such as ideation and will cease to be the abstractions that they otherwise tend to be. Abstract ideas will not lead to totally different ways of looking at physical symptoms. But if we really learn to observe and, in particular, learn to recognize the completely different way in which a youngster's nature acquires labials, gutturals, or palatals, then we are furthermore able to recognize how the forces of ideation are actively engaged in the forming of the body during the first seven years. We learn to recognize the external physical manifestations of soul-spiritual principles.

We learn to realize how the nature of the will becomes localized in the nature of the larynx. We discover how the will floods into human speech. Then will is developed and ideation no longer remains an abstraction, but something that we observe through the actual processes of life. Just as we observe the force of gravity in water rushing down a mountain, or the speed of flowing water through the pull of gravity and the resistance to it, so we learn to recognize how, from week to week, the physical body develops through the activity of soul and spiritual forces. We begin to trace the working of soul and spirit forces in physical substances. [*The Renewal of Education*, lecture of April 20, 1920.]

Reading and observing

When we teach children something that requires observation or that they experience in reading, we heavily tax the gray matter of their brains. A delicate metabolic process then occurs in the human being and spreads out in a subtle manner over the entire organism. Just when we think we are occupying the children in a most spiritual way, we really exercise a powerful influence on their bodily, physical nature. When the children are observing, reading, or listening to a story, their metabolism is invaded. Strong demands are being made on it. This is what we might call the impression the spiritual makes on the bodily nature. What we develop as children when we observe something or listen to a story, has to be incorporated, as it were, into our bodily nature. Something like a bodily phantom has to develop that becomes part of the whole organism. Minute amounts of salts are deposited in the organism. One must not picture this too coarsely, but the whole organism is, as it were, permeated by a salt phantom. Then the need arises for this phantom to be dissolved again by the metabolism.

Such is the process we evoke when we get children to read or listen to a story. We think we are appealing to their soul and spirit; in reality we are taxing their metabolism most of all. We must have this in mind when we prepare our lessons. We shall have to see to it that what we tell the children or what we ask them to read is formulated in such a way that it is incontestable from two points of view.

The first point is that the subject matter arouses the children's interest, that they follow everything with a certain interest. When interest is active in the soul, it is always accompanied by a subtle feeling of enjoyment. The enjoyment expresses itself physically in a fine glandular secretion, which then absorbs the salt-depositing process that had been started. We must try never to bore children; we must avoid teaching them something that they may find tedious. Otherwise, no feelings of interest will be aroused; the undissolved salt is produced and distributed throughout the body, and this may lead later on in life to all kinds of digestive troubles. We have to take this into consideration especially with girls. When they become prone to migraine, it is often the result of one-sided cramming with all manner of facts they have to learn, without these having been expressed in such a way that the children enjoyed them. For then there is a tendency for tiny little spikes to form throughout the body that are never properly dissolved. These are matters that should really not be overlooked.

And now for the second pitfall: Here we come up against the difficulty of there being so little time for all we have to do. We really should see to it that the reading material contained in current manuals—and they are enough to drive you up a wall—are not used by us. I regret to say I have seen readers being used in our classes in which some of the selected passages are simply appalling.

We must never forget that we are preparing the children for life, even physically, for their whole life. When we present them with the trivial stuff generally to be found in these reading manuals, we are forming their finer organs in the direction of the former so that, later on, they will turn out to be, not complete human beings but narrow-minded persons, hopelessly limited in outlook. We must realize how much we affect the whole development of children through reading, through teaching them to read. It becomes evident later on.

I would therefore beg you to try as far as possible to collect your reading material yourselves from classical literature or from wherever. Make your own selection, and do not trust the readers in current use; these, almost without exception, are atrocious and should play as insignificant a part as possible. It is of course a good deal more trouble to search through books and collect your own material; but it is an absolute necessity for us to take particular care with the selection of passages for children's reading. After all, the whole purpose of our Waldorf School is to do things differently from the way they used to be done. And we simply must make sure that no harm is being done to the children in their reading lessons, or in listening to stories, or in natural history lessons, no harm in either of the two directions indicated. [*Education for Adolescents*, lecture of June 15, 1921.

Zoology

Here too we must establish the relationship of the form of an animal to that of the human being. Comparative embryology shows that the embryos of animals with backbones closely resemble human embryos. At the beginning, for instance, the wing of a bird still has the form of an arm with hands and five finger-like lines. Later on, the skeleton of the bird's wing becomes specialized out of this basic human form. In comparison with the evolving forms of animals, human development is not specialized, as if summing up all animal forms.[35]

If we were to go still farther back, say to the time prior to [the Greek philosopher] Thales, one would find that, in the mystery schools and among those who taught in them, there still existed a clear insight, a perception that emerges in Plato's esoteric writings and came to expression in the following way. "Logic, what is it? Nothing but zoology! Zoology is logic come alive. For when zoology assumes a spiritually abstract form for which we as human beings are predisposed—something that comes to expression in the animal kingdom and is mutually harmonized in us—then the living interplay of thoughts begins to stir in us humans. It is the doings of the animal kingdom in our play of thoughts, and logic is zoology." Plato's insights were followed by the Socratic teachings of Aristotle, and in them no awareness existed of these deeper connections. People engaged in abstract logic; the living relationship of elective affinity was replaced by the relationship of intellectual judgment, the abstract connections between one concept and another as expressed in the logic of Aristotle. This logic can drive a person who tries to work with it to despair, because one can get no handle on it.

Thus we feel, think, and form images of concepts, because what spreads out in the animal kingdom outside is actually borne by us inside. We grow together with the world in quite a new way when we develop this idea. Human will and feelings acquire a new kind of life. We become conscious of our kinship with the kingdoms of nature. And we begin gradually to sense what it means that the astral is active in us, not merely something etheric.

If, instead of acquiring the abstract concepts so prevalent today, we let ourselves be stimulated by the contemplation of positive forms, this will teach us how to observe the fourteen- or fifteen-year-olds when we confront them in class. For through what we have received in this way

192

inwardly, our eyes and ears will be guided to how we conduct ourselves in the next lesson. Only this will stimulate our observation for what confronts us in the fourteen- and fifteen-year-old human beings. If we do not acquire such observational skills, if we do not permeate ourselves with such spiritual science that reaches all the way into feeling, we stand in front of the young people like the ox confronting Sunday after he has been feeding on grass all week—as people used to say when I was young.

This is what we have to bring into our whole culture, into civilization, into science. Only this way will science become a reality, not merely a sum of names, mere nominalism. Then it will enkindle and stimulate something real in us, and that will help us observe human beings for what they are. I am not suggesting we should craftily focus on a person and make notes of what he/she is like. True observation approaches us on its own. We form a judgment concerning each single youngster. We need not express it, for we have it within us, alive and flexible. Then we can lift it up into consciousness; and we conduct ourselves in class in accordance with the many separate judgments that are alive and a-move within us, in the same way as the whole animal world is alive and a-move in the true thought-forms. Imagine if we had to know all this, if we had to understand how a lion devours a lamb. Suppose we had to lift all this up into consciousness! [*Education for Adolescents,* lecture of June 18, 1921.]

On the differentiation of the sexes

Outwardly, we begin to detect in both boys and girls in the teens something that is not easily explainable from their individual development hitherto. It is indeed quite often in sharp contrast to the character they have shown earlier but does display a certain common, general element, and begins with the process of sexual maturation. In teenage boys, it can be the years of boorish, ill-mannered behavior; in girls it takes a rather different form. These years definitely originate in the peculiar inner experience that the astral body encounters at this time—and with it also the ego, though the latter has, of course, not yet come to full development. The astral body is trying to relate in the right way to the experiences that are being undergone by the physical system, and thereby to the whole surrounding world. Just because it is a search for the right relationship between subjective and objective elements, this gives rise to a kind of struggle in the human being, which accounts for the contradiction that youngsters of this age often present. For you will, in fact, sometimes hardly recognize children when they have entered upon this time of life.

The external characteristics of this awkward stage in boys are familiar to all, and there is no need for me to give any detailed description of them. What we must do, however, is to enter upon a careful study of these characteristics and get to know their real nature, for we shall find them to be of immense importance for education.

The first thing to be understood is that the astral body has more significance in girls than it does in boys. This holds true all through life; and because of it, the female organism has a stronger inclination towards the cosmos. Much that is in fact part of the secrets of the cosmos is revealed in the female nature. The astral body of a woman is in itself more highly differentiated, more delicately organized than the astral body of a man. In a certain sense, the latter is less structured, less differentiated, even cruder.

By comparison, the development of a girl between the ages of thirteen or fourteen and twenty or twenty-one is such that her ego is strongly influenced by what is forming in her astral body. One sees how her ego is gradually being absorbed, as it were, by the astral body. Eventually, at the age of twenty or twenty-one, a powerful reaction occurs, and the girl makes a supreme effort to reach her own I, to attain egohood.

It is essentially different in boys. Their astral body does not draw in the ego nearly as much. Although the ego remains concealed and is not properly active as yet, it endures throughout these years from age fourteen to twenty or twenty-one without being strongly influenced by the astral body. Just because the ego endures and remains unabsorbed during this age while, at the same time, it is not yet independent, boys may more easily become hypocrites or sneaks than girls. Girls of this age will more readily acquire an element of freedom, an attitude that inclines to outward presence. Due to the particular relation between ego and astral body that obtains in boys during the years of adolescence, especially in boys with deep feeling, something of an inclination to withdraw from life can be noted.

Boys will certainly make friends; they seek contact with others, but there is nevertheless the desire to become introverted a little with special thoughts or emotions. Withdrawal into themselves is especially characteristic of boys who have rather deeper natures, and the teacher (no matter whether it is a man or a woman) can have an exceedingly good influence on boys of this age by delicately entering into what I may call the secret that every such boy conceals in his soul. As teachers, we must not touch upon it too strongly,but we can show by our whole demeanor that we presuppose such a secret. It is somewhat like a love of withdrawing into their own selves. And if this love of withdrawal into himself does not appear in boys of this age, that should really put us on our guard. Boys in whom this obvious or slight inclination to draw back into themselves is not present—and it is noticeable to a conscientious teacher—need careful watching. We must realize that something is amiss that bears looking into, something that may lead to difficulties or abnormalities in later life.

In the case of girls, it is quite different. The differences are quite subtle; one has to acquire a certain gift of observation to detect them. In girls, the ego is more or less absorbed by the astral. On this account, the girl lives less within herself. For the ego-permeated astral body penetrates and lives more in the etheric body, enters deeply into it, and consequently into the girl's whole demeanor, into her very movements and gestures. In fact, we do find that where girls are undergoing right and normal development, they are ready at this age to take a stand in life; there is a certain sureness and confidence in the way they come forward and seek recognition. They become emphatic in their personality and do not draw back into themselves.

To face the world frankly and freely is the natural attitude for girls at this time of life. This may be coupled with somewhat egotistical feelings, with wanting to show off, with proving themselves in the world regarding their own individual character. We must recognize that it is characteristic for girls to have this free demeanor and to feel the importance of showing what they are worth. In extreme cases, this leads to flirtation and vanity; some girls are not content with expressing themselves merely through their soul qualities, but through what can be added as outer adornments. It is interesting to observe how, from the fourteenth or fifteenth year on, something that in the trivial sense leads to vanity and love of finery, can appear as a delicate aesthetic feeling in girls of this age.

All this is ultimately due to the special relationship the astral body and the absorbed ego enter into with the etheric body, something that outwardly manifests in changes of how the girl walks and carries herself, of how she holds her head high. In the extreme, this leads to arrogance, and so on. These matters should in fact be observed with an eye for the artistic.

When we consider these differences between boys and girls, and we have the good fortune of teaching them together, we shall understand how much can be achieved through tactfully dealing with a mixed class. When handling boys and girls together, teachers who are aware of their responsibilities will still differentiate between them in certain respects. They will, for example, need to differentiate between the ways in which the subjective nature of the boys and girls has developed in regard to the external world. For at this stage in life, the task is to bring the subjective element into a relationship with one's own body—the etheric and the physical body. This presupposes that one has attained a corresponding relationship to the external world. Teachers can work throughout all the years of school with this goal in mind. What proves to be particularly important at the age of puberty must be our concern throughout.

For, while we teach, we must see to it that the children receive impressions that are of a moral or religious kind, something that has frequently been discussed among us. And then they should likewise receive impressions and ideas that relate to an appreciation of beauty, to art, to an aesthetic view of the world. It becomes specially important when youngsters reach the age of thirteen, fourteen, and fifteen that we have stimulated ideas and feelings of this nature in them throughout their earlier school years.

A child in whom no feelings for beauty have been aroused, who has not been taught to see the world from an aesthetic point of view, will tend to become sensual, perhaps even erotic as a teenager. There is no better way of restraining eroticism than by a healthy development of the aesthetic sense for what is noble and beautiful in nature. When you guide children to feel the beauty and glory of a sunrise and sunset, to be sensitive to the beauty of flowers and to the majesty of a thunderstorm, when, in short, you develop in them the aesthetic sense, you are doing far more for them than if they are given sexual instruction that nowadays cannot be offered early enough and is often carried to absurd lengths. A feeling for beauty, an aesthetic approach to the world—these confine the erotic nature within its proper limits. As human beings learn to perceive the world in all its beauty, they learn to confront their own body in a free way; they learn not to be oppressed by it. And that is what eroticism is—to be oppressed and tormented by one's own body.

It is equally important at this age for children to have developed certain moral and religious feelings. Such feelings always have a strengthening effect upon astral body and ego. The latter grow weak if there has been little development of religious and moral impulses. If they are not developed, the child becomes sluggish—even as if paralyzed in body. And this will show itself particularly at the age with which we are dealing; lack of moral and ethical impulses will manifest outwardly in an irregularity in sexual life.

In all this preparation for the age of puberty, we have to take account also of the differences between boys and girls. For the girl, the moral and ethical impressions we form for her should incline to the aesthetic. Special consideration must be given to present moral and religious directions so that the girl finds them exceedingly attractive, that she experiences aesthetic enjoyment in the moral, the good, and the religious ideas she has assimilated. She should feel gladness in the knowledge that the world is permeated with the supersensible; her imagination should be richly supplied with pictures that are expressive of the divine that fills the world, expressive also of the beauty that is revealed in human beings when they are good and moral.

For boys, on the other hand, it is necessary to awaken in them perceptions that tend more toward the power inherent in the religious and ethical life. While we should drive the religious and moral impulses all the way into the eyes in girls, in boys we should preferably drive the religious and beautiful impulses into their spiritedness, into the sense of power that radiates from their inner nature. It goes without saying that we must not push this to extremes, imagining we are to train girls to become aesthetic felines, and boys to become bullies—as they would if we were to incite their egotism by appealing to all sorts of sensations of power. While we do right to arouse a sense of their own power in boys, this must be in association with the good, the beautiful, and the religious.

We must prevent girls in their teens from becoming superficial, mere spurious devotees of beauty. We must prevent teenage boys from developing into young hooligans. These are the dangers that beset the critical period of adolescence. And we need to be fully aware of the fact that these tendencies exist in one direction or the other, even while the children are still in elementary school. In the case of girls, much has to be conveyed in such a direction that they find pleasure in the good, and that religious ideas make a certain aesthetic impression on them. In the case of boys we should appeal to them somewhat in the following way: Look here, my boy, if you do this, your muscles will develop and you will become a fine, strong fellow! In such ways, boys must even be roused to a sense of being permeated by the divine within them.

Now, these qualities that appear in boys and girls are deeply and delicately embedded in human nature. Observation of the girl reveals that the ego is being absorbed by the astral body. Naturally, all this is described in a rather basic, overt manner; but that will enable you to form a true picture of what is taking place. Something is contained in this soul-spiritual process that can be compared with the physical process of blushing. A girl's whole development at this time may be called a blushing of soul and spirit; the penetration of the ego into the astral body is, in effect, a kind of blushing.

The situation is different in boys Here, the ego is less lively; but on the other hand, it does not absorb itself—with the result that we find in boys a pallor of soul and spirit. This is quite noticeable, and is always present. We must not allow ourselves to be deceived in this regard by physical appearance. If a teenage girl becomes pale, it is absolutely consistent with the fact that she blushes in soul and spirit. A teenage boy may turn into a young rascal and readily become over-excited, but that does not prevent his turning pale in soul and spirit.

Fundamentally speaking, these conditions are an expression of human nature for what takes possession of the whole human being at this time of life: the sense of bashfulness or embarrassment. This sensation pervades the whole of human nature at this time. It arises from the perception that girls as well as boys now have to receive something into their individual life that must be kept secret. They must carry secrets within their inner being. This is the nature of feeling bashful. This sense of bashfulness enters even into the most unconscious phase of soul-spiritual life.

As teachers, if we have the feeling that we must keep the knowledge of this to ourselves and treat it with respect; if we deal with boys and girls with that delicate sensitivity for their inwardly present bashfulness, it will have its effect. There is no need for words; it is the unspoken influence of one human being on another that is effective as we move about among the children, conscious of the presence within them of something they are anxious to protect as one would an unopened flower-bud. The very presence of this feeling of respect in the teacher will have an immense educational influence.

It is really strange how the external symptoms that show themselves in a child of this age are all traceable to this sense of bashfulness—which is often so modified as to be turned almost into its opposite. The girl who is blushing in soul and spirit and conceals her true being, puts herself forward, faces the world. What is indeed so strange in human nature is that externally people of this age manifest the very opposite of what is at work within. It is the plucky, forceful demeanor, drawing attention to herself, not putting up with anything, the insistence: I must be treated justly! Anyone who has taught in a girls' boarding school will know how girls begin to grow dissatisfied and demand to be treated justly. They feel emancipated, they will "jolly well give it to him!" They have their own thoughts, such as "They don't need us." All this is really nothing but the reverse side of what rests deep within their soul life quite unconsciously as a kind of bashfulness.

Again, with boys, you will find the same. The loutish behavior during the first part of adolescence and the more surly churlishness during the second half of this age—all the rather rough and rude behavior that we meet with so often in boys in their teens—is again nothing but the desire not to bring out into the open what they really are. What a boy does want is to make contact with the external world; and in his efforts to attain it, he behaves as clumsily as possible; he sprawls in a chair. One is not what one is, one is different. We should not forget that, through his individuality, a boy of this age is not what he really is. In point of fact, at this age, a boy is an imitator. While a child is a natural imitator in the first seven years of its life, the teenage boy now sets out to imitate, first one person, then another. He is ever so pleased if he can make a good impression by imitating someone else's manner or action. He will try to walk like someone else. He will model his way of speaking on the speaking of another. He will copy the rudeness of another, or again, try to be as refined and courteous as some other person. All this is an attempt to connect with the world, something that comes to expression particularly during these years of awkward behavior. At bottom, it is the embarrassment of laying bare his real self before the world, a withdrawal into himself that makes him appear different from what he really is. [*Education for Adolescents,* lecture of June 16, 1921.]

In dealing with the frequently mentioned subject of sexuality, an additional segment is quoted here from Rudolf Steiner's lecture of July 22, 1923 [in *Three Perspectives on Anthroposophy*]:

The ultimate foundation of love lies in the spirit-interwoven ego that submerges into the human physical and etheric organism. To recognize the spirituality of love in a particular case, means to recognize the spirit altogether. Whoever recognizes love recognizes the spirit. But in cognizing love one has to penetrate into the inner spirit-experience of love. Particularly in this regard, our civilization has become lost in the falsest possible direction.

Memory is a weaving and living in the soul's inner region, and distinctions are not so clear and deep for our perception. Only mystical spirits like Swedenborg, Meister Eckhart, Johannes Tauler, sensed the weaving and living of the eternal spirit in recollection as they submerged in their memories. They spoke of the kindling little spark that lights up in human beings when they become conscious in their recollections of the fact that, in the latter, there lives the same substance microcosmically that works and weaves outside in the creative formative forces, dreamlike forces that lie at the basis of all world existence. There, things are not as clear.

But they become clear when we pass on to the third stage, when we see how, in the third stage, our civilization has misunderstood the originally spiritual being and weaving of love. As a matter of course, everything spiritual has its outer sense perceptible form, for spirit penetrates into the physical element. It becomes embodied in the physical. If spirit then forgets its own self, if it is aware only of the physical element, it then believes that what is spirit-stimulated is merely stimulated by the physical. Our time lives in this delusion. It does not recognize love. It only fantasizes about love, indeed lies regarding love. In reality it only knows eroticism when thinking about love. I do not want to say that lonely persons do not experience love, for in their subconscious feeling, their unconscious will, they deny the spirit much less than they do in their thinking. But when present civilization thinks about love, it only speaks the word love—but it actually talks about eroticism. We can indeed say that if we check through our current literature and find where the word love is used, the word eroticism should actually stand in its place. For it is only this that our thinking, steeped as it is in materialism, knows of love. It is denial of the spirit that turns the power of love into erotic power. Not only has the genius of love been replaced, I should say, by its lower servant, eroticism, but in many instances, its counter-image, the demon of love, has entered in. And the demon of love appears when God-willed forces, normally at work in the human being, are taken over by human thinking, are torn loose from spirituality by intellectuality.

The descending path runs as follows: One knows the genius of love; one has spirit-pervaded love. One knows the lower servant, eroticism, but one falls into the clutches of the demon of love. And the genius of love has its demon in the interpretation, not in the actual form itself, but in the interpretation of sexuality in our present civilization. No longer do people today speak merely of eroticism when approaching the question of love; they speak only of sexuality!

It is safe to say that many goals of today's so-called sex education are included in the current talk about sexuality. And in this present-day intellectualized speaking about sexuality lives the demonology of love. Even as the genius whom our age should follow appears at another level as its demon, because the demon appears where one denies the angel, so it is in this area, where spirit in its most intimate form, in the form of love, is meant to appear. Frequently our present age prays to the demon of love instead of to the genius of love, and mistakes the spirituality of love for the demonology of love in sexuality.

Particularly in this area, the most complete misunderstanding can naturally come about. For what originally lives in sexuality is permeated by spiritual love. But humanity can fall from the level of spirit-penetrated love. And it falls most easily in our intellectualistic age. For if the intellect

200

assumes the form that I spoke of yesterday, the spiritual element of love will be forgotten; only its outermost expression is taken into consideration.

I could say that it is within the power of human beings to deny the very essence of their being. They deny it when they sink down from the genius of love to the demon of sexuality. In saying this, I most certainly understand the sort of feeling concerning these matters, a feeling prevalent in our present time.

Music and singing

Just as the ether body works at freeing itself in order to become independent at the time of the change of teeth, so does the astral body work in order to become independent at puberty. The ether body is a sculptor, the astral body a musician. Its structure is formed by the very essence of music. What proceeds in the human being from the astral body and is projected into form is purely musical in its nature. Anyone able to grasp this knows that, in order to understand the human being, a further level of teacher-training must be directed toward developing receptivity toward an inner musical conception of the world. Those who are unmusical understand nothing whatever about the formation of the human astral body, for it is fashioned out of music. If, therefore, we study ancient civilizations that were built up out of inner musical intuition, if we enter into such Oriental epochs of culture in which even language was imbued with music, we shall find a musical conception of the world entering even into the forms of architecture.

This changed as early as in Greece, and now, particularly in the West, it has become quite different, for we have entered an age when emphasis is laid on the mechanical and mathematical. In the Goetheanum at Dornach an attempt was made to return to this again. Musicians have certainly sensed the music underlying the forms of the Goetheanum. But, generally speaking, there is little understanding for such things today.

It is therefore necessary that we should gain in this way a concrete understanding of the human being and reach the point at which we are able to grasp the fact that the human physiological and anatomical form is a musical creation insofar as it stems from the astral body. Think how intimately the musical element is connected with the processes of breathing and the circulation of the blood. Human beingss are a musical instrument in respect of their breathing and blood circulation. And if you take the ratio between breathing and blood circulation: 18 breaths a minute, 72 pulse beats a minute, you arrive at a rate of 4:1. Of course this varies individually in many ways, but by and large you find that human beings have an inner musical structure. The ratio of 4:1 is the expression of an inner rhythmical relationship that is revealed in the whole human organization, a rhythm in which humans want to live through their own being. In olden times, the scansion of verses was arranged so that the line was regulated by the breath and the metrical foot by the circulation.

$$- \cup \cup - \cup \cup | - \cup \cup - \cup \cup$$

Dactyl, Dactyl, Caesura, Dactyl, Dactyl: four in one. The line is expressive of the human being.

But what human beings express in language is expressed still earlier in their form. Whoever understands human beings from a musical aspect knows that sound, actual tones are working within them. What is located in my back where the shoulder blades meet, what begins there and takes on form, shaping my whole human organism, are those human forms that are constituted out of the prime or key-note. When it continues to the upper arm, the form changes over to the second. In the lower arm, we come to the third. Because there is a major and a minor third—not a major and minor second—we have one bone in the upper arm, but two in the lower arm, the radius and the ulna; these correspond to the major and minor third. The notes of the scale are found in all this; we are formed according to it. And those who only study the human being in an external way do not know that the human form is shaped out of musical tones. Coming to the hand, we have the fourth and fifth, and then, in the experience of free movement, we go right out of ourselves; then, as it were, we take hold of our outer nature. This is the reason for the peculiar feeling we have in hearing sixths and sevenths, enhanced especially when experiencing them in the movements of eurythmy. Just bear in mind that the use of the third makes its appearance comparatively late in the development of music. The experience of the third is an inward one; with the third we come into an inner relationship with ourselves, whereas if we live in the seventh we experience most fully how we go out into the world beyond ourselves. The experience of surrendering lives especially strongly in the seventh.

Just as we experience the inherent nature of music, so the forms of our body are shaped out of music itself. If a teacher therefore wishes to be a good music teacher, he or she will make a point of teaching singing to the children from the very beginning of their school life. This must be done; he or she must understand as an actual fact that song becomes emancipated, for the astral body has previously sung and has brought forth the forms of the human body. Now, the astral body becomes emancipated between the change of teeth and puberty. And what emerges out of the essence of music forms humankind and makes them independent beings. No wonder, then, that the music teacher who understands these things, who knows that human beings are permeated through and through with music, will quite naturally allow this knowledge to enrich the singing lesson and the teaching of instrumental music. This is why we try not only to introduce singing as early as possible into the education of children, but to allow those with sufficient aptitude to learn how to play a musical instrument, so that they have the opportunity really to grasp the musical element that lives in their form as it emancipates. [*Human Values in Education*, lecture of July 24, 1924.]

For listening to music has a specifically healing influence upon the role that the head has to assume in the organism; while actual singing has a healing influence upon what the body has to do for the head. Human beings would turn out to be far healthier if we could do all that we should do in education. [*Education for Adolescents*, lecture of June 15, 1921.]

What we must chiefly consider in this connection is how the breathing works together with the whole nervous system. Indeed, it is quite special how breathing works together with the whole nervous system in the human organism. As teacher and educator we should have the greatest sensitivity for this; only then will we be able to teach correctly. Here, then, the air enters the body, distributes itself, goes up through the spinal column (see drawing), spreads out in the brain, touches the nerve fibers everywhere,

goes down again and pursues paths by which it can then be ejected as carbon dioxide. In this way, the nervous system is constantly being worked upon by the inhaled air that spreads out, goes up through the spinal column, spreads out again, becomes permeated with carbon, returns again and is exhaled.

It is only during the course of the first school period, between the changing of teeth and puberty, that the astral body carries this whole process of breathing, which passes along the nerve fibers right into the physical body, so that, during this time when the astral body gradually finds its way into the physical body with the help of the inhaled air, it plays upon something that is stretched across like strings of an instrument in the center of the body, that is, upon the spinal column. Our nerves are really like a kind of lyre, a musical instrument, an inner musical instrument that resounds up into the head.

This process begins, of course, before the change of teeth, but at that time the astral body is only loosely connected with the physical body. It is between the change of teeth and puberty that the astral body really begins to play upon the single nerve fibers with the inhaled air, like a violin bow on the strings.

You will be fostering all this if you give the child plenty of opportunity to sing. You must have a feeling that, while singing, the child is a musical instrument. You must stand before your children, to whom you are teaching singing or music, with the clear feeling that every single child is a musical instrument and inwardly senses the pleasant feeling of sounds.

You see, sounds are brought about by the particular way the breath is circulated. That is inner music. To begin with, in the first seven years of life, the child learns everything by imitation, but now the child should learn to sing out of the inward joy experienced in building up melodies and rhythms. To show you the kind of inner picture you should have in your mind when you stand before your class in a singing lesson, I should like to use a comparison that may seem a little crude, but will make clear to you what I mean. I do not know how many of you, but I hope most, have at some time been able to watch a herd of cows who were feeding and are now lying in the meadow digesting their food.

This digestive process of a herd of cows is indeed a marvelous thing. In the cow, a kind of image of the whole world is present. The cow digests her food; the digested food substances pass over into the blood vessels and lymphatic vessels, and during this whole process of digestion and nourishment the cow has a sensation of well-being which is at the same time knowledge.

During the process of digestion, every cow has a wonderful aura in which the whole world is mirrored. It is the most beautiful thing one can see, a herd of cows lying in the meadow digesting their food, and in this process of digestion comprehending the whole world. With us humans, all this has sunk into the subconscious, so that the head can reflect what the body, perceiving itself, digests.

We are really in a bad way as human beings, because the head prevents us from truly experiencing the lovely things that cows, for example, experience. We should know much more of the world if we could experience the digestive process, for instance. We should, of course, have to experience it with the feeling of knowledge, not with the feeling that human beings have when they remain in the subconscious in their digestive process. This is simply to make clear what I want to say. I do not wish to imply that we now have to raise the process of digestion into consciousness in our teaching, but I want to show that there is something that should really be present at a higher level in the child—this sense of well-being evoked by the course of inner intonation. Imagine what would happen if the violin could feel what is going on within it! We only listen to the violin; it is outside us; we are ignorant of the whole origin of tone and only hear the outward sense impression of it. But if the violin could feel how each string vibrates with the next one, it would have the most blissful experiences, provided of course that the music is good. So you must let the child have these little experiences of bliss, so that you really call forth a feeling for music in the whole organism, and you yourself must find real joy in it. Of course one must have at least some understanding of music. But an essential part of teaching is this artistic element that I have just explained.

On this account it is essential (for the inner processes of life between the change of teeth and puberty demand it) to give the children lessons in music right from the very beginning, and at first, as far as possible, to accustom them to sing little songs, quite empirically without any kind of theory. But they must be well sung. Then you can use the simpler songs from which the children can gradually learn what melody, rhythm, and beat are, and so on; but first you must accustom the children to sing little songs as a whole, and to play a little too, as far as that is possible. Unless there is clearly no bent at all in this direction, every Waldorf school child begins to learn some instrument when he or she enters school; as I say, as far as circumstances allow, each child should learn to play an instrument. As early as possible, the children should come to feel what it means for their own musical being to flow over into the objective instrument, for which purpose the piano, which should really only be a kind of memorizing instrument, is of course the worst possible thing for the child. Another kind of instrument should be chosen, if possible, one that can be blown upon. Here one must of course have a great deal of artistic tact and, I was going to say, a great deal of authority too. If you can, you should choose a wind instrument, as the children will learn most from this and will thereby gradually come to understand music. Admittedly, it can be a hair-raising experience when the children begin to blow. But, on the other hand, it is a wonderful thing in the child's life when this whole configuration of the air, which otherwise is enclosed and held along the nerve-fibers, can now be extended and guided. The human being feels the whole organism being enlarged. Processes that are otherwise only within the organism are carried over into the outside world. A similar thing happens when the child learns the violin, when the actual processes, the music that is within, is directly carried over and the child feels how the music within passes over into the strings through the bow.

But remember, you should begin giving these music and singing lessons as early as possible. For it is of very great importance that you not only make all of your teaching artistic, but that you also begin teaching the more specifically artistic subjects—painting, modeling, and music—as soon as the children come to school, and that you see to it that the children really come to possess all these things as an inward treasure. [*The Kingdom of Childhood*, lecture of August 18, 1924.]

Eurythmy

There will be no difficulties for children to learn eurythmy if they are healthy, for in eurythmy they simply express their own being; they want to make their own being a reality. This is why, in addition to gymnastics, eurythmy has been included in the curriculum as an obligatory subject from the first grade right through to the upper classes.

Eurythmy has arisen out of the whole human being, out of physical body, etheric body, and astral body; it can only be studied by means of an anthroposophical knowledge of human beings. Gymnastics today are directed physiologically in a one-sided way toward the physical body; and because physiology cannot do otherwise, certain principles of vitality are introduced. By means of gymnastics, however, we do not educate complete human beings, only partial ones. Nothing is implied against gymnastics by saying so, but their importance is over-estimated nowadays. This is why eurythmy should be offered side by side with gymnastics in education today. [*Human Values in Education*, lecture of July 20. 1924.]

We are not prepared to be as brazen as a man who once came up to me after I had made some introductory remarks concerning a eurythmy performance in Dornach, where I had mentioned gymnastics and spoken of their hygienic significance. This man declared that, as a physiologist, he could not favor gymnastics at all; neither had they any educational value whatever in his view. In fact, gymnastics were for him the most harmful pursuit one could imagine. He did not consider it a means of education but sheer barbarism. Well, one cannot fly in the face of present day public opinion in that way; we should be fiercely attacked at once—as happens anyway today. But just think how gymnastics and exercise—activities that go no further than the physical body (in the literal and lowest sense of the term)—are idolized today in all their forms, whether it be the strongly physical, the super-physical, or the sub-physical, whether it be the Swedish or the German variety.

Every one of these varieties starts off by regarding the human entity as a being of body only, that is to say, of body according to the inferior conception of the body that has been formulated in this materialistic age, not according to the conception I referred to. One proceeds like this: A human being should assume a certain posture; this pose is outlined. The back must not be curved inward too much; the chest must be pulled out in a certain way; the arms and hands must be moved in a particular way—so that the overall carriage has an exactly defined character. There is no thought here of the human being, only of a fabricated human model. We could make a drawing of it, or we could form it out of papier-mâché. All the instructions given in Swedish gymnastics for posture could be followed in such a papier-mâché model. Then one can use human beings as if they were shapeless sacks and tell them to imitate the model. In executing such a procedure, one has nothing to do with the actual human element, one deals with a figure made of papier-mâché, a model that contains everything that Swedish or German gymnastics demand. Without troubling to think of anything else that may be contained in the human being, one then tells a person to take up a certain stance, go through various exercises, and so on. The only problem is that nobody took into account that one confronts a human being.

The reason this whole matter is so objectionable—basically, it is villainous—despite its impact on our so-called civilization, is because the human being has no place in it even in a practical sense. Neutral science has already excluded human beings in theory, but here, in gymnastics and exercise, they are excluded in actual practice. They are made into mimics of a model. And that is no goal for education. We must see to it that children assume a posture in gymnastics that they experience inwardly. It is the same with movements we require them to make. They should be movements that the children experience inwardly.

Take, for example, the function of breathing. We must know that, when inhaling, children should be brought to the point of feeling something like a faint suggestion of some nice-tasting food that slips down past their palate. The experience should not go as far as an actual perception of taste; there should be a faint suggestion of it, just enough for children to be able to feel, as they inhale, that they can sense something of the world's verdure. You should try to have them say, What is the color of what I breathe in? And you will discover that at the moment children arrive at a correct sensation of breathing, they will experience something like a natural, greenish color. You will know that you have achieved something if you have been able to bring children to feel that their inhaled breath has a greenish color. And then you will always find that, of their own accord, their bodies will take up the right position for inhaling. Children's inner experience will lead them unfailingly to hold their body correctly. Then you can go on to exercises.

Similarly, you can bring children to the point of a corresponding experience with breathing out. The moment they begin to feel, in exhaling: I do think that inwardly I'm really a fit person! The moment they sense their exhalation as if they are fit, as if they feel their own strength, and as if they wished to communicate their strength to the world in breathing out, they will moreover experience the corresponding movement of the abdomen in breathing out, the movements in the limbs, the carriage of the head, the position of the arms as something absolutely in harmony with themselves. When once children have entered fully into the feeling of breathing out, they will experience the right movements within.

Now, here, we have the human being within, we really have the human being before us. We do not treat him or her like a sack of flour, pulling him or her into shape in imitation of what a papier-mâché model is doing. We move together with the child's soul that draws the physical and bodily element along with it. Out of the children themselves, we bring up the bodily movements that accord with their own inner experience.

I have taken breathing as an example. We could start from some other activities that children can feel: movements of the arms or of the legs, running, etc., or even their posture. Each time, we have to find and develop the inner soul experience, which the bodily-physical organism demands on its own. Here we have reached the point where we can bring exercise and gymnastics into an immediate connection with eurythmy. And that is just what we need to do.

Eurythmy brings a soul-spiritual element directly to expression. It pervades all human movements with soul and spirit. It takes as its starting-point what human beings have worked for and attained soul-spiritually throughout the course of humanity's evolution. But the physical-bodily nature can likewise be experienced spiritually. One can experience breathing or the metabolism, if one takes one's development far enough in this direction. You can do that and feel and perceive yourself. You can sense what is going on in your physical, bodily nature. And then, what a child receives on a higher level as eurythmy may rightly be followed by gymnastics. One can certainly create a bridge between eurythmy and gymnastics. But these exercises should only be done as follows: We should take what children do in gymnastics and, based on experiencing the bodily-physical nature as well as experiencing the soul-spiritual, allow them to adjust the bodily-physical to what they experience.

It is, of course, necessary for us to learn a great deal as we teach in this fashion. We must steadily occupy ourselves with these conceptions, if we wish to utilize them ourselves, but especially if we want to apply them to our lessons. They are hard to retain in memory. It is almost the same as is the case with mathematicians and their mathematical formulas. They cannot remember the formulas but can reconstruct them at a moment's notice. And it is the same for us with these conceptions we form about the human being's body of flesh and blood, of soul and spirit. We always have to call them vividly to mind again. But that very fact is quite beneficial for us. For when we work based on our full humanity, it has a stimulating effect on the children.

You will always find that when you have to put a great deal of work into your preparation of the lesson, when you have had to wrestle with the subject, the children learn far more. For then they learn in an altogether different way from what they would learn if you had been one of those superior, self-confident teachers who casually make their preparation. I have even known some who would quickly glance over the subject matter of the lesson while they were slowly walking to school! It makes a profound difference to our teaching when we ourselves have personally wrestled beforehand with the subject matters, and not just those that need to be communicated, but those that are part of the skills; with these too, we should struggle.

Spiritual connections exist in life. Suppose you want children to sing a certain song. If you have first listened to the song inwardly yourself, then it works more strongly on the children as they learn it than it would have if you had not heard it first in your mind. Such connections do exist; the spiritual world does indeed move and work within the physical world. We must utilize this influence of the spiritual world, particularly in education, in lessons, and for instance, in religious instruction. When preparing the latter, for example, and you yourselves are in a natural, pious mood, this religion lesson will have an influence on the children. If you fail to develop the right mood, not much will result from the lesson for the children. [*Education for Adolescents,* lecture of June 13, 1921.]

In our etheric body, we constantly have the tendency to practice eurythmy; that is something the etheric body simply does of its own accord. Eurythmy is nothing less than gleaning all the movements from what the etheric body wants to do. It really makes these motions, and is only prevented from doing them when we cause the physical body to execute them. When we cause them to be executed by the physical body, these movements are held back in the etheric body; in turn, they work back upon us, and thereby have a healing effect. [*Balance in Teaching,* lecture of September 16, 1920.}

When people do eurythmy, it is a fact that this has benefits for the lives of both eurythmists and those who watch; both significantly profit from it. In those who are themselves eurythmists, their physical organism is fashioned by the eurythmic movements into a suitable organ of receptivity for the spiritual world, because the movements strive downward out of the spiritual world. Eurythmists become receiving-organs, as it were, for the processes of the spiritual world by preparing their bodies for them. In the spectators of eurythmy, all the movements that pertain to their astral body and ego are intensified by the eurythmic motions. If you could suddenly wake up during the night following a eurythmy performance you would find that you had retained much more in you than if you had heard a sonata at an evening concert and had then awakened in the night; this effect appears to a still higher degree in eurythmy. It strengthens the soul by letting it find its way into the supersensible more vividly. [*Balance in Teaching,* lecture of September 21, 1920.]

Eurythmy and singing

Eurythmy and singing work in a certain opposite sense [from what was discussed earlier]. An altogether different organic process takes place. In all the organs of the body that are here called into activity, the spiritual is present to a marked degree. When you lead children in eurythmy, they move and, in the course of these movements, the spiritual that is in the limbs streams upward out of the organs. It is a deliverance of the spiritual, when we let children do eurythmy or singing. The spiritual, with which the limbs are full to overflowing, is redeemed, released. This is the actual process; what we accomplish is an actual drawing forth of the child's spiritual nature. Now, when the child stops doing the exercises, the spiritual that we have called forth is waiting to be used, so to speak. (I explained this to you yesterday in another connection.) In turn, the spiritual is waiting to be secured. You see, I spiritualize children when I let them do gymnastics, eurythmy, or singing. They have become quite different beings; they have more of the spiritual in them than before. But this spiritual element in them wants to be secured, wants to remain with them; and we may not divert it.

There is a very simple way of doing this. After the children have done eurythmy, exercises, or singing, we let them remain quiet for just a short while. We let the whole group rest a little, trying to make sure that during this time—even if it has to be for just a few minutes—quiet is maintained. The older the children, the greater is the need for this pause. We really should take this into consideration. Otherwise, on the following day, what we need for our work with the children will not be there. It is never good to hurry them away after a lesson of this kind; we should always let them remain quiet for a while.

In following this advice, you will be acting in accordance with a universal principle. People generate all manner of theories about matter and spirit. But a higher principle is in fact at the bottom of both matter and spirit. One can actually say that when this higher principle is brought to rest, it is matter; when it is brought into movement, it is spirit. And because it is a very lofty principle, we can certainly apply it to human beings. Through rest, you create within yourself a means of holding the spiritual that has been released in the way I explained; you fit it, as it were, into a scheme or plan. And now that it is precipitated and settled, you can make use of it. It is well just to know about such a thing as this, for it will help you to discover any number of possibilities in other areas that will help you conduct yourself appropriately in regard to children. [*Education for Adolescents*, lecture of June 15, 1921.]

Arithmetic and morality

A child is inclined toward the basic elements of arithmetic at quite an early age. But particularly in arithmetic, we can observe how, all too easily, an intellectual element can enter the child. Mathematics as such is not completely alien to human beings at any age. It develops out of human nature; mathematical calculations are not as foreign to human faculties as are written characters in a succeeding [incarnation in a new] civilization. Yet it is exceedingly important that arithmetic lessons are introduced to children in the right way. And only a person who can survey the whole of human life from a certain spiritual standpoint can really determine this.

Now, arithmetic and moral principles are two domains that logically seem very far removed from one another: Ordinarily, arithmetic lessons are not linked to moral principles, because no obvious logical connection appears between them. But it is apparent to one who looks at the matter, not logically but in a life-filled manner, that the child who has had the right introduction to arithmetic will have quite a different sense of moral responsibility at a later age than does the child who has not. The following may seem extremely paradoxical to you, but since I am speaking of realities, not of the illusions current in our age, I shall not be afraid to appear paradoxical, for truth often appears paradoxical in our age. If people had known how to permeate the soul with mathematics in the right way during the past decades, we would not have Bolshevism in Eastern Europe now. This is the result of inner perception—of what one perceives inwardly—namely, with what kind of forces the faculty expressed in arithmetic becomes connected, forces which likewise take hold of morality in human beings .

You will understand this even better if I give you a small illustration of the principle of arithmetic teaching. It is common nowadays to start arithmetic by the adding of one thing to another. But just think how foreign a thing it is to the human mind to add one pea to another and with each addition to have a new name. The transition from one to two, and then to three—this counting is quite an arbitrary activity for the human being. But it is possible to count in another way. And we find this when we go back a little in human history. Originally people did not count by putting one pea, one unit next to another, in order to bring about something new which, at least for the soul life, has little connection with what was there before. No, people counted more or less in the following way. They would say : What we have in life is always a whole—something to be grasped as a whole. The most diverse things can constitute a unity. If I have a large number of people in front of me, that can be a unit. Or if I have a single person in front of me, he/she is then a unit. A unit, in reality, is a purely relative thing. And I keep this in mind if I count in the following way:

1		1	2		1	2	3

and so on, that is, when I divide the whole, start with the unit, and seek the parts in the unit as multiplicity. This was indeed the original view of counting. Unit was always the whole, and in the whole, one sought for the parts. People did not think of numbers as arising by the addition of one and one; numbers were conceived as belonging to the whole and proceeding organically from the whole.

When we apply this to the teaching of arithmetic, we come to the following: Instead of placing one bean after another in front of children, we place a whole heap of beans before them. The heap of beans constitutes the whole. And from this we make our start. Now we explain to the children: I have a pile of beans—or if you like, so that it appeals more to the children's imagination, pile of apples—and three children of different ages who need different amounts to eat, and we want to do something that applies to actual life. What shall we do? We can, for instance, divide the pile of apples, and we say: Here are three parts, and we get the child to see that the sum is the same as the three parts. The sum equals the three parts. That is to say, in addition, we do not proceed from the parts and arrive at the sum. We start with the sum and proceed to the parts. Thus, in order to gain living understanding of addition we start with the whole and proceed to the addenda, to the parts. For addition is concerned primarily with the sum and its parts; the parts that must be contained in the sum in one way or another.

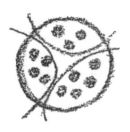

In this way it is possible to help children enter into life with the ability to grasp the whole, not always to proceed from less to larger. This has an extraordinarily strong influence on the child's whole soul. When children have learned to add things together, it gives rise to the moral disposition that develops the trend to be greedy. In proceeding from the whole to the parts, and in treating multiplication similarly, children have less of a tendency to develop acquisitiveness; rather, they develop what, in the sense of the Platonic worldview, can be called thoughtfulness, moderation in the noblest sense of the word. And moral likes and dislikes are intimately bound up with the manner in which one has learned to deal with numbers. At first glance, there seems to be no logical connection between the treatment of numbers and moral ideas, so little indeed that one who only wishes to think in an intellectual manner may well scorn the idea if you mention it. It may seen absurd to him or her. We can also well understand that people may laugh at the idea that one should proceed from the sum instead of from the parts in addition. But when you see the true connections in life you know that logically most remote things are often exceedingly near in reality.

Thus, what emerges from children's souls through working with numbers will greatly affect the way they will show interest in us when we try to offer them moral examples by which they are supposed to develop likes or dislikes, sympathy or antipathy, good or evil. We shall find that

214

children are susceptible to goodness when we have dealt with them accordingly in teaching them numbers in the way described. [*The Spiritual Ground of Education*, lecture of August 21, 1922.]

Physics and intellectuality

It is important that actual intellectual study [Rudolf Steiner has "actual mineralizing study," referring to what he had mentioned earlier. Trans.] is not taken up before the ages of eleven and twelve, that history should be taught pictorially until this age. Only then do you begin to consider cause and effect in history by means of a comprehensive historical view that allows children to attain broad outlooks. You will become convinced of the validity of this method in all areas, for if you bring causality into the description of processes too early, you find that the children do not listen to you. But if you do so at the right moment, their inward joy and eager participation come to meet you.

It is really impossible to teach at all without this inward participation on the part of the children. In all respects we must consider how to educate children; we must be aware how we actually send them out into life at puberty. Even among those who then become young ladies and gentlemen and continue at high school level with their education—in the Waldorf School we go beyond the elementary school grades all the way to high school and graduation—we have twelve grades and students up to age eighteen or nineteen and even further. We must be aware that, following puberty, we deal with human beings who really have "gone out into life," and we confront them quite differently from the way we did before. We must strive to educate human beings in such a way that the intellect, which awakens at puberty, can find its nourishment in the young person's own nature. If, earlier, a human being has stored up an inner treasure of riches in pictorial representation through imitation based on authority, then, at puberty, these inner riches can be transmuted into intellectual activity. He or she will now always be faced with the task of thinking about what he or she has earlier willed and felt. And we must take the very greatest care that this intellectual thinking does not appear too early in the lessons and in education. For human beings cannot arrive at an experience of freedom if we try to drill it into them; it only comes about by awakening in them of itself. But it must not awaken in poverty of soul. If young people earlier have acquired nothing through imitation and imagery which can then rise up into their thinking out of the depths of soul, then, when the young person's thinking should develop at puberty, they will find nothing within themselves to further their own growth. Their thinking then reaches out into emptiness. This makes them irresolute. Just at the time when they ought really to have found a degree of security in themselves, they become involved in all sorts of mischief. In these awkward years of adolescence they will imitate all kinds of things that please them (usually it is something that does not please those who have a more utilitarian point of view), and they imitate these things now because, when they were children, nothing was held up to them that could in a life-fashioning way have been imitated correctly. So it is that we see many young people after puberty running around, seeking support here or there, and thereby deadening their inner experience of freedom.

At every stage in life, we must see to it that we do not educate for this stage alone, but for the whole of earthly human life, and indeed beyond. For the most beautiful way to arrive at an understanding of the immortal human entity is to experience on one's own, following puberty, how what had been poured into one's soul through imitation in the form of pictures now becomes emancipated from the soul and rises up into the spirit. And then one feels how it passes from activity in time into eternal activity, which then advances through birth and death. It is just this welling up of what was poured into the human soul in education in the right way that gives human beings an experience of immortality, for, above all, one clearly experiences that one existed prior to descending to the physical world. And what we imitate out of our religious feeling and take into ourselves as pictures, unites with what we were before we came down into the physical world; thus we come to an inner experience of the essence of immortality. I use the word "immortality" based on its current use, but even where people do still believe in it, it is really only half of the matter. It is only out of certain egoistic feelings that we talk about actually existing immortality, meaning, the fact that we do not perish at death but continue on. But we do not speak about the other side, about "unbornness." Ancient, instinctively illuminated people still knew about these two sides of eternity: immortality and unbornness. Only one who can understand both understands eternity. This eternity will be experienced when education is properly conducted. Here, we once again face a fact where materialism should not be considered in accordance with its theoretical side. [*Practical Advice to Teachers*, lecture of April 17, 1924.]

The view of historical impulses in humanity and the view of physical impulses of nature in the human organism are related to one another. True humanness lives in impulses of history, but what is summed up in these impulses lives as external historical process that, in turn, affects the human being. When you describe the human eye, you describe an activity of external nature that in turn works in human beings. Both processes require the same powers of comprehension, and this comprehension only starts to develop at about age twelve. It is therefore necessary to arrange the curriculum for children during the period between the ages of nine and twelve in a way that will include lessons on the simple concepts of physics necessary for an understanding of the human being itself, this in addition to natural history. But the application of the laws of physics on the human being should wait until the twelfth year, in the same way that stories concerning history should be told up to the twelfth year in order then to be transformed into actual history.

My explanations so far refer to the way subjects are introduced. Of course we can then continue to enlarge on physics after the twelfth year. But neither physics nor natural history should be started before the ninth year, and neither history nor lessons involving physiology, that is descriptions of human functions, should start before the twelfth year is completed. If you take into account that comprehension is something that blossoms not only in human intellect, but always includes feelings and will, you will find that what I have just said is not too foreign to you. When people do not take such things into account, it is because they have succumbed to illusions. You can present historical or physiological facts before the twelfth year in a makeshift way to the human intellect, but by doing so you spoil human nature; strictly speaking, you make it unsuitable for the whole of life. Between the ninth and twelfth year, for example, you can gradually introduce the concepts of refraction, and the formulation of images through lenses or other instruments. You could perhaps discuss the way an opera glass works with the nine- to twelve-year-olds. You can furthermore talk with them about the way a clock works and explore the difference between a pendulum clock and a pocket watch, and anything like this. But before they reach their twelfth year, you should not describe to them how refraction and image formation can also be applied to the human eye.

All this will have provided you with points of reference from which you can learn how the material that is to be taught should be arranged in the curriculum so that the capacities of the children are developed in the right way. And there is more to be observed from this point of view. It is to a certain extent important that we should not move too far away from life in our lessons, though on the other hand, we should not take excessive account of the trivialities of life either. To say to children: "What do you wear on your feet?"and expect them to answer: "A pair of boots." "What are the boots for?" "For me to put on." is called by some teachers an object lesson, which in reality is nothing but a triviality. The kind of object lessons sometimes described in educational books bore the children terribly in their subconscious, and as a result, a great deal in them is damaged. To remain too close to life in this way and constantly to bring things to awareness that could quite well remain in the unconscious, to bring activities that are merely habitual too much into consciousness, is something we should not let ourselves in for. On the other hand, we need not lose all contact with life and teach the children empty abstractions too early. This will be especially important with regard to physics lessons. Indeed, physics lessons will in any case create opportunities for closely combining things near to life with things that in the first instance are rather remote from external life. You should therefore take care to develop concepts of physics from life itself. You should do as much as your inventiveness will allow to let children experience things, for instance how, after we have lit the stove in our classroom, the floor remains cold even when the air near the ceiling is quite warm. You thus draw their attention to a fact of life, and starting from here, you then continue to explain that of course the air around the stove gets warm first and not the air near the ceiling, but that warm air always rises upward and that this makes the cold air move down. So you must describe the process as follows: The air first gets warm down below round the stove, then it rises to the ceiling, making the cold air move down, and that is why a room is still cold around the feet even when the air near the ceiling has been warm for some time. In this way you have started from a fact of life and from there you can now seek the transition to the fact that warm air expands and cold air contracts. Now, that statement takes you further away from life. Another example is when you discuss the lever in physics. It is not good just to present the abstract lever. Start with a pair of scales and move on from there to the lever. Start with something that is used in everyday life and proceed from there to whatever can be thought out from it in physics.

Now I cannot conceal from you that a certain amount of what is included in our concepts of physics wreaks havoc in the child and that a great deal depends on how you as teachers know what is right and endeavor to be mature in your judgments. You cannot avoid saying to the older children: Here you have an electrostatic generator, a frictional electrostatic generator. I can produce electricity by rubbing certain objects, but I must first wipe the objects carefully because they have to be quite dry. If they are wet, the experiment will not work, and no electricity will be generated. Then you enlarge on the reasons why electricity cannot be produced with wet instruments. You go on to explain how lightning occurs, pointing out that it likewise is an electrical process. Now many people

218

maintain that the clouds rub against one another and that this friction brings about lightning as an electrical discharge. The children may perhaps believe this because the teacher also believes it. But, in their subconscious, something special takes place of which they are, of course, unaware. They says to themselves: Well, my teacher wipes the instruments before rubbing then to make electricity to make sure that they are not wet, and then tells me that if clouds rub together, electricity is made. But clouds are wet! The children notice such inconsistencies. And much of the disunity in life stems from the fact that children are told such contradictions. These contradictions ought to arise outside in the world; in our thinking they have no place! But because human knowledge and recognition is too shallow today, such contradictions that really rend the unconscious inner human nature, continually crop up in what we tell the children and later young people. Therefore we must at least take care that what we bring consciously to the children does not contain too much of what in their subconscious they picture differently. It will not be our task as teachers to eliminate from science such things as the nonsense that is maintained concerning the link between lightning and electricity in physics. But when we deal with more obvious things, we should always keep in mind that we influence not only the children's conscious but their subconscious nature as well. How can we take their subconscious nature into consideration?

We can do so as teachers only by becoming more and more the kind of people who do not adjust things in order to make them understandable for the child. I have mentioned in another connection what this involves. You must develop in yourselves capacities that allow you, the moment you enter upon the subject with the children, to become as absorbed by the subject as the child is by the lesson, regardless of what the subject is that you are teaching. You should not allow yourselves to be filled with the thought: Of course I know a great deal more, but I am arranging it to suit the children; I make myself quite superior to the children and prepare everything I want to say to then so that it will be suitable for them. No! You must have the ability to transform yourselves in such a way that the children literally wake up through your lesson and that you yourselves become a child with the children, but not in a childish way. [*Practical Advice to Teachers*, lecture of August 29, 1919.]

Threefoldness of the human organism and the interaction of science, art, and religion

In conclusion, we will touch on a basic precept of Waldorf education that is connected with everything mentioned here as the physiological effects of the individual subjects:

As I was saying, religion, art, and science are spoken about today as though they were entirely unrelated. This was not the case in ancient times of human evolution. They were a complete unity. Mystery centers existed in those ages that were likewise centers for education and culture, centers dedicated at one and the same time to the cultivation of religion, art, and science. For then, the knowledge that was imparted consisted of pictures, representations, and mental images of the spiritual world. These were received in such an intuitive and comprehensive way that they were transformed into external sense-perceptible symbols and thereby became the basis of ritual ceremonies Science was embodied in religions, as was art; for what was taken from the sphere of knowledge and given external form had to be beautiful. Thus, in those times, divine truth, moral goodness, and sense-perceptible beauty existed in the mystery centers as a unity comprised of religion, art, and science. It was only later that this unity split up and became science, religion, and art, each existing by and for itself. In our time this separation has reached its culmination point. Things which are essentially united have become divided in the course of cultural development. As human beings, however, we are predisposed to experience the three in their oneness and not regard them as separate. We can only experience religious science, scientific religion, and artistic idealism in unity, otherwise we are inwardly torn asunder. For this reason, where this division, this differentiation has reached the highest level, it has become imperative to rediscover the connection between these three domains. And we shall see how, in our teaching, we can bring art, religion, and science to children in a unified form. We shall see how children respond in a living way to this compilation of religion, art, and science, how it is in harmony with their own inner nature. I therefore had to point out again and again in no uncertain terms that we must strive to educate children out of a knowledge that they in truth are beings with aesthetic potentials; and we should try to point out how, in the very first years of life, children express themselves in a naturally religious way.

All these things, the harmonious combining of religion, art, and science, must now be grasped in the right way and their value recognized in those teaching methods about which we have yet to speak. [*Human Values in Education*, lecture of July 23, 1924.]

We need nothing more than a spiritual life that is fully rooted once again in the world, a spiritual life where books are written out of real life, work into life, and are impulses, means and ways for life. We must get away from libraries. Of all places, in spiritual life we must enter real life. And we must have an educational life that does not proceed according to rules, but in accordance with the children who are actually present, and according to an insight into the human being. Based on the latter, such an education will come to know children, and from the individual child will figure out what is to be done, every day, every week, every year.

We need a political and legal life in which a person faces a person, where those things are judged that lie within the competence of everybody, regardless of a person's profession or station in life. Those matters in which all people are equal belong to this political and legal life.

If spiritual or cultural life is taken the way I described it, what else will be part of it? Gradually the administration of capital will by itself move from the economic to the cultural life. However much we rail today against capitalism, we cannot do anything about it; we need it. Our concern is not with the existence of capital or capitalism, but the social forces active in capital and capitalism. Capitalism arose out of the inventive gifts of humanity. It arose out of the spiritual sphere through the division of labor and intellectual knowledge. Because I did not want to present a utopia, in my book, *Social Renewal*, I described as an illustration how this flow of capital into the spiritual sphere of the social organism might perhaps come about: Take a man who first amassed capital and now has capital working for him. He himself is engaged in the work that his capital generates. Just as we deal today with books, the rights of which pass, over a period of years, to the benefit of all, so arrangements could likewise be made for a transfer of capital. I did not state this as a utopian view, but said that things might possibly be arranged so that capital assumes a flow and, instead of stagnating everywhere, enters the blood circulation of social life. All my statements are meant as illustrations, not as dogma. They are not utopian concepts. I only wanted to describe something that may perhaps come about through an association.

But something completely different might likewise happen. A person whose thinking is imbued with life does not set down dogmas that are supposed to be put into practice; he or she reckons with human beings who, out of their own contexts, produce purposeful social actions, if they are integrated into the social organism in the right way. Everywhere we count on people, not on dogmas. Still I was forced to realize that there was no discussion at all about the real intentions of my book, *Social Renewal*. Instead, people asked: How does one manage to transfer capital to the most capable individual after a certain number of years? People do not want reality? they long for utopias. But it is this in particular that speaks against the unprejudiced acceptance of the impulse such as we encounter in the threefold social order. Once the political, legal life can unfold properly, one of its main concerns will be with human labor.

The work of a person is completely entangled in the economic life today. It is not taken as something that is determined between one human being and another. In an article about the social questions written around 1905, I wanted to show that with today's division of labor, work is reduced to a commodity as it flows into the remainder of the social organism. Our labor has merely an apparent value for ourselves. Only what the others are doing for us has value, whereas what we are doing is meant to be of value to the others. This has already been achieved in the realm of technology, but our morality has not yet caught up with technology. Within the social order of today we can technically not make anything for ourselves, not even a jacket. But even if we made it ourselves, it would cost as much in the total social structure as if it had been made by somebody else. The price of the jacket is determined by society. It is a figment of the imagination to think that the jacket which the tailor makes for himself is cheaper. It could be calculated in numbers and would appear cheaper. But if it were listed as part of a general balance sheet, we would realize that as little as we can jump out of our own skin, as little can we alter or eliminate economic life by making our own clothes. Even the garment that we have made for ourselves must be paid for in the general balance sheet. Labor is what one person produces for the other. It cannot be determined by how much production time is needed in the factory. The value put on labor leads us most definitely into the realm of law, into the political, legal life. That this is not an outdated idea can be seen by the fact that labor everywhere is protected and subjected to labor laws. But today, these laws are not even half-measures, but quarter-measures. They can only take full effect if a proper threefold social organism comes into being. For only then will one human being face another human being. Only then will labor be regulated correctly, when human dignity speaks out of the encounters with human dignity, out of the element in which all human beings are competent to speak.

Then you may say: Well, there won't be sufficient labor eventually, if labor is evaluated democratically in this way. Indeed, this is one of the areas where social life leads us into the general development of humanity.

Economic life must not determine human labor. Economic life must be enclosed within the boundaries set by nature and by democratically determined labor laws. Just as no committee can decide how many rainy days there are to be in 1923 so that the economy will run on course that year, just as we have to accept rainy days as something given, something given by nature, so the independent economic life will have to reckon with something given, with a specified amount of labor which is determined by the political, legal sphere. I can mention this only in general terms simply to characterize matters.

In the economic part of the social organism, associations will exist in which, based on their life's experience, consumers, producers, and traders will arrive at an associative judgment—not an individual judgment that has no significance at all. With the small beginnings existing today, this cannot be achieved. But these small beginnings prove that unconsciously people have the intention of going in this direction. Cooperatives, trade unions, all sorts of communities are founded. But if today you form a cooperative alongside the rest of the social structure, it will either have to grow into the rest of the social structure, have the same prices and the same marketing practices, or perish. The process of creating our threefold social order is concerned not with the creation of new realities based on utopian thoughts, but with coming to grips with the currently existing institutions, with those who consume and those who produce, the entrepreneur. Without newly establishing institutions, all that now exists is to be integrated into associations. So we should not ask: How are new associations to be founded? but, How can the existing economic organizations and institutions be integrated into associations? First and foremost, based on the economic experience within these associations, one proper result can then come about, namely, an economic circulation, a cash flow, consisting of capital for production, loans, and donations. No proper social organism can exist that does not contain these three. This in turn actually gives rise to a social order, just as a healthy organism gives rise to fitness in human life. However much people may rail against it, gifts and charitable foundations must exist today. We only kid ourselves when we say that a healthy social organism requires no donated funds. We pay our taxes. And taxes are only a roundabout way of making gifts for funding schools and other institutions.

People ought to have a social order in which they always realize how things are going and do not kid themselves. If the social life can gradually be led out of its present state—in which everything is contained in one big entangled jumble—something akin to the blood circulation in a healthy human organism will be achieved, the circulation of money as purchase money, loan money, and gift money. People will then see how, on the one hand, they are linked through trade circulation, production, and earnings with invested money, which, by way of loans, pays dividends and passes over into production and how, on the other side, they are linked with gift moneys that must flow into the free cultural life.

Only in this way can people participate in the social course of events, if everybody can see how life develops in the free association. Then health can enter the social organism. Abstract thought is incompatible with the idea of the threefold order. Only living thinking counts here. [*The Spiritual Ground of Education*, lecture of August 29, 1922.]

CHAPTER 9

School Physicians' Reports

Child Study

The following are examples of the child study in Waldorf schools. It is one of the central tasks of the school physician to moderate and take part in this discussion. In these discussions with the teachers, a descriptive picture of each student is painstakingly worked out, in order to support the healthy development of the child. Every teacher, also parents, can request such an intensive consultation. It takes place within the framework of a special meeting or a faculty meeting. As Rudolf Steiner stated [*Human Values in Education*, lecture of July 21, 1924]:

I know that many people will say: If you assert that human beings, in addition to their physical body, consist of supersensible members—etheric body, astral body, and ego-organization—it follows that only someone who is clairvoyant and able to perceive these supersensible members of human nature can be a teacher. But this is not the case. Everything perceived through imagination, inspiration, and intuition, as described in my books, can be examined and assessed by observing the child's physical organization, because it comes to expression everywhere in this physical organization.

It is certainly possible for teachers or educators who carry out their profession in a truly loving way, basing their teaching on a comprehensive insight into the human being, to speak in the following way about a given case: This child is completely fit in regard to the ego, astral body, and even the etheric body. But the physical body shows signs of hardening, of stiffening, and the child is therefore unable to develop the faculties that were created as potentials in the spiritual realm, because the physical body is a hindrance. Rudolf Steiner, *Human Values in Education,* lecture of July 21, 1924.]

When we go back into earlier epochs of history, to early Grecian times, we find that the words "educator" and "healer" were very closely connected, for people knew that when human beings enter earthly life they are beings who as yet have not attained their full development; they are beings who must first be brought to full development. This is what is sound in the conception of the Fall of Man, for people actually enter earthly existence as subhuman beings. If they were not subhuman beings, we should no more need to educate them than we have to teach the spider to weave webs when grown. Human beings must be educated and taught everything before they are brought to full humanness. And if it has been rightly adjudged that we must first lead human beings in body, soul, and spirit to become truly human, then we will furthermore understand that this must be achieved according to the same laws by which an abnormally working human nature must be brought back on the right track. To heal a person whose intact humanity has been damaged is a task that is similar to education. It is only when, once more, we come to recognize the natural and spiritual relationship between these two activities that we shall be able to fructify our education in the right way by an ethical physiology. [*The Roots of Education,* lecture of April 17, 1924.]

If, in the following, several specific possibilities for advancing healthy development are being addressed, one danger should be mentioned as well. It is the danger of turning the child into a pathological case. This must be avoided under all circumstances. Rather, it is a matter of supporting and developing faculties, potentials. The point is that every child can learn—just as adults must work all their lives on developing their capacities.

[In the following reports, the physician or teacher is referred to as *she* and the child as *he,* when gender is not specified.]

Child Study

Methods of Child Study
Johannes Bockemühl

After many years of practice in clinical child psychiatry, medical care in various curative homes and remedial schools, and from activities of school physicians at Waldorf schools, the child study has become the very essence of our social and medical work. Properly understood, it is a methodically practiced path for all who enter into a therapeutic-educational, or nurturing relationship with a child or patient. Here we will go into some questions that are connected with such a study and pool our experiences.

This kind of study can be led by one teacher alone, or by a smaller or larger group of colleagues, if the direction is fundamentally agreed upon by all the participants. Variations in the way this is carried out are naturally determined by the child's age.

The frequently posed question of whether the child ought to be physically present depends on the maturity of the teachers' or therapeutic group that is to conduct this study. If the group is composed of people from several quite different backgrounds [teachers, doctors, therapists], it makes sense, of course, for the participants to try to create a collective viewpoint so that a common, objective basis can be laid. This presupposes exercising a particular inner attitude towards the child. This can be a first focal point in the study.

How is a child perceived? Will he or she be improved or harmed through such a discussion? Aside from the attitude of the group, this also depends on the skill and experience of the trusted individual who introduces the child into the group (for instance, the class teacher, teacher's aid, or therapist). A class teacher, for example, could in a playful manner involve the child in a game activity that is familiar from activities in class; an older student might perhaps comment on the work for the year, or could present his or her questions. It goes without saying that, depending on the student's age, each case gives rise to a quite different awareness of the situation. In every single case, therefore, individual forms of such a discussion should be discovered.

It is frequently revealing to invite the parents, perhaps even the grandparents, to the conversation. In no way can the presentation of a child's case be carried out in a small circle without informing and having permission from the parents. In some instances, the physician may even have to be released from professional confidentiality.

The child and the parents will most likely participate only up to the end of the first stage of the discussion. Parents have a right to receive a clear picture as to the outcome and suggested therapeutic measures (see *Conversation with Parents* pages 233-237).

Steps of a Child Study

Step 1. First Encounter or First Impressions

During the initial encounter with the child, one's attention can be directed to two things: on the one hand, to the overview of what has been perceived in the child's nature; on the other, to one's own attitude and approach in this encounter. Along with the attempt to describe the first impressions, it becomes clear how complex and almost impossible it is to give a simple description of what is happening. It challenges us to prepare ourselves to totally engage our powers of observation.

This first impression requires, above all, awe and wonder on the part of the observers. They try to open themselves up and to stimulate all their senses. This is not achieved point by point, but rather in the sense of an alert open mind and reverential listening. Trying to hold the following perspective can help:

Everything that I encounter has occurred in the course of the child's life, and within it future developments are contained. What meets me at present are merely the physical and the soul-spiritual sounding together. The momentary encounter shows me the compressed image of the total biography. Everywhere I see indications of the spirit's working; without the physical, the spiritual cannot be brought to realization.

The inner attitude therefore is to have an open, unprejudiced mind, and to respect the other person.

Step 2. Seeking Out Various Views

(As a rule, playing with a child can end at this point. Perhaps the parents could express their view regarding the child; then they and the child leave the discussion.)

The observers now direct their interest to the perceivable details. They try to form the most accurate description and characterization of what they perceive. It can be the face, for instance, the form of the head, the shape of the ears, the gait, the figure, the hands, the hair, language, and so forth, which can be chosen as areas of observation. Descriptions should purposely be without interpretation or judgment. We should strive for this in the strictest sense of a natural-scientific exercise. It becomes clear that in this way of working the group strives to eliminate any prejudice. But a force of love is thereby awakened as well, which is dedicated to detail. This step includes a description of the case history, the environment, and reports from the various subject teachers or other groups. Our inner attitude following this should be recollection of the experiences and taking it all in.

Step 3. Questioning the Various Views—Forming an Image

Out of the view-gathering, we arrive at the question: What do these different perspectives taken as a whole tell us? The observers begin to put together a picture by fitting the individual views together. This is a joint artistic process of considering, moving, and weighing impressions and thoughts. When the views are compared, they are amplified or contradicted. Tensions can arise in us; the child becomes a riddle for us, a question—sometimes even an insoluble one. It is important not to become fixed immediately on some sort of law or image; instead, we fit together the individual observations, making a joint effort to strive for comprehension, to work on producing an overall image. The inner attitude here can be described as weighing and comparing.

Step 4. *Sensing the Laws*

The image or images we have gained can awaken in us a sense for the law or regulating factor through which an underlying principle or impulse can manifest. Here, on the one hand, we see the group's creative, disciplined interaction with an anthroposophical understanding of the human being. On the other hand, one can observe what the individual has achieved esoterically through inner discipline.

In a concrete case, the group should determine jointly which viewpoint should be used as the basis of the current study. For instance, the lawfulness of a polarity can be chosen as a focus on how a principle manifests in the human constitution. Such polarities or contrasts might be:

- cosmic/earthly
- synthetic/analytic dominance of forces: anabolic/catabolic; round/radial
- threefold functions: nerve-sense system / heart and circulatory system / metabolic-limb system
- fourfold constitution: ego organization / astral body / etheric body / physical body

- the seven-fold state of the ether body: breathing /warming / nourishing / secreting / conserving / growing / producing
- the twelve-fold state of the sense organs
- aspects of development (the seven-year-phases)

In any case, the focus of the presentation should be determined. It is important for the group to carry an attitude of listening to the inner movement, and to feel the responsibility connected with this process. This step can lead to an individual diagnosis based on a livingly experienced understanding of the human being. This step is an assessment, a descriptive diagnosis.

Step 5. Resonance of Processes as Therapeutic Impulse

If the principle at work in the human being in the particular illness or challenge now becomes discernible, then related processes or principles working in nature can awaken in us as a kind of resonance. Silver and lead, evening and morning, cold and warm—for example—could thus become therapeutic polarities in this active, creative phase. Out of the individual views of teachers, therapists, and doctors, a common perspective is formed as a starting point for developing a therapeutic plan for the child, the patient. Here we deal, at least in part, with an intuitive event. These considerations should lead to a joint decision by the teachers, doctor, and therapists.

Step 6. Application

Once the therapeutic ideas have been compiled, we find ways of implementing the therapeutic measures and assign responsibility for care. Particular attention should be paid to the weight of responsibility and the will to help.

Step 7. *Gesture of Thankfulness*

To complete the diagnostic-therapeutic path, and to raise into consciousness again aspects of the biography and an appreciation for the individuality, time should be devoted to bringing an expression of gratitude centered on this human being and the efforts made on his or her behalf. As a conclusion, the moment of the first encounter should be recalled.

Epilogue:

If one works in this way, something on the order of various breathing processes result on their own from the relationship between observer, therapist, and child. At one point, we turn our attention to the child; following that, we assume a contemplative attitude. Again, we focus on the whole of the impression, or, once again, on the detail. The sequence of views and their images are gathered and concentrated; then we turn our attention once more to nature in order to seek out principles within ourselves that result from the diagnosis, and so on. Experience shows that what we have outlined here requires considerable training and cooperation within the group. This is why the whole course of the child study frequently remains incomplete. But what matters here is that the child study has the nature of a practice. These moments are important when we succeed in concentrating healing forces that can aid the child. The whole effort will therefore be as helpful for the child as it will be for the group.

As to time, to prepare for an orderly course of events, one needs to plan on about two hours. One can take notes as an exercise during the second step in order to strive for resolute attentiveness.

Conversation with the Parents

In my practice as a school physician, in curative and medical work, but particularly in clinical child psychiatry, the conversation with parents of individual children has become more and more important for me in the course of the last thirty years. Parents know their children better than anyone else, although perhaps from a particular perspective. At any rate, they are generally in more intimate contact with the child than we doctors, teachers, or any other people are. Thus, in the beginning, parents are the hereditary mediators between the child and other people. They are the ones who by their very nature are in a position to give the child confidence, protection, and guidance in regard to the world he enters. That is a good thing; it should always be called to mind and receive our respectful attention. It is, however, a task that parents nowadays often neglect.

To begin with, parents must be viewed as competent. They are specialists on the subject of their child. Even when we have to assess actions of parents from the viewpoint of our experience, nonetheless, they have spent time with and know their child. Parents make a strong mark in the course of the child's development, through experience, through their habits, through the circumstances of their lives, and most decisively through their personality. This is the reason why parents can frequently give the very best information about their child, if we only ask them with interest and really listen to them. Even when parents are not able to offer good information, we can nevertheless learn a great deal from their demeanor, their style, their way of speaking to each other in regard to the milieu in which the child lives. On occasion, the most delicate perceptions can be reported to us, perceptions that may easily appear to us to be exaggerated, prejudiced, or overly sensitive. Yet, even in an often quite awkward presentation, they can be indicative for an understanding of the child.

During the conversation, the parents should increasingly be in a frame of mind where they can express their questions confidently, where they notice that they are understood and where they might receive new viewpoints, where they sense the responsibility that they themselves have in regard to their child. If one succeeds in creating an atmosphere in which the child himself becomes describable as a person, both parents and physician can find a new perspective that does justice to the child. The goal should be to loosen the often too closely and subjectively colored relationship to the child so as to enable the parents to gain distance from their problems and to describe the child anew in such a way that his nature becomes objectively decipherable out of the phenomena.

The physician has to go in a different direction. To begin with, she keeps her distance. In the encounter with both child and parents, she should do all she can not to intrude on the meeting with too quickly formed prejudices, technical know-how, the diagnostic repertoire, and so on. While keeping some distance, she maintains awe and respect for the dignity of this child whom she may perhaps be meeting for the first time and whose confidence has to be won, if a meaningful or creative result of this meeting is to come about.

Thus, parents, physicians, therapists, and teachers can produce a kind of respect- and trust-filled atmosphere into which—in the perception of those who are present but better yet in person—the child can enter.

Our therapeutic conversations, for example, in the framework of a Waldorf School—perhaps planned by the class teacher, a remedial teacher, a therapist or a therapeutic eurythmist, but quite often also by subject teachers—always include parents or at least the mother. Frequently the reason for the conversation is some kind of health problem, some sort of developmental discrepancy, a critical situation, difficulty in learning, or a social problem. As a matter of principle, we cannot help or propose help if the parents are unable to agree to the educational or therapeutic measure. In this regard too, parents must be viewed as being competent, for they are indeed involved in the process of education. They have to experience this task in ever new ways, and have to be able to support the gestures of assistance on the part of the school. It is, for instance, extraordinarily important whether an exercise is taken up at home and cultivated in an understanding way, or whether the parents feel bypassed in their competence by the school's efforts at help, and therefore are not able inwardly to accept it.

The conversations with parents and teachers have the common goal, first of all, to learn to read the child, so to speak. This means, to observe in a sympathetic way all that the child shows in the way of gestalt-phenomena: expressions of movement, speech, voice, skills, sense activities, social characteristics, schoolwork and artistic activities, gifts, and manner of behavior. It means to decipher their common elements that the child demonstrates, quite beyond and independent of our feelings, habits of behavior, our inhibitions and expectations. If a proper image is successfully produced here, relief can frequently be experienced that eliminates a good deal of emotion, misunderstanding, and controversy that work between human beings. This allows for a new way of seeing things out of which help and assistance can be developed.

This is likewise the point where the child senses deliverance out of many relationship tensions. He notices that he is of interest to the adults, that they are really making an effort to understand him. Finally, the child feels understood and senses help in his own understanding of himself.

The conversation with the parents—if at all possible in the presence of the child—often leads to an indirect resolution of hardened positions between parents and teachers, positions that sometimes have accumulated over the course of many years and may have led to antagonistic confrontations. Caught in the middle, the child can suffer or may have learned to play both sides against each other. Here, it is important for the school physician to remain objective, to take sides neither with parents nor teachers, but always to make the attempt to describe the situation based on a comprehensive knowledge of the human being including insights gained through anthroposophy, and furthermore, to develop and make clear as part of the diagnostic picture the potential contributions by parents, teachers, therapists, and even those of the physician. Here we have to find a pictorial language, comprehensible to all and yet based on a thorough understanding of the nature of the human being, that in the end can lead to the organizing of the educational, therapeutic, and medical measures for the child.

Such a conversation has been successful if the parents, seeing new approaches for solutions, are prepared to cooperate, and conclude the conversation filled with hope. This is most important for the continuation of an educational, therapeutic process. This atmosphere of growing confidence, the reality of the encounter, is quite a decisive factor that must be developed in an artistic fashion. The riddle of the child has to be called up anew in all the participants, otherwise no successful healing effect will be attained.

Actually, the course of such a conversation with the parent serves the purpose of penetrating the nature of the child so intensely that the realm of the spirit can be unlocked, enabling therapeutic intuitions (more modestly, ideas) to occur.

How is this arranged in regard to the timing? It would be desirable if, prior to the conversation, the parents were to present or in short sentences note down highlights of the child's development, the prevailing conditions at home, and any questions they might have. Questions can also be compiled from teachers and therapists. Still, is better to develop all these matters together in conversation, because prejudices can then be prevented.

Furthermore, it is most important that school notebooks, results of crafts or needlework lessons, the work of the year, therapeutic eurythmy exercises, class verses, the playing of flutes, and other such things are presented, so that the broadest possible picture of the child comes about and his abilities can be demonstrated. This is in any case

236

a much better approach than choosing the child's disciplinary transgressions as the theme, in which case the child feels from the first to be on trial. These things too must be discussed, but that should only be undertaken when an objective level has been found, a level from which even the child learns to view his own misdeed with different eyes.

In cases of kleptomania or aggressive behavior, the circle of those participating in the conversation should under certain circumstances be kept very small, because the elements of consternation have frequently narrowed down the picture considerably, and an understanding often can no longer be successfully attained. Such a conversation can then not be handled within the time span of a single school hour. At another time, further conversations alone with the child, with only the parents, or alone with the teacher must be scheduled. In principle, living conditions frequently have to be examined much further so as to recognize details of behavior. In such a case, I often have to refer the child to my own medical practice and spend a good deal of time in order to fit together more precisely a picture from the daily habits of the people involved, so that I can help to direct the subsequent biographical steps the child should take.

The conversation with parents and therapists can become an exercise for objective individual insight, whereby the relationship of trust, the child's individuality, and the immediately present situation determine the course that the processes will take.

Child Study in Education and Therapeutic Education
Wolfgang Goebel

The conversations among a child's caregivers will here be called child study. The goal of such caregivers is to be better able to help the child with his difficulties in life through understanding him better. Initially, I became acquainted with this kind of child study about thirty-five years ago in the first home of the therapeutic Camphill movement at Aberdeen, Scotland. Later, in somewhat altered forms and under different conditions, I continued to gather experience in a German Waldorf school for children and young people with various disabilities, in a school for teenagers who have learning disabilities, in a larger Waldorf school, and finally in the psychiatric ward of a children's hospital. All these enterprises were based on anthroposophy.

As an example, I shall attempt to outline what a child study can be, then mention the broader anthroposophical foundations, the possible metamorphoses of such conversations, their preparation and follow-up, and finally what such conversations should not be. In conclusion, a kind of historical comparison should give us an idea of the value and weight such discussions can have for a therapeutic education community and those who are cared for there.

In a curative home, all the co-workers meet once a week as a group after the children have gone to bed. For a whole week, everyone has known which child's turn it will be today. Those who did not know him well have taken a closer look in passing. The group-caretaker responsible for the child begins with a characterizing remark that is supposed to call to mind the image of the child for all participants. For instance: In the morning, B., with her thick black hair and broad smile, comes up to me in her heavy, awkward manner of walking and whispers in my ear, "Today is Wednesday. My name is Bertha." Then, the whole appearance of the child is described: form, movement, proportions, physiognomy, head shape, body and extremities in all detail, the color of the eyes, the shape of the ears, the condition of the teeth, the shape of hand and foot, also the handshake and walk. The attentive participants can thus reconstruct the image of this child, add previously unnoticed details, and allow a quite open and mobile picture to take shape. This is then supplemented from many sides by reports about details of sleeping and waking rhythms, eating, drinking, and excretion habits, as well as participation in the various phases of the rhythm of the day.

Here, other participants in the group add observations from their own sphere of activity: the teacher from the school, the therapists from their specialties, perhaps the gardener and the cook from brief but typical encounters with the child. This way, the moods and attitudes in which the child lives are called to mind—also his power of perception, his interests and the extent of his reserve, his joys and sorrows, his sympathies and antipathies, and the problems that brought this particular child to be chosen as the subject of the conversation.

Through the different descriptions, the picture has assumed a deeper dimension. Now it is possible to have a look at where the child comes from, out of what kind of conditions, which influences had an impact on his past—whether it be illnesses, social influences, or other things. Finally, the physician in attendance will perhaps add the medical aspect to this picture.

If the conversation up till now has been quite focused, it may be good to follow it by a brief silence. For now the participants ponder their astonishment concerning hitherto unknown aspects that now fit into the overall picture. If participants are lucky, they reach the point where they sense: So that is what you, B., want to express with your life.

As a rule, some of the participants now make suggestions concerning how they might deal differently with the child in the future—applying different therapy, teaching him differently, and treating him medically in other ways. Naturally, it is also possible that misunderstandings arise and corrections must be brought to bear. Misunderstandings are easily corrected if all participants are in agreement concerning the goal of such a child study. Participants report again and again that in the course of the next few days such a child, even before anything was done differently, already made a different impression in the direction of progress or an improvement of sorts.

The participants in the conversation may have at their disposal to a greater or lesser degree, the following perspectives gained through anthroposophy:

Human polarities

- The threefoldness of the human organism: nerve-sense system, rhythmic system, and metabolic-limb system. (*Foundations of Human Experience.*)

- The fourfold state of the incarnated human being: ego-organization, astral body, etheric body, and physical body. (Rudolf Steiner/Ita Wegman, *Fundamentals of Therapy.*)

- the polarities of the human being: relationships of head and limbs to the cosmos and earth; connection between elements of physical body with soul-spiritual elements; restricted imagination and lack of imagination. (*Education for Adolescents*, lectures of June 13 and 15, 1921.)

- predominance of nerve-sense system or metabolic-limb system—classified under large-headed and small-headed phenomena. (*Faculty Meetings with Rudolf Steiner*, meeting of February 6, 1923.)

- juvenile hysterical or epileptic constitution; sulfur-rich and sulfur-poor organization; weak-minded and mentally overactive organization. (*Education for Special Needs*, lectures of June 28 and 30, 1924.)

Medical polarities:

- hysterical and neurasthenic [debilitating nervous] constitution. (*Spiritual Science and Medicine*, lecture of March 22, 1920.)

- inability to fall asleep, inability to awaken. (*Spiritual Scientific Aspects of Therapy*, lectures of April 13 and 14, 1921.)

Temperaments:

- choleric, sanguine, phlegmatic, melancholic.[36]

Recognizing the members of the human being through observation:

- for instance: imagination, inspiration, intuition, or Goethe's way of perceiving and the kingdoms of nature (*The Mystery of the Trinity*, lecture of July 28, 1922.)

What we have received from anthroposophy and made our own can be fruitful in the conversation if it characterizes the child in an accurate way without classifying him.

Child study may be conducted differently in different institutions. In a school for children with mental challenges, the discussion was carried out as the first part of the weekly meeting in the early afternoon; the children were sent home early on this day. As a rule, following this discussion, further lengthy and tiring meeting topics are taken up. Therefore it is better not to begin with the child's problems, but with a concentrated description of his physical appearance. Inasmuch as the physical identity of the child is described, his individuality is more closely approached than if one hears merely of all too typical psychological/soul difficulties in dealing with the child.

This temptation is even greater in a regular Waldorf school, because child studies are frequently done only in cases of extreme behavioral disturbances—or teachers do not have the desirable level of practice to conduct the discussion in a hygienic manner.

Things are different in a school with small classes only for children with learning difficulties. Here, the positive attitude of the group of teachers (under the direction of then school physician, Johannes Bockemühl) was brought about through the fact that the child and his parents were invited to attend the discussion. First, under the guidance of his class teacher, the child could demonstrate what he could do, perhaps a couple of eurythmy exercises. Then he was taken outside. Next, a conversation ensued with the parents in which the joint attempt was made to create an image of the child. This enabled the parents to be trustful because they sensed that nothing but loving interest prevailed concerning the child's positive development. It was therefore not a problem to ask the parents to wait outside during the last part of the conversation. In the subsequent internal conversation among the teachers, an understanding grew for the possible contributions by the parents. The teachers were able to consider how to include their efforts in a positive way. In conclusion, the parents were informed about the results of the conversations.

The school physician readily finds parallels to her own activity in this type of situation. For it is only possible for her to consult successfully with parents and teachers when she creates an image of the child that they can confirm—an image, they may have to admit, that one hopes will contain additional, new, previously unknown elements. To the degree that consensus comes about through this, positive future perspectives become possible. To be sure, it soon becomes noticeable that parents can be properly supportive only if they can understand the educational, medical, and artistic/therapeutic measures and can accept the people who carry them out.

The example above was of a young child who lived with the caregivers; the parents were far away, having placed the child completely in the hands of this group of people. In the following examples, parents and teachers share more equally the responsibility for the child's positive development. Older children who are becoming independent increasingly have the feeling that nothing goes well unless they are included. The first germinal beginnings of this independence are rooted in the human organization along with the developmental step taken by a child between the ages of nine and ten (a step sometimes designated by Rudolf Steiner as the Crossing of the Rubicon).[37] Initially the child is then easily wounded and in strong need of support. Through difficult personal experiences, and increasingly through the influences of modern civilization and education, premature intellectual awareness or inhibitions can appear that are expressed in serious, disturbed, or chaotic behavior and must be heeded in special ways.

From the aspect of family participation in therapy, the experience has been reported that problems of the most varied kinds can only be satisfactorily resolved when, according to their own stage of development, the children are drawn into and included in the conversations. This applies particularly to problems that arise between students and teachers. New possibilities come up here when, under the expert direction of a third party in whom all those involved in a problem at school have confidence, open conversations take place in which everyone can frankly express his or her experiences, moods, and intentions. Genuine meetings of the mind thus take place, and future cooperation comes about.

A child study has to be adjusted to the problems that arise. In curative homes, the co-workers talk together and report on how they view the child while he is asleep. Thus, almost unintentionally, they work on a kind of positive thought-configuration of this human being that is supported by an interested and loving understanding of his particular characteristics. The therapeutic ideas that then arise are proof of how this positive image moves by itself toward further development, and the participants in the conversation begin to recognize their own share and place in it. This is quite different in schools. Where alert participation is possible in regard to the totally different problems here, the endeavor should be made to achieve it. Such participation is of benefit if the inner attitude is both objective and sympathetically observant and tolerant. Sleeping on the process that has been set in motion by all participants in both curative and regular schools is equally important, because, in sleep, confirmations and sources of strength open up for the direction that is being pursued.

Bringing the ideas into practice

The reports included here from the school physicians' work were obtained as the result of a questionnaire circulated among school physicians. They answer questions concerning the scope of the work, particular problems, and the financing involved. They give insight into how physicians actually work at Waldorf schools.

Job-description of the physician at Engelberg
Wolfgang Kersten
published in *Der Merkurstab* [The staff of Mercury], March 1996.

Outline of the School Physician's Tasks

For Students	For Teachers/School	For Parents
Creating a course of therapy, follow-up	Child study Medical consultation	Consultations Parent evenings
Instruction in human biology	Psychological consultation	Lectures in kindergarten
Visiting classes Admission of students Psychological consultation Class-screenings for physical conditions First aid	Visiting classes Faculty meetings	

For Caregivers	For the School Organism	For the Public
Discussion of therapy	Lending a helping hand withsocial complexities	Lectures Workshops

Diagnosis

At the Waldorf School in Engelberg, the school physician is integrated into the school organism as a member of the faculty. He has an assignment corresponding to that of a full-time teacher in a Waldorf school. He teaches for 5.9 TWH (= Teacher's-Weekly-Hours)—normally four blocks, two in the ninth grades and two in the tenth grades. It is exclusively conducted as block instruction over a period of a whole block.

For the students, the school physician offers instruction on human biology in ninth and tenth grade. On occasion when a substitute teacher is needed, he teaches blocks on nutrition in seventh and eighth grade.

In the special subjects, the physician has conversations with parents, teachers, and upper grade students, and visits classes in curative eurythmy, eurythmy, sports, and other subjects. During periods when the school physician has no instruction scheduled, he visits the main lessons in grades one to eight, and screens all the students (in Baden-Wuerttemburg, at the beginning of school and in the fourth grade).

A large part of the time is dedicated to working on therapy, as well as follow-up, with the students. This includes a conversation between school physician and family doctor . The screening of all students at the beginning of school includes conversations with the teachers concerning admissions, and deliberation concerning rejections and special cases (that is, integration of children in need of special care).

Almost every recess in school is taken up with first-aid cases (usually minor ones, rarely serious injuries: stomach aches, headaches) treatment of which do not necessarily require the care of a physician, but are always opportune moments to get to know the students better.

Work for the teacher (i.e. for the school): In Engelberg, the school physician was urgently awaited and overloaded with all sorts of diverse tasks. This is surely the most exhausting but, for me, the most beautiful and challenging way to begin work. And this makes it particularly evident that an outline of the school physician's duties is a great help for the beginner in order to have at least something to go on in the stimulating and yet chaotic situation of being faced with overwhelming demands and requests. Despite this, it must be said at this point that every school assuredly requires its own school physician in accordance with its traditions, its local problems, its recently established or longstanding existence, and so on. A general outline of duties can therefore merely be a guideline that does not stand in the way of freely arranging one's tasks. Teachers expect a good deal from the school physician:

1. Help in recognizing students' problems, and possibly ensuing therapy, as well as advice on instructional measures that could be emphasized for a particular child.

2. Competent support in conversations with parents regarding questions of therapy, the need to attend a special school, and educational problems.

3. One-to-one consultation with colleagues, not only in regard to the school and faculty, but also for private psychological and marital problems.

4. Participation in faculty meetings, as well as in specific work with the faculty regarding pedagogical-medical problems, discussions with children, fundamental anthroposophical studies (the human senses; the media; drug addiction; academic maturity, etc.).

For the parents, the school physician is *the* individual to whom they flock as soon as the child runs into problems at school. At this point, it is appropriate to say a word about an important subject concerning doctors: professional discretion! In my experience, this commonly accepted obligation, which I have emphasized from the very beginning, offers protected space that all the groups in the school want to use. Here, students can discuss things they probably would not discuss with their family doctor (perhaps because of his or her lack of time). Teachers can seek advice here during personal or crisis situations with colleagues. Parents can express concerns that do not necessarily lead to actions fraught with consequences. Therapists can talk calmly about possible failures. Frequently, such a talk begins with the words, This is a professional conversation, isn't it? and then the explicit wish is expressed that the talk be confidential. If a child has fears about school, has learning difficulties or other problems, the parents come for advice, and to find help and understanding for their assumption that it is not only the child that is wrong, but that the teacher may perhaps be guilty as well. Problems concerning the child's upbringing and the parents' marital problems are important subjects for consultations (because in the end they always have an effect on the child).

An additional large domain of work with the parents is the special evenings for parents on the subjects of drugs, the media, puberty, violence, or the instruction in human biology and the therapies that are available at the school. Likewise, in the parent-teacher association, the school physician is frequently needed as a referee. Various other evenings with parents (such as introductory talks for new parents, therapies at the school) belong to the school physician's scope of tasks, likewise the issuing of invitations to speakers from outside the school.

In addition, the school physician is naturally the partner who has to be consulted when epidemics arise in a class, be they lice or chicken pox.

For the therapists, the school physician is the partner in the conversation dealing with the planning of therapies. Here we find the most medically-oriented tasks: diagnoses regarding the configuration of the higher human components and of the sense organism, but also regarding orthopedics or internal conditions. This, of course, always challenges the physician to develop an eye for prophylaxis [promoting health and preventing the spread of disease]. In fact, the relationship between school physician and caregivers has to do above all with the domain of prophylaxis. Rudolf Steiner directed Eugen Kolisko, the very first school physician at the original Waldorf school, primarily toward the most fundamental issues, for which it would be necessary *to know all the children in the school,* namely, problems of nutrition, abnormal posture, breathing irregularity, and so on. Here, the school physician has a splendid opportunity, working with therapists and family doctors, to recognize illnesses at their very inception and to prevent their outbreak.

Now, what illnesses and preconditions does the school physician have to deal with? First are the large number of behavioral problems, ranging from constitutional agitation—children who cause disturbances and provocations, those who have aggressive behavior—through chronic tiredness, to speech impediments, and a multitude of apparent partial learning disabilities. In addition, there are the more medical problems: bed wetting; children with posture, walking, and vision problems; chronic illnesses; headaches; orthodontic problems; more rarely occurring acute illnesses; and first aid.

In Engelberg, a two-hour therapy conference takes place every Wednesday. Participants are the three therapeutic eurythmists, the remedial or art therapist, and the physician. In this circle, class teachers report on their problem cases and therapeutic possibilities are discussed. Aside from this, Rudolf Steiner's book on curative education or other such material is studied. Other faculty members are also invited to this work.

For the general public, the school physician gives lectures on Waldorf education and its remedial effect, on problems of the media, on childhood diseases and their treatment, on the question Do illnesses have a purpose? and other subjects. The general public is mostly those who have connections to Waldorf kindergartens, holistic groups, and public schools.

My personal intention right from the beginning of my studies was to become a school physician at a Waldorf school. For this I visited a teacher training course in Berlin, and regularly took part in the school physicians' conferences in Dornach. Thus I represent the surely rare case of a medical doctor who has the professional wish to be a school physician. In our time when even physicians increasingly face the choice of not working at all—working in undesirable situations, or not working in the medical field at all—it makes good sense to draw the attention of university students or young physicians interested in anthroposophy to the vocation described above that has much to offer— particularly in regard to human interaction, urgently desired support, and integration into the organism of a Waldorf school. On the one hand, the physician should be asked to view this profession, which is equal to that of a teacher financially, as a prospect for the future. On the other hand, schools and teacher training programs should also take more notice of this necessity that is embedded in the conception of a Waldorf school, but is not properly recognized because of lack of funds.

This job description of the school physician in Engelberg is naturally influenced by the amount of work expected from the doctor. With reference to Rudolf Steiner's expectation that a school physician know all the children, in light of all the work that is assigned in school, it appears to me that a part-time physician or one who only occasionally visits the school would merely be able to handle a few of these areas of work. Truly getting to know the students (especially in a school with double classes in each grade) is surely out of the question. For this reason I feel the urgent need to establish positions of school physicians. Again and again, when I have had personal conversations with school physicians—who, aside from their busy practices, are kind enough to look after a school once or twice a week—they express a certain dissatisfaction with this position of an outsider, a position that prevents actual penetration into the school organism.

Regarding the concept of the school organism, I must make the following remark. During the years of my activity as a continually present school physician, the obligation, even necessity, to stand by at the side of this organism in a healing and helping way has become increasingly clear. Many disease-causing tendencies are inherent today in the social realm and affect the interaction between parents and teachers, teachers and students, teachers and co-workers, and teachers among themselves. Here too, a rich field of activity opens up for doctors and caregivers to lend a helping hand, if possible before the outbreak of conflicts, but at the very latest at the beginning of the illness.

To help teachers fulfill the task with which he charged them, namely, to educate the children to be healthy, Rudolf Steiner placed the school physician at their side. Soon thereafter, this was followed by therapeutic eurythmy. In an age of growing difficulties, this combination of education and medicine that is good for the children should not be degraded to the status of a financial problem, if each Waldorf school faculty is really aware of its mission to bring about health.

Qualifications. The professional foundations for the school physician consist of medical experience, an anthroposophical-educational bearing in life (many questions posed to the school physician relate directly to anthroposophy), enjoyment of teamwork and medical work predominantly carried out through conversations.

The occupation of *school physician* is really an official designation. But Rudolf Steiner introduced this position as a necessary constituent in the faculty of a Waldorf school. The reasons for this in 1919 appear to me to be future-oriented. Everywhere today, people cry for the cure after the fact. The concept of prevention as a physician's tool has been recognized very little by health insurance. The need for therapeutically supported help in education becomes more pressing every year. With the increase in broken marriages, stress-dominated family relationships, with ever-growing terror presented by the media, and more intensely threatening effects of environmental issues as well as other diverse pressures, children in the first seven years grow up actually crying out for help. Their urgent needs must be recognized in a loving way. Due to problem-laden children in their classes, but likewise due to the facts just mentioned, teachers have less and less energy at their disposal to meet and deal with the needs of the children through educational measures alone (which, if they correspond to the Waldorf school curriculum, do work in a health-benefiting way).

In view of this situation, I recognize how far-sighted the concept of the Waldorf school is, inasmuch as Rudolf Steiner integrated the therapeutic domain—school physician and caregivers—into the school from the very beginning. This was done to provide a healing education with the help of knowledgeable healers. In a similar way, he also integrated religious instruction as an indispensable subject into the school. And with this concept, he united the ancient triad of teacher, priest, and physician in a single task that, through this working together with the children, plants important seeds for the future in them. In the course of this activity, the significance of the verse that Rudolf Steiner gave in 1924 to medical students and young doctors in a circular letter [published in *Deepening the Art of Healing*] becomes ever clearer.

In ancient ages there lived in initiate souls
Powerfully the thought:
Every man, by nature, is ill.
Education was looked upon
As equal to the healing process,
Which, with maturity, brought the child
Health for the life
Of the fulfilled being of man.

Personally, the presentation by Dr. Steiner in the lecture of April 7, 1920 in *Health Care as a Social Issue*, has especially motivated me in my work:

In relation to health care or hygiene, one domain of social life in particular—that of education—will have to be most strongly influenced by such a knowledge of the human being. Without a comprehensive knowledge of human beings, we cannot really evaluate the consequences of allowing our children to sit in school with bent backs so that they never breathe properly, or the repercussions of never teaching children to speak the vowel or consonant sounds loudly, clearly, and in a well-articulated way. As a matter of fact, the whole of later life depends on whether the child in school breathes in the right way and whether he or she is taught to speak clearly and with good articulation. I say this merely by way of example, for the same thing applies to other realms. It is an illustration, however, of the specific application of general hygienic principles in the sphere of education. The whole social significance of hygiene is revealed in this example.

It is also apparent that, rather than further specialization, life demands that the specialized branches of knowledge be brought together to form a comprehensive view of life. We need something more than educational norms according to which the teacher is supposed to instruct the child. The teacher must realize what it means for her/him to help the child to speak clearly and articulately. She/he must realize what it will mean if children are allowed to catch their breath after only half a phrase has been spoken and the teacher does not see to it that all the air is used up in the phrase being uttered. There are, of course, many such principles and rules. A

253

proper appreciation and practice of them, however, will live in us only when we are able to measure their full significance for human life and social health; and only then will they give rise to a social impulse.

We need teachers who are able to educate children on the basis of a worldview that understands the true being of man. These were the thoughts underlying the course I gave to the teachers when the Waldorf School in Stuttgart was founded. All the principles of the art of education that were expressed in that course strive in the direction of turning the children who are being educated into human beings. We should make them into human beings in whom lungs, liver, heart, and stomach will be healthy in later life because, as children, they were helped to develop their life functions in the right way; because, in effect, the soul worked on them in the proper way.

This worldview will never give a materialistic interpretation to the ancient saying, "A healthy soul lives in a healthy body" (Mens sana in corpore sano). Interpreted materialistically, this means that if the body is healthy, if it has been made healthy by every possible physical method, then it will, of itself, be the bearer of a healthy soul. This is pure nonsense. The only true meaning is that a healthy body shows me that the force of a healthy soul has built it up, has molded it and made it healthy. A healthy body proves that an autonomous, healthy soul has worked in it. This is the true meaning of this saying, and only in this sense can it be an underlying principle of true hygiene. In other words, it is quite inadequate to have, in addition to teachers who merely work based on an abstract science of education, a school doctor who turns up every fortnight or so and goes through the school with no real idea of how to help. What we need is a living alliance between medical science and the art of education. We need an art of education that teaches the children in a way that is conducive to real health. This is what makes hygiene or health care a social issue, because a social issue is essentially an educational issue, and this, in turn, is essentially a medical issue, but only if medicine and hygiene are both fructified by spiritual science.

◆ ◆ ◆

In the fall of 1994, Wolfgang Kersten, along with Sebastian Junghans, who is the therapeutic eurythmist at the Waldorf School in

Engelberg, circulated a questionnaire regarding the presence of therapeutic support, as well as the availability of remedial help in the German Waldorf schools. Of the 156 questionnaires sent out, 75 were filled out and returned. This process was undertaken in cooperation with the Freie Hochschule für Pädagogik in Stuttgart and the Medical Section at the Goetheanum.

Results of the Questionnaire:

The 75 schools have a combined current enrollment of 34,350 students.

Of these, 5,255 regularly receive therapeutic treatment.

Approximately 400 annually receive short-term therapeutic treatment.

Fifty-two school physicians are engaged at the seventy-five schools.

Twenty-five schools have no school physician.

Of the school physicians, thirteen are employed full-time (18–24 TWH—teachers' weekly hours); two are part-time employment of 14–15 TWH; 3 are employed 9 to 11 TWH, and 34 are only sporadically at the schools (4–5 TWH or less).

The school physicians are paid as follows:
twenty-three on a teacher's salary,
twenty-five on other models: salary, expense account,
four on a volunteer basis.

Instruction in biology is given by three school physicians,
thirty-nine give no instruction at all,
nine give first aid courses.

Therapists and caregivers in the schools are divided into the following groups:

seventy therapeutic eurythmists,

thirty speech formation teachers (only some of whom are speech therapists),

ten art therapists,

six Bothmer gymnasts,

four curative teachers,

two psychologists,

1.5 music therapists,

1.5 masseurs,

1.5 school nurses,

1 chirophonetic therapist.

Ten schools have no therapy.

The remedial work shows the following:

fourteen schools have a full-time remedial teacher,

one school has a three-quarter-time remedial teacher ,

sixteen schools have a half-time remedial teacher,

three schools have remedial track classes,

three schools are exclusively directed toward therapeutic education,

twenty-four schools have no remedial support (neither remedial teacher nor remedial track).

The financing of the therapists is normally in accordance with the salary level of the teacher. Variations:

two schools request contributions for therapy (primarily from parents of children who need it),

ten schools take outside patients, for instance, operating a treatment center,

one school refers all its therapy to local therapists,

one school works with the Department of Juvenile Psychiatry at Herdecke [hospital],

seven schools have instituted a fund for the support of remedial work,

one school works with a local horseback-riding therapist,

one school works with a local chirophonetic practice,

two schools plan to set up a financially independent budget separate from the rest of the school.

Some schools have instituted special features:

additional examination of children in the second grade from preventive viewpoints including a dental checkup,

expanded rhythmic part of the main lesson (morning circle) for therapeutic exercises,

special examination in first grade for early detection of developmental problems of the lower senses [touch, life, movement, balance],

hexameter block in the fifth grade,

remedial work for dyslexia,

five schools (primarily from the new federal states of Germany) request support for building up a therapeutic track,

seven schools are looking for a school physician,

eight schools strongly feel the lack of adequate therapeutic support.

Evaluation:

In order to describe a situation and evaluate its strengths and weaknesses, a conception is needed as to what can be viewed as the ideal. If we look back at the beginnings of the [first] Waldorf school, we sees a school physician among the faculty of teachers, and soon after, the beginnings of therapeutic eurythmy and art therapy. Following Rudolf Steiner's advice, Karl Schubert set up a remedial class, and Rudolf Steiner himself gave diverse lectures about the therapeutic foundation of Waldorf education. He lectured about the proper relationship between waking and sleeping, about proper breathing, and the physiology of the senses. In the first circular letter to physicians [*Deepening the Art of Healing*, First Circular, March 11, 1924], he urgently challenged them to join the teachers in a common educational undertaking.

In regard to the ideas on therapy, the current situation indicates that overall in the Waldorf movement we now find ourselves in a worse position than at the beginning. Figuring the results of the questionnaire at their best, we have 104 school physicians at present among the 150 schools in Germany. This means that 30% of the schools have no school doctor. If we refigure the amount of work that is actually carried out, 150 schools have the equivalent of forty-eight full-time school physicians. This means that 60% of the schools are not provided for. All told, since only six school physicians are actually involved in teaching, the benefits of having doctors teach in the schools should at some time in the future be discussed at a conference. The ratio of forty-eight school physicians to approximately 70,000 students, one doctor to 1,458 students, should certainly be critically evaluated as to efficiency.

The number of children involved in therapy adds up at best to about 10,500. But the results of the questionnaire clearly show that the number of children in need of therapy is significantly higher, and that there is a significant shortage of therapists. The number of therapeutic caregivers should correlate meaningfully with the various therapies. Roughly figured, we see that one therapeutic caregiver has to have a case load of forty-two children. Therapeutic eurythmists have made a strong contribution already during their training, placing special emphasis on therapeutic school-eurythmy.

Twenty schools have no therapeutic caregiver. This is partly because of financial considerations and partly a function of the way the faculty views its responsibilities. The starting point of Waldorf school therapy is preventive; unfortunately, that of health insurance is not. Working with outside health care centers and other local therapists therefore becomes problematic, because treatment can only begin when the child has already fallen ill.

The situation in the remedial sector raises grave concern. Only forty-five full-time remedial teachers are available to the 150 schools. Six of these schools have a remedial track and six are exclusively remedial schools. Approximately forty-eight schools have no remedial program at all. Thus, only forty-five full-time co-workers remain for approximately ninety schools. Thus, aside from the above-mentioned ones, approximately fifty schools are woefully underprovided for in the remedial realm. It is a matter of serious concern if we ask ourselves whether even one remedial teacher is enough for one school. Viewed from this aspect, we have a catastrophic situation!

The task for the immediate future must be:

1. The possibility of a career as a school physician should be publicized more extensively, particularly to medical students. In teacher training colleges, students should be taught about the therapeutic basis of Waldorf education. For example, since 1997 at the Teacher Training in Stuttgart, one week per year is offered on therapy in the Waldorf school. Furthermore, the idea of therapy should be included in conferences for school business managers.

2. Proportional to the needs, full-time positions should be created for therapists at schools.

3. Building up a remedial program is an urgent need of Waldorf schools, particularly in view of the ever-increasing difficulty experienced by class teachers.

The Physician and Therapeutic Education

Hans Müller-Wiedemann

Hans Müller-Wiedemann was the physician at the Special School in Brachenreuth, Überlingen. He passed away in November 1997.

In the day schools oriented toward curative education, as well as in anthroposophical homes and homes for children in need of special care, the doctor's task is to work in the way described by Rudolf Steiner in the curative education course [*Education for Special Needs*]. Based on his or her medical insight, the doctor has to recognize the connection between the soul-spiritual element of a particular child and what is going on in the physical organism. Moreover, in a long-term therapeutic process of constitutional transformation, he or she has to help the children and young people to overcome hindrances and deviations in the way the components of their being relate to one another in the incarnation process. This involves an intense and regular cooperation with the teachers, the teaching group, the caregivers, and parents of the children—joint work that extends over many years. In the center of all this stands the institution of the so-called child study. Here, the physician must acquire specific insights into the ways the child's soul-spiritual forces of individuality interact with the body built up by hereditary forces (Rudolf Steiner called it the "model-body").

Naturally, an additional task of the physician is to treat children of such an institution in cases of acute illness or acute developmental crises, as well as treating those co-workers who wish to consult a doctor. Setting up regular appointments at the school or home has proved beneficial. Another diagnostic and therapeutic domain for the doctor is early outpatient support for disadvantaged children or those threatened by handicaps, wherever this kind of outpatient office can be connected to homes or schools.

The physician participates in the child study, as well as in discussions about the children that occur several times a week. In the latter, the necessary curative pedagogical and medical measures for each child have to be discussed and planned in correspondence with the child's particular developmental condition. In the faculty meeting and possibly also in auditing classroom instruction, the physician has the opportunity to work with the teachers and to respond to their questions. The same likewise applies in different forms to working with caregivers and teaching groups who naturally also participate regularly in the discussions and conferences on children.

The physician has important and extensive responsibilities for conversation, not only in connection with the admission of a child, but as an advisor who accompanies the relationships between child and parents, and renders medical assistance to the parents. Likewise, medical cooperation with the family physicians of children must be cultivated so that the parents can develop confidence in the mutually planned measures that are to benefit their child. The same naturally applies to contacts with other specialists (neurologists, orthopedists, and so on).

Speaking from experience, the different therapies used in curative settings are weighted differently in each patient's case. The exercises that are used in daily life by house parents and teachers in the home communities are of particular significance for anthroposophical curative education. Additional therapies are developed and applied either in single or group therapy. For example, in Brachenreuthe the following are now used: therapeutic eurythmy (speech and tone eurythmy), tone eurythmy group lessons (particularly for autistic children), strong(forte)-tone therapy (for children with weak muscle tone), "listening-space-therapy" (for restless children captivated by visual perceptions). Furthermore, there is group therapy with colored shadows (for children disturbed in various ways in connection with the rhythmic system), and individual therapies such as Bothmer gymnastics, speech exercises, body rubs with oil, rhythmic massage, baths (including temperature-raising baths), and physiotherapy.

Regarding integration of the physician into the life of the school—for example, in a clinical office in a home-school for special children—the physician's tasks include so many social and organizational responsibilities and activities that a full-time position in the institution seems to be necessary. Whether a physician—as has been attempted in some cases—wants to and can manage an outside practice in addition depends on a number of circumstances. This depends primarily on the vocational image that a therapeutically oriented school community develops about its doctor and vice versa. It appears that all possibilities have been tried from complete social integration of the work-activity to a looser, contractual time-limited cooperation of the physician. The so-called child study—in which all the co-workers participate in a spirit of communal striving for knowledge—has furthermore proved to be the socially uniting realm in which the will to heal can arise in each person. This will to heal can then be realized in the various individual fields of activity within an institution.

This social configuration of insights and abilities to which the doctor belongs, is the life force of the curative school physician. In such a relationship, the doctor will receive compensation in the sense of Rudolf Steiner's main social law—not in accordance with his or her performance but by becoming a member of an institution founded on that law. [The social law states: For a group of people who work together, the less the single person claims the fruits of his labor for himself, the more the group will benefit. This means, one gives these fruits to one's co-workers so that one's own needs are not met out of one's own achievements but out of the achievements of the others. From Rudolf Steiner, *Education of the Child.*] Of course, depending on the circumstances, all other forms of a physician's compensation should be available. Each institution has to include its physician in making these decisions. In any case, in Brachenreuthe, the agreements reached with the doctors who work there are in accordance with the main social law.

In conclusion, the physician also has teacher training tasks in a curative education home, as well as doing continuing education for house parents about wraps, baths, diets, and care of the sick.

Important themes for the school physician

The Public Work of a School Physician
Marina Kayser-Springorum
Marina Kayser-Springorum is the school physician at the Waldorf School in Hannover-Bothfeld.

Time and again, in dealing with parents and teachers, a strong need for an understanding of human development, particularly that of the child, becomes evident. Questions are raised concerning *health and illness*: How do I define health? How do I view illness—as a defect in need of repair; as a feeling of discomfort that must be eliminated as quickly as possible; or as a developmental opportunity that challenges an individual to experience it with the greatest possible karmic effect, attended by a physician who follows this process and offers his or her supportive medical and human capacities?

Then there are questions on *nutrition*: What part is played by sugar and animal protein in accelerating child development? What should a diet consist of that is suitable to the child at whatever age level? Questions can be raised concerning the composition of foods as well as their quality, and the point is to include aspects such as the child's temperament, constitution, health instability, or environmental damage.

Another subject is the problem of *left-handedness*. Where does it come from? Why do we encourage a left-handed child in a Waldorf school to learn to use the right hand in all that pertains to the school?

How do we deal with questions of *puberty*? In what way does the Waldorf school curriculum go into this area? What has educational significance in this phase of transition? What happens insofar as physiological development is concerned? What changes in the soul-spiritual domain? How do we deal with discrepancies and one-sidedness? How does the development differ between girls and boys? How do we stand in regard to the question of sex education?

Kindergarten parents and participants in a Waldorf teacher training are interested in questions of a child's *readiness for entering school*. How can I measure that? What developmental steps regarding the body—but likewise the etheric and soul elements—must have been completed so that a child is ready for school? Has he gathered enough experiences, has he sharpened his senses through many exercises, has he practiced social behavior in a group? Is he able to separate from his parents? Does he have the necessary faculty of concentration and faculty to learn, as well as perseverance to endure school in a healthy way without overtaxing himself? Has a part of the forces that worked formatively on the body been freed for learning? Has the child finished with the growth process necessary to attend school? Has the change of teeth begun? Have his bodily forces truly reached the periphery, all the way to the tips of fingers and toes? Has he been able to develop skill in gross as well as fine motor functions?

During kindergarten, it is important to answer questions regarding nonverbal education, imitation, and self-education of the adult?. But questions also come up in kindergarten concerning disturbances and delays in development, questions about the origin of delays and a timely diagnosis as well as proper measures for dealing with this. When is learning in a small group preferable to learning in a large class and why? How do we deal with so-called sexuality in the kindergarten—with something that by definition cannot exist as yet, but is called that again and again, and results in different styles of education?

How do we deal with *the media* for the kindergarten age, and also in the school years? What do the media produce and how can parents and teachers agree on a common way to proceed for the benefit of the children?

What significance do *childhood diseases* have for children's development? How should the risks be evaluated? In which domain of human nature does which childhood disease have its place, particularly in the sense of harmonization and further development? What does the threefoldness of the human organism signify? What is the significance of illness in regard to a human being's destiny?

These questions and many more are addressed to the school physician. They come from parents, the general public, the faculty, teacher training programs and continuing education courses, from the subjects offered in adult education and information from the professional medical organizations, from organizers who promote environmentally friendly and healthy life styles, and from the Waldorf kindergartens. These questions appeal to the physician to educate the general public, a task which he or she has in addition to all the others described in this book. This task should be recognized insofar as possible, because the school physician can function as the link between school and the public. Experiences from the most diverse segments of life could fructify each other, and ought to be made available if there is a need.

Uncertainty in the sphere of education is great, but also in the medical field. Nothing can be based any longer on tradition. There is no more instinctive knowledge about what is right and what is wrong. Everything must be thought out anew and reached through hard work done out of consciousness united with feeling so that actions can be taken out of conviction. If asked to do so, the school physician has to make his or her contribution to this process in one-on-one conversations, in the faculty meetings, and during parent evenings, so that we give the best possible service to the child.

The combination of educating and healing becomes clear at this point too. Self-discipline on the part of the adult can have a healing effect in two ways. If a mother controls her outbursts of rage, for instance, and learns to get a grip on her emotions through continuous work on herself and, along with that, her involuntary actions, her heart and circulatory system will find a certain balance, her breathing becomes more relaxed, the tendency toward asthma and heart-rhythm irregularities diminishes. This means that the balance tips more in the direction of health, equilibrium, or can even alternate between exertion and relaxation. In addition, the child can avoid shocks or fear of them, and fear-related inner reverberation will abate. This way the child is more settled inwardly, does not constantly have to react, and can turn to other matters in a calm, centered manner.

Healing is likewise achieved through an education that supports the child's age-specific developmental steps. This is accomplished partly through quite concrete methodological measures, for example, through the rhythm of block instruction, the threefold structure of the main lesson, through the rhythmic part of the main lesson, and so on. Many other examples could be cited about the extent to which Waldorf education is corrective education. Conversely, processes of illness and healing are genuine processes of education in the sense of soul-spiritual progress and the overcoming of weaknesses. The latter even implement processes of self-knowledge that would not have been possible without illness or would have taken much more time.

In the activity of the school physician, we thus observe a great many ways of penetrating educational and healing processes. This vocational activity can develop specifically through the mutual fructification of medical practice and school-related medicine, through being integrated in a faculty of teachers, through association with male and female students, through work with the general public, and purely on the basis of love of the child—of the human being as such.

Medical Examination for Entry Into a Waldorf School

Karl-Reinhard Kummer

Karl-Reinhard Kummer was the school physician at the Waldorf School in Karlsruhe from 1982–1996. This article was first published in *Der Merkurstab* [Staff of Mercury], June 1991.

One of the most important duties of a school physician is examining children who are about to enter school. This is handled differently from school to school, and the physician and teachers have somewhat different responsibilities. Examination of physical and mental fitness for school is essential, as is recognition of physical defects. Readiness for school is the main focus. Finding the correct time for entry into school determines a child's entire school experience and affects his or her whole development in the second and third seven-year periods. Excessive pressure threatens a child that enters school too early; lack of challenge and boredom result if a child is too old for a grade.

Some refer in jest to the maturation exam for kindergarten. What is correct is that certain capacities have to be present if a child is to enter school, but test-items are not essential for evaluating this readinessl. The validity of school entrance examinations is comprehensively described by Nickel.[38] The overall impression of a child's etheric development and condition is decisive for the Waldorf school physician. Particular examination parameters only lead to an overall assessment of the etheric aspects. One could therefore proceed quite differently from the sample examination described here.

Possible Procedure for a School Entry Medical Examination

The first moments of meeting the child are of special importance. In a school physicians' conference in 1980, Johannes Bockemühl formulated two questions concerning this: Where do you come from? Where are you going? Other questions are: How does the child face an unusual situation? How independent has he become? By means of a visual diagnosis, the physician sometimes has an immediate impression of the child's constitution type. Frequently, the transformation of his infant body is evident from the first moment. The significance of this first moment in such a threshold-to-school-age situation cannot be valued highly enough.

While the physician is noting down the medical history, the child can undress for the examination. While thus engaged, the physician can inconspicuously watch the dexterity of the fingers engaged in opening buttons, the child's equilibrium, or his perseverance.

A basic physical examination follows, along with weighing and measuring. The condition of the teeth, the changes of form [from the infant body], and physical development processes of the first seven-year period that have not yet happened (such as undescended testicles) are important. Of particular significance are the dominance, the right- or left-sidedness of eye and ear, hand and foot, as well as the functions of seeing and hearing. To determine the state of the child's eyes, have him look through a kaleidoscope. Ear dominance is apparent if the child holds a ticking watch up to the favored ear to hear the ticking. The red and green color-chart test and the stereo-test for hearing give indications concerning perceptions of more complex forms.

The motor function test includes hopping, balancing, and jumping-jack motions, as well as jumping rope. This is followed by throwing a ball a few times. Here, one should observe most of all how the child gets ready to catch and throw. From the preparatory facial expressions and other movements, one can see how far the child has come in mastering the process inwardly. In the case of children who are over six years old, one can try to test how they bounce the ball against the ground. Testing the motor functions does not take long with children who are coordinated, and this supplies essential information about school maturity. Simultaneously, the dominance of hands and feet becomes clear. Then the child gets dressed. The physician writes down his/her findings and once more makes observations on the behavior of the child as he dresses.

At this point then, the abilities in painting and other finger skills can be investigated more thoroughly. At the Waldorf School in Karlsruhe, this is the domain of the teachers. But it is important for a school physician to observe children as they paint zigzag lines, wavy lines or meandering lines. Possible future perceptive disorders become apparent here. It would naturally be better to allow children to paint an entire picture during the examination, but unfortunately there is usually not enough time for this.

Transformation of the Etheric Formative Forces

The doctor checks whether the inherited body of the first seven-year period is in the process of being transformed and whether, due to such a transformation, the preconditions for the awakening of thought- and memory-forces are present. Rudolf Steiner speaks repeatedly about the transformation of the growth forces: "It is of the greatest significance to know that the ordinary thought forces of human beings are the refined forces of growth and form." [Rudolf Steiner and Ita Wegman, *Fundamentals of Therapy*. See also Rudolf Steiner, *Introducing Anthroposophical Medicine*, lecture of April 7, 1920.]

Regarding the formative forces, Ernst Marti [*Das Ätherische* (The Etheric Elements), p. 108ff.] distinguishes between gestalt- or form-building forces, life-building forces, and substance-building forces. Here, the attempt is made to assign the phenomena present at the beginning of school to the child's thinking, feeling, and willing. The change in the physical form can most likely be assigned to the figure- and form-building forces. The awakening feeling for time and space, for rhythm and measure, as well as the forces of thinking can be attributed to the life-building forces. The substance-building forces no longer appear to participate significantly in the change of teeth.

I. Change of Teeth and Transformation of Body Form

These phenomena are generally summed up under the catch words *change of teeth* and *change of form*.[39] In deciding whether a child is ready to enter school, it is important to determine whether these changes have begun.

1. The change of teeth is readily perceivable. In some children, the milk-teeth in front have been shed as early as around age five. This may be viewed as an expression of these children's connection to their senses. The appearance of the molars, characteristically called the six-year molars, is more important. The descending of these teeth changes the shape of the jaw. Children in whom the teeth descend somewhat late often experience a late awakening of their conceptual and thought life.

2. The development of the chest region begins. That is to say, the middle parts begin to show special signs of growth: In the head, nose and sinuses enlarge. They move between the cerebral cranium and the jaw bones. In the trunk, the rib cage expands, and, around age nine, arches out more. In the arms and legs, the shafts of the bones grow, lengthening the limbs. (Growth occurs at the point where the head of the bone meets the shaft.)

3. A more pronounced configuration of the body begins to take place: Head, trunk, and limbs become more clearly differentiated from each other, whereas earlier the body appeared generally round.

4. In regard to movement, the last vestiges of the reflex-organization ought to have ceased, for instance, the reflex of spreading out the fingers while walking on tiptoe. The head attains its position of rest. The limbs become mobile in regard to each other and to the trunk. Several movements become possible simultaneously, for instance, in throwing a ball at a target. The movement of the trunk begins to assume a median position between the head's

resting position and the movements of the limbs. Several of these observations can be made the moment one first greets the child.

5. Listening to the change in heart sounds can be a means to judge the body's readiness for school according to Appenzeller's heart observations.[40]

II. Will Forces

A sign of readiness for school is the change that occurs in the will forces. The morning verse of the first four grades includes the words: "for learning and for work." [The literal translation of the German words would be: that I be hard-working and eager to learn. —trans.] One sign of readiness for school therefore is joy in learning and joy in something new. Even during the child's school-readiness examination, one can approach the child with new material. For example, many children learn how to jump rope during the examination, and proudly go home with a new skill. But if it is apparent that a child is not yet ready to begin school, one should be cautious.

Along with being mature enough to enter school, fewer of the child's will forces are directed toward building up the body. No longer do they merely have the goal of working on the body but also aim at working on the world. Nevertheless, until the age of puberty, these will forces are mainly in a receptive, soulfully harmonizing mode. It is important that mental imaging activity increasingly enters the sphere of the will. [See Rudolf Steiner,*Foundations of Human Experience*, lecture of August 26, 1919.] At the same time, will forces increasingly enter conception and thinking. This becomes evident in the child's persistence. Even when he is undressing prior to the medical examination, one can see whether a child is persistent or whether he has to be told repeatedly to continue. Many children lack persistence at the time of entering school despite possessing intelligence.

III. Forces of Feeling

1. Space Awareness

When ready for school, the child uses the lower senses [senses of life, touch, movement, and balance] in a more differentiated way. This is demonstrated by the child's behavior in space when you greet him. A child who enters the physician's room with a straight, upright posture is most likely mature enough for school. The child seems to permeate the space he has entered with consciousness. In his mind, he then feels at home within that space. However, since shy children often require more time to become accustomed to new surroundings, the physician should be rather cautious about arriving at an initial conclusion.

Consciousness in regard to space is demonstrated by the child's movements: He can only do jumping-jacks if he has a feeling for the space behind him. As a rule, children who are not yet mature enough for school do jumping-jacks somewhat in a squatting position, moving their arms and legs in front of their body. In this way, their limb movement remains within their field of vision. Along with his readiness for school, a child begins to develop an awareness of the space in back of him. Then he can do jumping-jacks in an upright position with arms and legs moving outward to the side, outside his field of vision. Similar things can be observed in jumping rope: An immature child often maintains a somewhat crouched, cramped, and forward bent posture. He is not yet able to guide the rope properly. Only when he is ready for school does the child have a perception of how the rope swings behind his body. Then you see how the child guides the rope while it is behind the body. Hopping likewise demonstrates mastery over the space in back. A child who is ready for school can even hop backwards while looking forward.

274

2. Sense of Rhythm and Beat

Along with the change of teeth, the relationship to rhythm and beat changes. There is a difference between the way the child behaves in regard to rhythm and beat before and after the change of teeth. Before, rhythm and beat was something that the child imitated, but it was transposed into a sculptural element. Afterward, it is transposed into an inner musical element. [Rudolf Steiner, *Soul Economy and Waldorf Education*, lecture of December 31, 1921.]

Rhythmic capabilities are used at every repetition. A child who is ready for school gladly and voluntarily carries out repetitions, for example the jumping-jack mentioned above. Sturdy children who are about seven years old often do the jumping-jack exercise not just once when asked, but five or six times in a row. This could be thought of as a little melody. For the observer it is possible to see how the musical forces have now become free and are expressed in the child's movement.

Rhythmic capabilities are preconditions for jumping rope, hopping, and throwing balls. The school physician has to check whether motor weaknesses are due to a lack of maturity or a disturbance in coordination.

Rhythmic and musical faculties are moreover put to use in certain drawing exercises such as the lines of roofs, a simple wavy line, the meandering wave line, or the zigzag meander pattern. When these patterns are merely copied line by line, the child loses the overview. Then he either cannot go on or draws some sort of pattern of his own.

One can attempt to associate patterns frequently used at the Waldorf school in Karlsruhe with certain forms of beats. A simple zigzag line can be associated with the two-beat rhythm, simple and reversed wave lines to the three-beat rhythm, and the angular meander-form to the four-beat rhythm.

Even in a child's speech, certain rhythmic capabilities can be observed. A child who is ready for school shows rhythmic capabilities by accenting words properly. These are comparable, for example, to what might be called the short in-between step in skipping. Every emphasis, or the beginning of it, should be understood as a rhythmic expression.

IV. Forces of Imagination and Forces of Thinking

1. Memory and pictorial thought

The precondition for thinking is the faculty of memory. Whereas the preschool child has associative memory, the child that is ready for school begins to have a concept for time and sequence. In the first seven-year period, mostly as a matter of habit, a child remembers and immediately forgets. A preschool child is asked: "Where were you yesterday?" Answer: "On vacation." Actually the vacation was three months ago, yesterday the child happened to be at the zoo. The remark, "But we were at the Zoo!" leads to recollection in the preschool child. One association follows another. School children have a memory in pictures. They would recall a walk in the pictorial sequence of events. Of course, it is likewise true that forces of memory are developed even by many preschool children. The capability of memory can therefore not always offer proof as to whether a child is mature enough for school.

Now thinking becomes pictorial. A school child has a picture of how something is or should be in order to be correct. This can be observed even by means of a simple visual test table. A stereo test or a color chart test can show it as well. A child will not just recognize something; he makes an effort to recognize the right thing that really corresponds to the figures pictured on the chart. A child who is ready for school is more likely to hesitate with an answer in certain circumstances rather than give a false reply.

2. *The question of style, the "how"*

The child who is ready for school asks *how* to do something, for instance, in hopping. He asks whether he should hop on one leg or two. You can moreover observe how a child follows processes. You see that when throwing a ball at him. The child attempts to throw the ball the same way the grownup did. In his thinking he is then no longer caught up in himself, but directed to the observed action or person.

The simple throwing of a ball makes it evident whether the child throws the ball randomly away from himself or whether he throws it toward a goal. Random throwing could be viewed as "throwing as such." In aimed throwing, the child is at the goal in his thoughts and no longer caught up in himself.

The same can be observed in catching the ball. When playing ball, the child who is ready for school mentally goes along with the one who throws the ball. At the moment of having the ball thrown at him, the child has inwardly caught the ball already (anticipation) in a manner of speaking.

The use of tools likewise demonstrates whether thought forces are already free, and able to participate in the child's surroundings. A child who shortens the jump rope to the proper length shows thought forces. Properly oriented behavior can likewise be observed when, in painting, the child divides up the various sections of drawing paper. The essential thing is that the child has an idea of how to proceed when he does something.

3. Correction of errors, "the right thing"

When the child has an idea of how to do something, he arrives at the point where he corrects his own mistakes. The child who is ready for school tries to carry out something in the right way according to what the action requires. In so doing, he begins to notice and to correct mistakes. When throwing a ball, the child attempts to throw more accurately and better each time. When copying form drawings, the child will improve and paint over a line that was drawn.

The child now has an inner perception of the previous throw or the original drawing, and he has an idea of how it should be. A child who corrects himself has an inner image of the procedure. He reaches the *essence* of a thing. One can likewise observe this when a child tries to follow a clapping rhythm, or a sung melody. Mentally, he begins to sense the form of something.

4. The encounter with something new

Unaccustomed activities are also instructive. If a ball is thrown down to the ground, a child who is not ready for school is surprised by this. He does not expect the ball to bounce back up from the ground. This is even the case when one has announced one's intention. After a child is ready for school, he has an inner picture of the course the ball is about to take. It is not until after the change of teeth that the child begins to grasp reality through percept and concept. [Rudolf Steiner, *The Philosophy of Freedom*.]

Conversely, prior to the change of teeth, a child illustrates the condition of perception without thinking. He observes the ball's course without being able to anticipate it, and reaches for the ball, not for the point where one can expect to catch it. If such a child catches the ball correctly, then this is based on habit or training, not on an inner participating experience.

5. *Synchronizing several activities*

Now a child begins to carry out several activities simultaneously. When he jumps rope, he can actually jump and swing the rope in a rhythmical fashion. This likewise includes activities involving a change of direction. Walking an 8, for example, is the combination of two circles with a crossover to the opposite direction of rotation. Simple crosses can be drawn even by a five-year-old preschool child. But to draw a proper 8 demands a much higher level of skill. One can tell children to walk an 8 on the floor; this shows whether an inner perception of the form is present. But this is too much for many children. Movements that cross over and reverse the direction of rotation can also appear in form drawing in the many continuous patterns.

6. *Motifs in children's pictures*

Some characteristic motifs turn up almost regularly in children's drawings: a doorknob, curtains on the windows, a flowerpot on the windowsill, or—for a boy— the steering wheel in a car. A child represents the world in the way it would be if complete.

7. Speech

We can only deal in a very summary form with the process of speech becoming free when a child reaches school age. [Rudolf Steiner, *Human Values in Education*, lecture of July 19, 1924.] At this point, children become reachable through speech. They can now follow directions given merely in words that are not accompanied by gestures, for example, placing the feet next to each other. Earlier, one has to make directing gestures or hand movements.

Overview

During the school entrance examination, the physician checks whether the etheric forces, which earlier had been active in building up the body, have become free. There is a change in thinking, feeling, and willing. The physician can observe this by means of specific phenomena that are obvious even from a regular medical examination. It is not a matter of going through a list of questions that are asked in a test. It has to do with the overall impression of the child's etheric condition of development.

Effects of Soccer on the Developing Human Being

Karl-Reinhard Kummer

Extract of an article published in *Erziehungskunst* [Art of Education], March 1997.

This article tries to answer the following questions: What are the educational aspects of soccer? Should playing soccer be prohibited during recess on a Waldorf school playground or not? What advice can be given to parents in regard to a soccer league?

Soccer has evidently been played for centuries, among the Assyrians, the Egyptians, in classical Greece and Rome. In the eleventh century in England, soccer was so popular that Henry II forbade it, for instead of practicing the martial disciplines of archery, people wasted time playing ball. This prohibition lasted for over 400 years in England. In Florence, the game of soccer reappeared at the beginning of the modern age. In 1831, it was again brought to life in the large English private schools of Eton, Westminster, Charterhouse, and Harrow and provided with a set of rules. In Germany, the first soccer league was founded in Hanover in 1878.

The interest in soccer has continued on into the present unabated, particularly in comparison with basketball, volleyball, or swimming. It has particular fascination for young males. Compared to other kinds of sports like skiing, snowboarding, tennis, rowing, and sailing, the necessary equipment is relatively inexpensive. Playing soccer is possible almost anywhere. For educational reasons soccer is not cultivated at Waldorf schools, but the discussion of pros and cons often seems to be led more by emotion than objectivity.

Educational aspects of game rules

Soccer has a firm set of rules. A few basic comments about games with rules and their educational significance are therefore necessary. The rules for team sports are frequently not educationally founded but stem merely from conventions that have evolved throughout history.

In their rigidity they actually correspond to the adult soul constitution. The external aspects of the rules can be seen, for example, in the present discussion about regulations for soccer during free time.

For children, on the other hand, rules are only educationally meaningful if they can inwardly agree to and experience them. In first through third grades, game rules result from a story the teacher tells, whereas, in fourth through sixth grades, rules are set by the teacher and are gradually refined. The origin of the rules is therefore experienced by the students themselves. In this way, up until about the seventh grade, children themselves gain their own treasure of experience of how rules come about and how one has to live with them. At this point the teacher can introduce even more complicated rules. It is educationally meaningful if one begins first with the basics and then works to refine them, according to the level of understanding of the classs. Along with this, one addresses causal thinking that begins at this stage.

Educational goals of team games

Kischnick[41] distinguishes three groups in ball games. Soccer, hockey, and rugby belong to the first group. In the second group—tennis and volleyball, the ball is exchanged between individual players and the team. A mediating element comes about. Softball and baseball belong in the third group in which one plays in teams, where the individual player has to pursue a certain line that can be compared to a test or trial.

With the objective of shooting the ball into the opponent's goal or, in basketball, into the basket, the game acquires a definite soul coloring of which one is frequently not aware. Soccer would be senseless without the opponent and without the intent of making goals and wanting to win. It is important to keep the ball under control and among one's own teammates. The opponent can thus be purposely misled, tricked, and overcome. The player works within a regulated hostile relationship to the opposing team. He aims at passing the ball past a defender into the opponent's space and into a position to shoot it through the goal. This requires an ability to react and to hold the overview, and an enthusiasm for competition. At the same time this paves the way for a group egoism which only after puberty can develop without damaging social consequences.

These egoistic and aggressive tendencies are ideally still alien to childhood, even though many children today show aggression in their behavior. This is due, on the one hand, to their souls' lacking a protective sheath, which causes them to be thin-skinned and highly sensitive. On the other hand, it is caused by the example of violent young people and television programs.

In her short version of the curriculum, Caroline von Heydebrand[42] refers to the unselfish soul attitude of children. In the years prior to puberty, children should therefore play games where they play with one another, not against an opponent. To be sure, children in the lower grades always measure their skillfulness, strength, and their resourcefulness against fellow students. In a friendly way, one checks whether the partner measures up to required tasks. Educationally, it has a different effect when children do this on their own, or whether this measuring of each other is raised to a principle by the rules of the game. Such principles are often allowed to become an attitude in life if they are introduced prior to the appropriate age. By playing soccer prior to puberty, children acquire a false set of values that drive them selfishly to achieve their own goals.

Comments on games played with the feet

It is a basic rule in soccer that a field player is not allowed to use his hands and arms. What is otherwise necessary and customary for work or play, namely the use of both hands, is strictly punishable in soccer.

Educationally speaking, this is questionable. The only player who can move like a human being and use his hands is the goal keeper.

From the educational perspective, the exclusion of the hands signifies a one-sidedness and lack of challenge. Playing ball with the hands, on the other hand, promotes the skill of the hand with its specifically human capacities. One plays more vigorously in space with the hands, for instance in handball or volleyball, whereas soccer is bound to a more horizontal level. In volleyball, the ball is thrown up into the air and is then caught in the air. The uplifted leg in soccer is against the rule. In most cases, the player first has to stop the ball on the ground with the foot if he wants to play further with a kick or a pass. Only advanced players can continue directly out of the air.

Because it is played almost exclusively with feet and legs, soccer tends toward offensive and aggressive movement—toward a brutalizing of movement. The player kicks more roughly with the foot than would be possible with the hand. The emphasis on the feet can have a detrimental effect on children who have difficulties in directing their movement. Playing soccer can increase the tendency in these children to dominate more highly skilled, technically advanced children by brute strength and intimidation, something that can easily place them in a socially problematic light. Children who are naturally gifted with a tendency toward harmonious movements are less exposed to this danger. On the other hand, it may be beneficial for children who are too head-oriented to learn to direct the energy of their movement into their feet.

The tremendous effect of one's own action can be fascinating. It is easy to kick a soccer ball fifty or sixty yards. It requires much greater effort to attain such distances with the hand. By excluding the natural impulse to play ball with the hands, soccer proves to be a sport that belongs to the age of youth. In the period between the ages of fourteen and twenty-one, it is necessary to accommodate oneself to the normal given facts of the surroundings in an individual way. In order to do this, one submits voluntarily to particular limitations such as the rule, for example, not to touch the ball with your hands.

Because use of the hands is prohibited, one has to put all the more effort into the skills of movement. The difficulty of this can be observed in people who were handicapped by dysmelia (thalidomide embryopathy). In soccer, it is not the harmonious movement per se that is required, but specialized, goal-oriented movement. Yet there have been certain soccer players who have played with a beautiful aesthetic touch—Franz Beckenbauer or Pelé, Uwe Seeler or Thomas Häßler—but they are definitely exceptions.

Because of this one-sidedness, children should only begin to play soccer when they can master harmonious forms of movement. This occurs usually around age twelve, when a certain level of maturity in breathing and circulation has been achieved. As we know, the harmony of movements begins to disappear at the time of puberty. The movements become more slack and undirected and more strongly determined by the mechanics of the skeleton. Only then is it sensible to train the muscles. [See Rudolf Steiner, *Soul Economy and Waldorf Education*, lecture of January 2, 1922.]

At what age is a league appropriate?

From the previous considerations it becomes clear that one should advise parents not to allow children of the lower grades to join a soccer league. In place of a league, parents are asked to participate in quite different activities such as afternoons of play, long hikes, or excursions. In this regard, Waldorf schools are quite dependent on the strong cooperation of the parent in order to address all the children if possible. It would be educationally senseless and wrong to prohibit a child from entering a sports league if one has nothing better to offer.

Teenagers, high school students, are concerned with experiencing the other human being, especially "on the edge." This can happen in league sports. In the middle grades, more general human experiences are predominant—for instance, love of animals.

In sports leagues, two specific problems frequently occur. Life in a league is often determined by the recreational behavior of the adults (league gatherings with smoking, alcohol, etc.). The other problem concerns children gifted for sports, who easily fall into the hands of ambitious trainers. The possibility to shape the child's body is greatest if one begins with intensive training long before puberty. Then it is possible to make use of the natural grace of movement of that age. Thus, many leading female sports figures, for example in gymnastics or swimming, are children insofar as their body is concerned, children who are prevented from entering normal puberty in order to keep them in top form.[43]

If parents seek out a sports club for their child, they should pay particular attention to whether the sports club intends to carry out a broad range of body work, rather than competing for honors in sports. Children who are gifted in this way should join a sports club only after age fourteen or fifteen. From the outset, there is less danger for children who are not gifted.

It is well known medically that even later on one has to set healthy limits for training. Sports are concerned merely with the physical aspect.[44] If pursued too one-sidedly, they destroy the physical. Beyond a certain healthy degree, any training leads to processes of degeneration. One finds bone fractures in long distance runners, degeneration of knees and hips, or absence of menstruation in outstanding sports women. From the fate of child athletes in totalitarian countries, we have learned that these degenerative processes occur most intensely and early when excessive training is imposed prior to puberty. Knowledge of these processes of maturation is extraordinarily limited.[45]

Comments on sports instruction

Rudolf Steiner compares eurythmy and gymnastics in numerous passages of his lectures on education. Eurythmy, as a soul-spiritual form of gymnastics, enlivens the whole human being, whereas gymnastics allows one to experience one's own physicality and the relationship to the external world. [*Practical Advice to Teachers*, lecture of August 25, 1919.] It was therefore natural for *Steiner* that both be taught in school. We can experience in the schools that, on the one hand, children need eurythmy more than ever. The number of clumsy children is increasing significantly, yet teaching eurythmy is becoming more and more difficult.

On the other hand, children are enthusiastic about sports, even though they have more difficulties because of their lack of motor skills. This confrontation with the physical and with physical movement in sports is part of the teenage years. It is therefore all the more important to offer children in the lower grades such good instruction in gymnastic games that the soul images coming from the teacher can guide them into skillful movement. Even relatively young children want to experience something here, as do the students in the upper grades. Ultimately, teenagers should be helped to advance so far physically that they reach the limits of their own abilities. Then they feel they are really being taken seriously. Waldorf schools should therefore make the effort to offer the best sports instruction possible. In the upper grades, for instance, the greatest emphasis should be placed on teaching the students good technique. Perhaps we should consider whether the term *gymnastics* is still appropriate today.

Erhard Fucke[46] writes that Steiner included stenography for a specific reason in the curriculum of the first Waldorf school. [*Grundlinien einer Pädagogik des Jugendalters* (Basic principles for pedagogy of teenagers), Stuttgart 1991.] He said it belonged to that time. Similarly, the question can be asked whether sports and soccer are not likewise part of the contemporary age. In any case, certain students can best be approached through gymnastics. Another question might be whether eurythmy could profit from particularly good instruction in gymnastics.

Soccer at the Waldorf school?

What is to be done in a practical sense with soccer? At a certain age, children begin to play soccer on their own. They are mostly sixth graders who kick the ball around after school. In the years before, this need is not so great, nor is it later on. This so-called problem therefore resolves itself in most cases.

It is important that teachers react in an educationally appropriate manner when children kick the ball on the school playground. Here, they cannot afford to be dogmatic. On the other hand, students have to experience that soccer is not desirable in a Waldorf school. All the teachers at school must support this attitude consistently and press it home, but also with humor. In so doing, kicking a tennis ball around may certainly be overlooked. Still, the students should be aware that the teacher has an eye on them and would stop a real soccer game right away. A teacher can moreover point to the danger of injury by kicking a few hard balls.

But what about the students in the high school? The specific prohibition of soccer at a Waldorf school is viewed by many high school students with incomprehension, for they want to be treated as different from the younger children. If they are prohibited from playing soccer, they become alienated from the school and its actual aim that students acquire the capability of free, independent decision-making. One should therefore consider whether it might not be possible to create free time for soccer at the upper level of the Waldorf school. After all, one can have confidence that, compared to other students, Waldorf school students are least of all endangered by soccer.

Further sources of information concerning the training of movement:

Rudolf Kischnick: *Was die Kinder spielen* [Games children play], Stuttgart 1982.

Karl König: *Sinnesentwicklung und Leibeserfahrung* [Sense development and body experience], Stuttgart 1978 (particularly the chapters by G. von Arnim: *Körperschema und Leibessinne* [The structure and senses of the body]).

Jochem Nietzold: *Geistige Strukturen sinnvollen Turnens* [Spiritual structures of meaningful gymnastics], Stuttgart 1978 (includes a large number of statements by Rudolf Steiner concerning gymnastics and sports).

Jochem Nietzold: *Freudiges Bewegen. Bewegungs- und Turnspiele für jung und alt* [Fun-filled movement: Movement and gymnastic games for young and old], Stuttgart 1988.

Simeon Pressel. *Bewegung ist Heilung*, [Movement is healing], Stuttgart 1984.

Peter Prömm: Bewegungsbild und menschliche Gestalt [The image of movement and the human form], Stuttgart 1978.

I am grateful to Johannes Hörner, Hanover, for sending some of the above references.

Dyslexia in the Waldorf School
A case report
Armin Husemann/Daniela Greif/Ernst Bücher
First published in *Erziehungskunst* [Art of education], 11th edition, 1994.

Manfred (not his real name) is in the third grade—an alert, gifted boy, age 8—who can work assiduously. He sings with a clear, beautiful voice; he can repeat stories in a lively way, but his style of painting is a bit hasty. His teacher is basically pleased with him. If one looks at his notebook, one notices tolerably formed script; nothing else conspicuous stands out. From the beginning, Manfred had difficulty with reading. Ever since dictation had begun in the lessons, he was completely helpless. It turned out that *he could not read anything at all of what he copied from the blackboard.* He corrected mistakes purely visually, imitating the forms of the letters. This discovery surprised both teacher and parents. His father took him to the special department for developmental problems in a pediatric clinic. Following a description of the diagnostic results, the report concluded as follows:

> In Raven's CPM test, a visual testing method (not using speech) that tests recognition of conformities with natural laws and the faculty of logical thought, Manfred attained an IQ of 102. It became obvious in the test that Manfred frequently could not properly recognize spatial relationships or a location in space. . . . Other than this, I could not find any indications for Manfred's difficulties. His EEG, which I took at the end to round out the diagnostic test, was completely normal. One must therefore conclude that Manfred has a constitutionally based predisposition for dyslexia. As a Waldorf student, Manfred can live with this partial weakness for the moment, but even in the Waldorf school (at the latest by next year) he will face great difficulties. I therefore recommend that you take him for treatment to the institute for dyslexics.

At this point the child was presented to me, the school physician. After I too had found that vision (optical test: E-hook test; color vision: Ishihara test; spatial vision: TNO test) as well as hearing (audiometry) was normal, I tested Manfred's relationship to speech and writing as follows:

Task	*Result*
—Separating syllables in speaking (for example: dishwasher dish-wash-er)	unable to do it
—Sound analysis in speaking -(For example: hand H–A–N–D)	unable to do it, except M, first sound of his name
—Sounding out letters chosen by him, then writing them down	about four-fifths were wrong
—Copying letters (small and capital letters, even from cursive writing)	perfect
—Saying words of his own choice, then writing them	unable to do it
—Copying of words (sentences)	perfect
—Sound dictation (phonetic, corresponding to the sound)	unable to do it
—Dictation of words, sentences	unable to do it
—Dictation of letters (by name of letter)	unable to do it
—Reading (letters, words, sentences)	unable to do it

The essential result was that, in the case of words that Manfred himself pronounced and whose content was completely familiar to him—such as ball, door, suitcase, blackboard, bike tire—he could neither *separate the syllables* nor indicate *the structure out of the single sounds* (the exception was the first sound of his own name, M). With an intact sense of hearing, seeing, and conception, Manfred did not yet have the *sense of sound* at his disposal.

Rudolf Steiner described this sense for the first time in 1910 [*Anthroposophy. A Fragment,* See also *Conferences with Teachers,* vol. 2]. Nowadays, the concept of phonemic awareness has been introduced into linguistics and recognized as a partial ability clearly separable from sense comprehension.[47] Here, as was word-blindness according to earlier authors,[48] it is understood as an accomplishment of integrative assimilation of other sense impressions like seeing, hearing, and the sense of motion, not, as does Rudolf Steiner, as an original *sense* activity.

Due to this weakness in his sense of sound, Manfred had great difficulty with the fact that while consonants have a sound-form of their own (phoneme), as letters they bear names that are not identical with the sound of speech. In the case of just a few letters whose names he impressed on his mind, he placed the names of the letters in place of the sounds during attempts at reading. (In the case of the word *ball,* he made an attempt, like BEE-A-EL-EL, and then was perplexed because there is no such word.)

According to Zimmermann, who examined 1422 Waldorf school students, the sound-sense disorder is one of the most important causes and types of dyslexia.[49]

In Manfred's case, we were faced with three questions:

1. How does the sense of sound develop?

2. How can we understand Manfred's undeveloped sound sense in terms of an anthroposophical understanding of the human being?

3. What therapy can promote the development of the sense of sound?

1. Thoughts on the development of the sense of sound

The acquisition of speech is preceded by learning to walk and to stand. Not until the breathing musculature of the shoulder girdle and, above all, of the larynx are freed from working on locomotion, does sound forming become possible. Even simple self- observation shows that the closure of the glottis in the larynx is the precondition for exertion of strength in the trunk and in the region of the shoulder girdle. If you cause someone who is carrying a heavy weight to burst out laughing, you force him or her to put down the load. Why? As soon as the rib muscles, the muscles of the abdominal wall and the solar plexus, are set in motion by laughter, the muscles attached to the trunk in the back, the abdomen, and the arms lose their firm grip; you can have *either* the moving of a weight (in the case of the small child's standing upright, the weight of its own body), *or* the motion of speech. And because, in the second year, the arms are freed for gestures and the larynx musculature for development of sounds, the child initially learns the sound forming movements through *imitation*. Along with this, the faculty of perception for sound formulation is developed. For someone who hears a language silently *imitates* the sound motions that are heard, not only with the organs of speech but also with the most delicate forms of motions in the entire body, motions that were first discovered through analysis of high speed film images. These micro-motions of the musculature of the whole head, trunk, and limbs are precisely allocated to the single forms of sound: "As early as the first day of life, the newborn human being moves in precise and sustained segments of movement that are synchronous with the articulated structure of adult speech."[50]

It is clear that a metamorphosed, inwardly deepened activity of movement is the basis of the sense of sound. The fact that these movements elude ordinary physical perception and only by sophisticated technical means are made physically perceptible signifies that we are dealing with movements that are essentially part of the *inner impulse of movement,* that they are movements which outwardly and physically are not manifested at all, or merely in a germinal way. Expressed in anthroposophical terminology, these movements that serve the perception of sound occur mainly in the etheric body. They are in the independent life-organization that integrates the physical substances into the laws that sustain life and endows the physical body with the movement of growth as well as muscular movement.

The inner, silent, imitating movements of the *speech organs* that appear only faintly in the physical body but primarily occur in the etheric body are carried by the eustachian tubes toward the sound heard in the middle ear, according to Rudolf Steiner [*Faculty Meetings with Rudolf Steiner,* meeting of December 5, 1922]. In addition, we have to keep in mind that the etheric body also carries out movements of its own that are not accessible to physical observation but can only be perceived by spiritual scientific means of investigation [Rudolf Steiner, *How to Know Higher Worlds,*].

This means that the sound form that is heard is taken hold of by the imperceptible imitating movements of the larynx and the other speech organs. Figuratively speaking, etheric arms and hands in the eustachian tubes bear the sound gesture to the ear.

Thus, a process of "eurythmisizing" (the creation of sound-forms) by the larynx toward the ear lies at the basis of the sense of sound, a process that must be imagined as being in resonance with the above described micro-movements of the body's entire system of movements. In connection with this, Ernst Bücher was able to make a most significant observation in Manfred's case (see Remedial Instruction, p. 300). In order to be able to recognize sounds, Manfred had to go through a phase where he spontaneously made an externally visible but silent imitating sound-forming motion and after that could indicate the sound correctly. [See Alfred Baur, *Healing Sounds*.]

2. How can Manfred's underdevelopment of the sense of sound be understood according to an anthroposophical view of the human being?

Manfred's motor-organization showed two weaknesses. For one, Manfred had remained a *toe-walker* until he was in third grade. For another, in the limb system of the head, meaning, in the region of the jaw, he had a *cross-bite*, that is, the upper jaw did not completely overlap the teeth of the lower jaw. This corresponded to a slight underbite (a protruding lower jaw). These characteristics contradict each other. Walking on the toes shows an overreaction of the forces of the nerve-and-sense system. Such children are pulled upward, so to speak, too strongly. They are gripped too powerfully by the head's elevating forces, which are in opposition to gravity. The cross-bite, conversely, is an image of a hidden difficulty in the upper senses-system [speech, hearing, thought, perception of the ego of the other] to integrate the system of movement (lower jaw) fully into itself.

Both phenomena point to the fact that the mediating function between metabolic-and-limb system and the nerve-and-senses system is disturbed. Looked at from the level of the senses, a weakness of the sense of self-movement lies at the basis of walking on the toes. The child has too little awareness of the motions of the limbs in that he does not place down the heel and roll forward on the ball of the foot.

Here, if we consider a significant *event when Manfred was two years old,* his sound-sense-weakness becomes more comprehensible. From the time he was a year and a half old until the age of two, the boy suffered through a difficult and prolonged case of bronchitis that led to a halt and set-back of his whole development. After several futile therapeutic attempts, sudden improvement and complete healing occurred after Manfred coughed up a large mucous plug. In looking back, the father, himself a physician, felt that they were dealing with some sort of foreign object that had become lodged in the windpipe. Between the ages of one and two, when a child is completely dedicated to learning language, we have an *obstruction in the respiration,* in that rhythmic pulsing which, as mentioned above, facilitates *the metamorphosis of the motion of the limbs into the motion of speech.*

3. Which therapy can help develop the sense of sound?

The function described above of the sense of sound as a silent larynx motion and sound-forming movement, and the metamorphosis of the sense of sound from the sense of self-movement that Rudolf Steiner describes [*Anthroposophy. A Fragment.* and *Faculty Meetings with Rudolf Steiner*], led us to perceive *therapeutic eurythmy* as the appropriate therapy because eurythmy returns the movement of speech in full consciousness back to the movement of the limbs. Additionally, in remedial education, a way was worked out to access the forms of the letters of the alphabet out of movement. J. Hein also called attention to the significance of the schooling of movement for treating and preventing dyslexia.[51] R. Braumiller pointed to the significance of the sense of balance with dyslexia.[52] The total connection of uprightness, speech movement, and eurythmy was worked out in detail with respect to anthropology and education by Gisbert Husemann.[53]

Armin Husemann

Therapeutic Eurythmy

The following description presupposes knowledge of eurythmy and the anthroposophical medical basis for curative eurythmy. Manfred began with curative eurythmy on January 11, 1993. He came daily until May 28, 1993. One treatment lasted about 20 minutes. There were breaks in the rhythm due to pre-Lent vacation (one week) and Easter vacation (three weeks).

The therapeutic eurythmy plan outlined by the school physician had two parts. First, exercises were done to stimulate the metamorphosis of the sense of movement into the sense of sound. In the second part, speech-related exercises were undertaken in regard to the sound gestures of the whole alphabet.

We began with the accelerated therapeutic eurythmy IAO so as to dissolve the above-mentioned blockage in the rhythmic system [Rudolf Steiner, *Curative Eurythmy*, lecture of April 12, 1921]. This was followed by various rhythmical stepping and stamping exercises as a therapeutic response to the tendency of walking on the toes.

Next, the letter B was exercised, first with the arms, then with the legs, then with the arms and one leg in the standing position and then in walking. We also worked on L and M. The series B-L-M resulted from the idea that, from the stimulation of the kidney (B), which is to be looked at as a kind of breathing organ in the blood system of the metabolism, a path is created to the exhalation from the lungs (L-M). Or formulated differently, the metamorphosis out of the experience of self- movement into the sense of sound, which has not been executed, can be simulated by L and M, if one bears in mind the L movement that inverts the lower half of human nature into the upper half. M promotes exhalation and therewith the path of breathing from the metabolism up to the head. Thus, in L, one takes hold of the kidney-breathing stimulated in B and leads it to the upper senses system of the human being through M. (B-L-M-N would also be conceivable).

Following this, the exercises below were carried out with a copper rod.

1. Letting the rod roll from the hand to the shoulder and again back to the hand, first on the inside of the arm across the palm of the hand to the fingertips, then down the outer side of the arm over the back of the hand up to the fingertips.

2. "Waterfall"

Both of these are intended to arouse and stimulate the sense of movement from *outside* as a supplement to the previous process of the series BLM. The outer movement of the rod is here controlled by means of the sense of touch and the sense of balance.

Ten minutes later, the second part of the treatment was begun. We now exercised:

1. the eurythmy movements for the sound of his own name. Every sound was carefully introduced and exercised separately. This gradually passed over into doing the sounds eurythmically in a flowing manner one after the other (writing the name). In this manner, the forms of the letters are intensified inwardly by the sense of movement;

2. speaking the syllables of his name forward and with each syllable taking a step forward. Then backwards: Man–fred / derf–nam. This arouses the sense of sound that is otherwise covered over by the content of the meaning. Later, we extended this to the single sounds : m-a-n-f-r-e-d / d-e-r-f-n-a-m

Course of the therapeutic eurythmy treatment: Rhythmic stamping was very hard for Manfred. His step was subdued, hardly audible. It took eight weeks before he was able to stamp loudly and clearly.

The eurythmy movements at the beginning of the treatment were straight, wooden, stiff. The bending and the rounding of the letter B was scarcely possible. In the course of the treatment it became somewhat better, and the motions became more differentiated. Differences between lightness and heaviness, the drawing together and spreading apart in connection with the L, the flowing motion with M became visible in a rudimentary way, and the movements as a whole became somewhat more fluid. Nonetheless, the entire tendency was still clearly ray-like or pointed; when walking, Manfred still balanced himself on his toes.

In doing the syllables by walking forward and backward, Manfred made obvious progress. Out of the initial chaos, clearly separated syllables began to emerge. In the end, Manfred mastered the walking of the single syllables and likewise the letters to perfection. Coordinating the movements of sound with the spoken sounds was something he learned fairly well, though not entirely without errors.

Daniela Greif

Remedial Instruction

Along with Manfred, two other boys from third and fourth grade attended, who likewise were unable to recognize various sounds and therefore could not read. The above-described situation led us to the following exercises which, for quite some time, each of the three children carried out alone for approximately half an hour daily during the main lesson time.

We began with the sounds of their names. The children, following their noses, hopped the form of a letter—-making it as large as possible—on the floor. With each hop, the corresponding sound was clearly and distinctly spoken by the child. Daily, the exercises were changed a little. The forms of the letters were gradually made smaller in various ways: with small steps, on tip toe, walking on the heels, with the hand in the air, with chalk on the board, with the nose on the wall, writing them with the shoulder, the knee, the feet, likewise forming them with the body and with their fingers (to the extent this is possible). At the end of each exercise, the child spoke the sound clearly and precisely.

Now a letter was written on the children's backs. They were supposed to search out the form, then speak the sound and—with or without looking—write it down. Here too, they were led from the large to the small scale (the "blind" sign strengthens the consciousness for the path of the line). This increased all the way to the spelling of complete words.

Dynamic drawing was also included as a support.

At the same time we made an effort to strengthen the *power of memory*: We practiced speaking sentences word for word, series of words and numbers, later on nonsense words, syllable by syllable, and finally words, sound by sound, forwards and backwards, and for every word we took a step.

Step-step-step-step (forward)				Step-step-step step (backward)			
the	man	is	good	good	is	man	the
blue	red	yellow	green	green	yellow	red	blue
two	seven	one	three	three	one	seven	two
gra	no	lis	pu	pu	lis	no	gra
D	R	A	B	B	A	R	D

Since two of the children were scarcely able to distinguish G and K, B and P, as well as T and D, we worked on corresponding *speech exercises*. This way, the children gradually succeeded in combining the letter's form (precipitated as it is out of movement) with its sound, and the sound with the form, and to remember both as well.

After some sounds had been worked on and learned, and it became possible to form quite simple words such as BAT, BAD, BED, we began to write these down and even to read them. The children repeated the spoken word and wrote it down, saying the individual sounds out loud. Again, they read it first while saying the sounds one after the other, then they combined the first with the second sound, then combined the first two with the third, and so on.

It was evident that some sounds were recognized only by means of the position of the lips, the tongue and teeth, through the process of forming them, perhaps even by the muscular tension in the body. When Manfred uttered the word, BEAR, and was supposed to say which sound it started with, he formed his lips correspondingly, listened and probed within himself, and then knew that it was a B.

By moving letters around, exchanging them or adding more letters, we discovered new words in a playful manner:

dog   —   dig

dog   —   hog

dot   —   dog   —   god

dig   —   dog   —   go   —   good

Good dog!

The children were delighted with each word that they discovered for themselves. This remedial instruction was done in two six-week sessions..

Ernst Bücher

Reviewing the results of the therapies with the class teacher and parents.

After four months of treatment, Manfred had made significant progress.

- He had learned to separate words into syllables.

- He could analyze syllables by sound.

- He had begun reading independently with great eagerness.

Now (in April of 1994), Manfred is scarcely behind in reading and dictation as compared with the class average. We are quite sure that the rapid improvements are due, first of all, to the *daily* exercises in therapeutic eurythmy and remedial instruction, but secondly, to the fact that both therapies were closely harmonized with each other. The other two pupils that were mentioned have likewise impressively improved their recognition of sounds and their reading ability through this therapy.

Perhaps this report can encourage colleagues at other Waldorf schools to try this out. It goes without saying that it will have to be further developed. Unfortunately it was not possible for us to take into account the experiences of various other therapeutic procedures that have been developed to this date in as thorough a way as would be appropriate in this case report.

Anorexia nervosa[54]
Gisbert Husemann

In 1981, British author Sheila MacLeod published a case history of her own illness. Its original title was *The Art of Starvation*.

When she was fourteen to fifteen years old, Sheila MacLeod experienced what many young women at the beginning of puberty go through today, something that appears to insinuate itself like an actual temptation. They begin to starve themselves, find satisfaction in doing this, and some even starve themselves to death. This strange soul reaction to the tendencies of puberty meets with great interest in many young people today. The following excerpts from the case history make it clear what sort of problem we are dealing with.

Sheila MacLeod was born in 1939 on the Scottish island of Lewis (outer Hebrides), the daughter of a teacher who had the clear intention of training her for a particular career. As a student on full scholarship, she studied English literature, kept a daily diary, and experienced sickening factors in school, family, and society such that, in reaction, she felt that her feminine independence was being blocked, put in question, and suffocated. She paradoxically experienced the weight reduction of her body as a defense mechanism in the desperate struggle to maintain her existence. She recovered from the first bout of anorexia. During a relapse, she wrote her first novel, *Snow White's Conversations with Herself*. Sheila MacLeod is married and lives with her sons in London. We are dealing here with a case history written down in retrospect by the patient, an experienced, educated woman.

She reports concerning her time as a boarding school student: "Everything I said was invented. I lied about the size, the architectural style, and location of my parents house" —as well as about the social position of her parents. She replied to questions about how she would amuse herself during vacation with "a list of movies, dances, fox hunts, organized hunts, . . . whereas I was not even allowed to go to the movies, never had been to a dance and didn't even know how such hunts are arranged."

Then her underwear came back from the laundry with the note, "Quite soiled." She had not been properly advised at home about the onset of menstruation. Now, everything that was connected with this in the way of bodily symptoms—spots on her summer dress, cramps, pains—made her hate the bodily processes of puberty to which all these signs pointed. "I was short and thin, physically mobile, mentally awake, aroused maternal affection; that made it possible to overlook my impudent behavior. When I looked into the mirror, I saw someone who appeared to me disgustingly fat." At this time she did not yet become anorexic. She decided to ignore everything and: "I wholly and definitely decided I would become a poetess." She anticipated a lofty calling. It soon became apparent that this idea of a profession hardly fit into her real world. The crisis could initially be overcome by her high goal that satisfied her soul. At her home, Sheila MacLeod had been under absolute authority, for her father expected her to show no interest in anything except the subjects of instruction and learning. In the boarding school, the schedule for the entire day, from seven in the morning until nine o'clock at night, was divided in hours and minutes so carefully that she theoretically had half an hour free time. There was no unpressured time available for her. The authority of the family continued outwardly in this daily timetable and deeply affected her psychic needs and conceptions. "In my subconscious I wanted to be grown up, but at the same time I was firmly determined not to become adult."

What the world had to offer in the way of models horrified her and was unachievable. Instead of confiding in a teacher, kicking up a row and having to be corrected, she was dissatisfied in her searching desire for the world, and this very desire turned negative. "I did the one thing that I was able to do; I became anorexic." It was less a firm decision than a shifting in the soul body, in the astral body, in the opposite direction, away from the world. The imagined calling pulled the body along with it.

Diary: "I had to go to the doctor—no games, more rest, milk, butter, cream! There is really nothing wrong with me. . . . The housemother put a glass of milk in front of me. Yuck! . . . Had to take butter, but did not eat it." The battle had begun and was to last for another year. 97.9 pounds down to 92.4 pounds.

Anorexia gave her the illusion that she controlled herself—her body and her standing in the community as well as her biological processes. The paradoxical feeling of achievement arose "that instead of becoming grown up, I was developing backward." The biological process of menstruation had stopped. I was no longer a woman. . . . In the idealized world of childhood to which I attempted to return, there was neither death nor sexuality. . . ." Conclusion: "An anorexic is not simply a girl or young woman who does not eat and who can be considered cured when she begins to eat again. It is a matter of someone who does not know how she can survive other than by not eating."

Markus Treichler: "Astral forces chaotically shift around in the body and lead to the phenomenology of anorexia—stomach cramps, flatulence, even kleptomania—all signs of a perverted ingesting of the environment.[55] Here, I should like to make reference to Goethe's novel, *Wahlverwandtschaften* [Kindred Souls]. Viewed from the medical, psychological standpoint, the way in which Goethe allows Ottilie—who stands between two partners whose marriages are about to fail—to starve herself to death, is absolutely classic and unique. A naive reader may even feel the situation is creepy, for the novelist reports the action like someone conducting a scientific experiment, keeping minutes of the attempt calculated in advance. Morality does not appear on stage; it works. It works in a sheath that envelops everyone. This was as far as Goethe could go until, in the Mystery Dramas by Rudolf Steiner, morality became revealed as karma and reincarnation.

What happens in the novel? Ottilie stops eating and successfully convinces Nanny not to betray her. Because it tastes so good, Nanny herself eats all the food. Ottilie remains undetected. Finally she sinks down onto the sofa. The unsuspecting physician orders that she be served beef consommé, which Ottilie refuses with great disgust. The tremors when the cup is merely lifted up to her mouth cause the doctor to ply Nanny urgently and earnestly with questions until she confesses to everything. When Charlotte's husband Edward enters and, tearfully taking the hands of his beloved, says, "Good, good! I will follow you beyond. There we will speak in different tongues!" Ottilie answers, "Promise me to live!" "I promise," he calls out, but he only calls after her; she has just then passed over. Ottilie has starved herself to death. Nobody can describe this so accurately who has not personally observed it.

Now we will discuss these two case histories, their physiology, their pathological disturbance, and the therapy. The curves of the LH-secretion out of the pituitary gland of a 77.4 lb. girl of sixteen with anorexia nervosa, indicate clearly that the secretion stops during the time of the disease (see upper curve), that the secretion has started up again in the healing phase, ceases once more during a relapse (third curve from the top), finally becomes normal again (fourth curve down). The fourth curve shows that of the adult.

Those who suffer from this illness withdraw themselves so far from the body that the hormones of the pituitary gland are no longer secreted. In the same connection, one recognizes the withdrawal of the menses and other symptoms.

In the following medical-educational indications, we become acquainted with one of the numerous hygienic-therapeutic measures in school instruction that Rudolf Steiner recommended to the teachers. In all this, the school physician's task is to translate her medical knowledge into instructional measures. A pathological case is

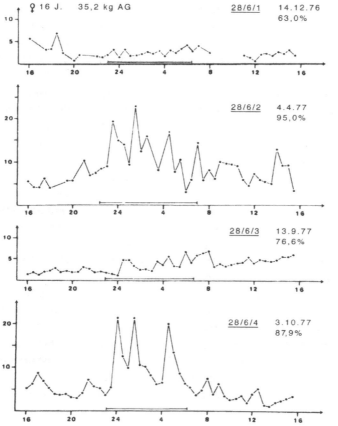

Cycle of spontaneous LH secretion in a girl suffering from anorexia nervosa:
1. in fully developed phase
2. in complete remission
3. during recurrence
4. during renewed improvement
(J.R. Bierich, Pubertät, Verhandlg. Ges. Naturf. und Ärzte [Puberty: Discussions by Association of Scientists and Physicians], Berlin/Heidelberg/New York: Springer Verlag, 1981.)

an aid in grasping the normal relationships, for out of illness we receive a one-sided clarification of what lies at the basis of good health. As Rudolf Steiner said in *Education for Adolescents* [lecture of June 15, 1921]:

I should like to add that in regard to the musical element it is also good if teachers acquire an idea of how their children are constituted in this direction, whether they are poor or rich in imagination—hence, with this transference to memory . When children are poor in imagination, and have a difficult time bringing up their conceptions, one gets them involved more in playing instrumental music. In turn, those children who are rich in imagination, are easily bothered by their imaginations, even in an extreme sense, they should be involved more in singing. It would be ideal if we were able to arrange it -naturally we would need the proper space for that - that we could get the children occupied simultaneously with both playing music and singing. If these two aspects of music, the listening to and making music, which could have such a significant influence on children, work in and through each other, they have a tremendously harmonizing affect. It might even be possible to alternate the activities. That would be most significant in instruction, if one could have one half of the children singing while the other half listens, and then the other way round. This is most desirable and should be cultivated. For listening to music has a healing, hygienic affect on *what the head ought to do in the rest of the human organism*. When you sing, it works in a healing way on what the body is to do to the head. Human beings would become much healthier if everything could be done that ought to be done in instruction.

The pituitary gland lies at the base of the skull close to the center in a small, bony indentation; it weighs approximately 0.6 grams [.021 oz]. Many functions of the rest of the organism depend on the secretions of this little endocrine gland. In the first place, it is the growth of the body and the reproductive organs that respond to the hormone of this gland in the head. This makes the unusual expression "what the head ought to do in the rest of the human organism" comprehensible.

The relationship of the head to the organism is disturbed; the pituitary gland does not work; the organism is wasting away because any appetite is paralyzed. The patient has withdrawn from her body. She has no appetite or desire to come down into the organism, and instead rejects it. She finds satisfaction in this Luciferic attitude. Here, hearing and experiencing music are most suitable, like a medication, without appeal to insight. It unites mere living in the senses once again with feeling and deepens hearing into musical sensitivity—from the head into the rhythmic system. Singing offers the possibility of drawing closer to the metabolic-and-limb system from hearing and breathing. Hearing is divided into two aspects:

1. Perception present only in the organ of hearing as a sense process.

2. Hearing that is drawn into breathing as a musical experience. Hearing in the head penetrates, through breathing, into the entire human being. This is what the head does for the rest of the body. Music therapy is indicated for anorexia nervosa.

This is a fine example of how internal medicine, enriched by education, becomes a new form of hygiene. This, in turn, shows how medical art is transformed into educational art and therapy and is thereby spiritualized. Further recommendations of music therapy are found, for instance, in a cycle of education lectures in 1920 [*Balance in Teaching*, lecture of September 22, 1920. The indications in this paragraph likewise are from this group of lectures.]. A child who is inclined to daydreaming should be treated primarily by educational means, through *recollecting the musical element*—meaning, development of *tone memory*. A child who walks heavily should be guided toward *instantaneous hearing,*—less to tone memory. These suggestions are mentioned here because they contain original musical therapy measures. They should be particularly helpful to school physicians.

Johannes Bockemühl[56] suggested the following artistic therapy for anorexia nervosa:

> Painting in polar colors and doing E and L in curative eurythmy. Both the color polarity and the sounds focus on the same thing as the music therapy we discussed. The E belongs to the head functions and the L streams upward. Thus, in the colors, in the music and in "the word" one has the same principle throughout. This principle leads from the formative life forces to the vibrations of the soul, and right up to the ego.[57]

Glimpse into the Work of a Child Psychiatrist and School Physician
Johannes Bockemühl

Overcoming fear—one human being helping another

Out of the profusion of illnesses conditioned by fear, we will look at the aspect of developmental delay during childhood and the teens. Background histories and possible psychiatric treatments will be discussed. The first cases are of two children on the verge of puberty, who are suffering from anxiety, with various symptoms. We will then take up a basic description of fear, phenomena of fear, and a therapeutic guideline.

It is not our inner task to define the concept of fear here, nor to interpret fear symptoms. Out of our experience and conviction, it is helpful to try to characterize carefully and to study the unique emotions and feelings that have been described to us. We should not separate ourselves from what we perceive, or focus on what we have learned from previous case studies. Instead, we should learn to decipher the picture we have been given as a life- and soul-situation in its biographical context. Furthermore, in each case, we should "suffer along with" the weight of experienced emotions and their point of origin. In this connection, Rudolf Steiner said in *Education for Special Needs* [lecture of June 26, 1924]:

> Not until you have reached the point where such a symptomatic phenomenon turns into an objective picture, where you view it with a certain composure as an objective picture and do not develop anything except compassion, will the corresponding soul mood be present that places us in the right way by the side of the child.

First Example

M. is 15 and a half years old; with his height of 144 cm (about 4 feet, 8 inches) and weighing 35 kilos (77 pounds), he looks like a linnet.

He came to us because of his severe panic attacks of suffocation (pnigophobia) with tic-like spasms of the whole body. Certain segments of his prior history are significant. M. is the last of four children in a family who keep very much to themselves. The father is an introvert, timid and melancholic to the point of occasional depression, but he pursues his profession conscientiously. The mother is defenseless, light-hearted, and overly concerned. With a smile, she says, "It was a catastrophe to come here with M." The older sister is an actress. The oldest brother experienced an anxiety-filled phase of hypochondria prior to puberty (fear of going to the toilet, among other things). The other brother who is four years older has disabilities and lives in a protective village environment. Among other things, this brother caused a lot of concern during the first fourteen months of his life because of extreme difficulties in feeding him.

M. was born after this brother. Right after his birth, a blood transfusion had to be done because of severe jaundice. Otherwise his development initially proceeded without incident. He had a sunny, cheerful disposition. He continued to develop without any undue problems. He attended a Waldorf kindergarten and then became a student in a Waldorf school located elsewhere. He did not learn to ride a bicycle until he was eight-and-a-half years old (out of fear). He did not like to do gymnastics (for anything could happen to him there). He learned to read and write, but slowly. Starting with third grade, he was considered a dwarf; he was never taken seriously, and while he was accepted, he was made fun of and teased. He tried to make friends, but found nobody. Since that time he thinks school is boring.

Half a year prior to admittance into our facility, he began to twitch with his shoulders, often adopted exaggerated inhaling positions, with spasms of the whole body and face—deathly pallor, racing pulse, desperation, attacks of screaming, anxious clinging to something, fear of suffocation. In between these, he suffered from renewed states of fear. He frequently could not attend school. Medical treatments for these conditions had been ineffective, but he carried twenty-nine little medicine bottles of various sizes and contents with him in a cloth bag to which he clung during his bouts of despair. He believed he could not survive without the protective proximity of a physician. These tic-like phenomena and states of panic caused anxiety, consternation, helplessness, and disconcertion among those around him and increased the apprehension and over-protection which had already been established through the past history in the family and school.

Second Example

The second description is given by A., a fifteen-year-old girl, the oldest of three siblings. She writes: I actually hate to voice my own opinion, because it could be weird, and others who get wind of it would begin to laugh when they see me, because I have such weird thoughts. I would like to be healthy again, not think constantly of food, but live quite normally. But I simply can't imagine saying on the spur of the moment, I'll eat with you. Then I'd have a bad conscience for having given in. Sometimes I think, If I now start eating, I have a future. But I don't want one! I am totally afraid of it! When I go home again, I have to enter a new grade in school, and I don't have anything anymore with which to call attention to myself! Then, I am probably only important if I can help. Besides, my friends go away so often, meet with other people, and talk about God and the world. And I am again on the sideline because I don't have the nerve to say anything. And how will it be when school is over? How is my whole life going to go on? I think, through not eating, I can forget my future. Then I always have somebody who decides for me. I am simply not left to my own devices. Moreover, I don't want to grow up. Well, later on, I would like to have children and everything else, but always later, later, later. That is still an eternity away; why should I be grown-up now? I believe this is also one of the main reasons why I want to lose weight. My sisters are proud of growing up; for me it's the end of the world. But I believe this is what it is: If I were to eat, I would be one of many—lined with butter! This is how I get attention! I'd rather put up with the other children being cross with me than to resume eating. When I think these things, I don't even think of the fact that the other way I would be free of this fear and the mental pressure. I think of how I can get through the day without retaining much within— and again, that I could have fun in life. But I simply have no faith..

These examples appear to be quite different. The boy actually remains in an overly awake state of inhaling; the girl stops her whole further development into puberty. The first description shows itself to us as a tic-disease; the other as addiction to weight loss. In both, a greatly intensified consciousness has intruded that is marked by deep anxiety. In both youngsters, all development, even physical development, is stopped. Both experience extreme anguish.

Anybody, not only a patient, knows and experiences anxiety, and yet it is something that is extremely subjective emotionally. The emotions are as varied as are human beings and the circumstances of their lives. A whole collection of related emotions gather—for example, worries, shock, depression, compulsion, isolation, mood shifts, panic, and problems with relationships. Everybody's experience shows that fear rises beyond the pure level of emotions and penetrates into waking consciousness. First, intensified, often self-protective attention grows (vigilance). Then consciousness is sharpened to avoid fear, to avoid situations that cause fear. Conceptions develop of what might be approaching, apprehensions but also idealized illusions. Finally, fear of continued fear arises. But feelings can also be experienced physically: nausea, vomiting, loss of appetite, tensions, heart palpitations and arrhythmia, blushing and pallor, chills and heat waves, but also dryness of mouth, sweaty hands, diarrhea or constipation, and problems of urination can occur.

How can such symptoms appear? To answer that, we must first study some basic laws of development. As early as during the incarnation process of the human entity, when it descends from the spiritual world into the body that has been prepared by heredity, this human entity has to confront completely new, physical circumstances. Life begins, and with it, earthly existence. Only after being born, when the human entity communicates with the world through its body (its organism of nerves and senses)—through breathing and eating—does it awaken to the world. The world directly affects the human being, and it affects the world. At the same time, the prenatal consciousness of the spiritual world becomes dimmed on this side and finally is completely forgotten.

In the course of a human being's development, numerous "births" occur in a variety of transformations, often in small, day-by-day steps, sometimes more obviously in greater steps of development. One of the most important steps in acquiring the full human state is the one when one learns not only to penetrate into himself and beyond himself into his environment, but further into the spiritual core of other human beings. Then, in perceiving the I of the other person— this is a most complex, extensive perception—one knows: Here are human beings, individuals who have their very own being, just as I do. This perception of the other I occurs in a natural way early on with the first smile, which means that the child realizes: Here there is kinship. I have perceived something spiritual directly (in most cases in the mother), something spiritual that has evolved from a common origin.

Although frequently overlooked, such events of births or developmental demands are decisive for the essential, existential feeling of every human being: Here I am no stranger, here I am understood, here I feel at home. If such moments do not occur, if no ego is encountered by the ego-sense which any human being can develop, or if such moments are damaged through shocks, experiences at the wrong time, for example, misuse or abuse, or even coldness of soul or irony, a person's whole existence and earthly development can be threatened.

The spirit-kinship of the human being with the supersensible, spiritual world must remain intact throughout the course of life, even if ever so unconsciously, if further human development is not to suffer fundamental damage. Incarnation or security, in the sense here described, is a constant passageway to new spaces; it is threshold experience, sense experience and spirit perception. Such events are frequently traversed unnoticed in the most varied ways between birth and death.

What can be experienced in passing from space to space, from level to level? How does one go across? Voluntarily? Under constraint? Too early, too late? What awaits me? What do I expect? Does one go into a pantry? Into a cellar? Am I prepared? What are the experiences I have had so far?

It is in the nature of human beings and their evolutionary capabilities that they progress from world to world, from space to space, from realm to realm. But what happens at the crossings? What happens, for example, when people are buried by debris or by an avalanche; what happens during terrible accidents, in initiation experiences, during catastrophes of war, in natural disasters, day after day, a thousand times? Threshold crossings take place—elevations and extensions of consciousness. They are states of fear as well as initiations. They are in each case exceptional events, even if they are not survived. Such events are always possibilities to call forth the ego to new panoramic insights, to greater capabilities of integration, if such a step is surmountable. Doubt of one's ability to master the situation and come out alive often goes hand in hand with fear. In our two examples of developmental thresholds, this question is posed. Doubt of the ego's identity despite all developmental transformation, particularly avoidance of such a step through escape or backsliding, are results of fear that has not been overcome.

Do I remain the same despite all the changes of life circumstances? Is my identity maintained in my experiences or am I placed in question as an entity? Is my earthly existence threatened? Am I sure of myself? Do I have the faint feeling that I can change myself? Such profound presentiments are always dimly in our minds. All these crossings into new life-situations contain freedom and commitment, liberation and confinement. Fear is a mental side effect of every new development and calls into our awareness the threshold of a crossing.

The birth of the physical body itself is an existence-bestowing event, but at the same time it is both life-threatening and consciousness-arousing—narrow passage and liberation, primal fear and primal liberation. How is the transition managed? Some trials and challenges come in the form of childhood diseases or developmental crises and disturbances.

The more foreign the transition, the more powerful its effect on the human being, the greater the challenge to the ego to maintain and strengthen its existence in daily life. In the emotions of the soul, this struggle is mirrored as fear, among many other things. Fear is not an affair of the ego; it is the soul-reflection of the tension and connection of spirit with body. Steps of overcoming transitions are steps of overcoming fear.

From infancy, all the events of the day—even the smallest that have to be mastered—are significant exercises, for example: having to join the circle in kindergarten, to keep one's mouth shut at the dinner table, to go to school alone, to do something one does not feel like doing. Such challenges can produce negative emotions, even fear. It depends on the extent to which the human individuality is present, can maintain an overview, arrange the function of the body and adjust to the new conditions. This faculty depends quite significantly on one's habits of allowing change to occur, of tolerating unpleasantness and facing up to challenges. If a child has had practice in this, overcoming of tasks or hindrances becomes a source of joy that strengthens the soul's sense of security, which increases the ability to bear burdens.

It depends on the experiences, the certainty, the acquired abilities, and the sensibility of the individual person, whether fear comes to expression in illness at all, or impedes development. Fear does not appear all of a sudden in a soul where the ego has developed the overview, the power of integration to surmount ordinary life situations. But in a full retreat, in avoidance, or in wantonness, fear is no longer perceived. Attainment of new developmental levels progresses in waves of expectation and fear, of overcoming and liberation. This is true for human beings, right down into their physiology.

It is the great task of elementary education, and of a truly human education, to lead to such a delicate, dynamic equilibrium. The kinds of expectations that surround the physical birth of a child—the very first threshold event—are therefore decisive. It is all-important how the first narrow passage is experienced by the surrounding human beings and the child itself, as fear—it has even been called primal angst—or as liberation. Here, the attitude of the parents long before the birth is especially significant. If pregnancy, for example, follows one or even several miscarriages or stillbirths, or if it occurs following the birth of a child with disabilities (as in the first example), or after a miscarriage that had threatened this pregnancy, the child may be expected and received with special and most anxious, vulnerable feelings. Thus, any irregular heart sound, any change in skin color (dyschromia), any apprehensive and worrisome atmosphere, any uncertainty, any exaggerated precaution against possible dangers, can have an impeding effect on the child's healthy development. This tendency can easily be perpetuated by promoting explanations and intellectual knowledge. For mother or parents, this produces a problem child. Other factors—an increased awareness of health, sex education at the wrong time, shocks or overwhelming experiences,

318

perhaps a divorce, alcoholism of the parents, a one-sided intellectual way of addressing a child, a faulty diet—can significantly hinder a child's courageous, unbiased security from which to move forward into the future. Thus, an anxious, reflective and often doubt-filled attitude in relation to the child's significant adults and the environment is introduced and promoted. If such a basic attitude continues (and it is not possible to develop a deeper, more courageous, understanding comprehension for the educational development), the stream of pulsing life in mental and physical growth is hindered, stopped, or interrupted. Then rhythmic function disturbances appear, for example:

Disturbances of concentration and rest

Disturbances of sensory functions (abnormal perceptions)

Heart rhythm disturbances, metabolic disorders, conditions of collapse (possible hyper-ventilation fits), breathing disorders

Digestive disorders (constipation and tendency to diarrhea)

Sleep disorders

Growth and developmental delays

Depressions, in extreme cases with tendency to suicide

But we also know how all these widely divergent symptoms and fears disappear when it becomes possible to lead the child confidently to surmount the tasks and challenges of the future. One must be willing to take some risks, to not be too fixed, to let some unexpected things happen and be experienced, guided by the child's age and by the diagnosis.

The art of psychotherapy, guiding and accompanying the process of mental balancing, requires presence of mind and an ability to deal with disturbances that may either impede development or over-accelerate it. The goal of psychotherapy is to create a framework in which an older child or teenager can experience freedom.

When we use such therapy individually, comprehending it as developmental assistance in the course of a biography, we must reckon with the essential core of the human being, the "I" that to begin with, depending on age, organizes and centers a person only incompletely. Only the I is in a position to bestow order on the human organism's developmental course, to readjust disorders, and to create a fitting, rhythmic/dynamic balance. We cannot force anything; we can only offer help. This endeavor is characterized by Karl König as follows:

> Only one human being helping another—the encounter of I with I—becoming aware of the other individuality, . . . simply the face-to-face encounter between two personalities creates the possibility that brings healing to our threatened innermost human essence.[58]

When the therapist has found certainty in the survival of an individuality as a continuing reality, he or she will consider other influences that have to be termed spiritual. These also affect the origin of fear and the unfolding of the personality. To this must be added the influence of the environment—of education, of civilization, of diet, and much else. In addition everything must be studied that in any way is connected to heredity, everything that plays into it in the way of traditions, family membership, expectation, ancestry. Even the question concerning life before birth or after death, possible life tasks, and the development of karma, must be posed. These influences naturally exceed the clearly evident circumstances of life and the merely physical and organic dimensions. Nevertheless, these overriding questions must always form the background of diagnosis and therapy.

The phenomenon of fear, however, has additional contemporary causes that have powerful significance in human evolution and individual destiny. It is the increasing darkening, the human being's condition of being cut off from spirit-affiliation, the ego's forgetting its kinship with God from birth onward, and with that the extinguishing and weakening of orientation for tasks, goals, redemptions, during earthly life. This is a cause of a Luciferic nature. The forgetting of one's earthly origin, of ancestry, history, of tradition and, with that, a loss of all ties and obligations is a result of Ahrimanic activity. Both powers, accompanying destiny as they do, and conditioned by the time in which we live, together bring about the incoherence, the disruption of our civilization, the rush and indistinctness of modern life in which the individual, who is an enduring individuality, has to pursue his or her path.

Because the tasks of psychotherapy are complex, there are characteristically no technical or mechanical means of support. Although psychotherapy is supported by other treatments that are no less effective, where reference is sought *directly* to the individual nature of the human being, the presence of mind, literally the spirit-presence, of the encounter is decisive, the alert activity of the ego sense, which in a conversation can light up now and then. With young people, having understanding conversations is essential to therapy, if it is honest and not routine or closed-minded. If the ego-sense of the young person is not completely inundated or underdeveloped, there is a possibility of striking a spark of understanding in the other. From that spark can grow a feeling of trust in the continuance of his or her existence, a sense of biography, of a mission in life or a decisive future step. Such an effort entails a significant overcoming of fear and building hope for the future—learning to find oneself in the present, to create space for the spirit-presence of the ego.

In dealing with such therapeutic encounters—which, in fact, can never be completely successful—it is not enough to have one meeting or only occasional office contacts. They must be part of several months of institutionalized treatment. Experience in these conversational encounters shows us that three steps are needed:

1. sympathetic understanding, the searching listening that is as unprejudiced as possible and takes the other person seriously;

2. searching for and pictorially discovering connections in the events of the past, and emotional orientation in the present situation;

3. finding and formulating tasks, designing one's own activities to practice, stimulating conceptions of the future, making plans and considering perspectives, developing age-appropriate independence.

These three steps usually go hand in hand with the general clinical phases of our treatments at the clinic:

1. phase of letting go of what is in the past, of what one is used to;

2. phase of integration and identification with the present situation (acceptance of treatment);

3. phase of stabilization of personality along with new orientation, the finding of perspectives, of trying them out with a view to the future.

To move on once again with individual development means to overcome fear, to manage steps. This can only succeed through one human being helping another.

Appendix

Of the two youngsters mentioned above, we need to report that, in M.'s case, the pathological conditions of fear with their severe symptoms of tics was healed completely within one year, that M. was able to integrate himself well with his old classmates. He has furthermore continued to develop positively in his physical growth.

A. accurately recorded her feelings in writing, something few of her age will do. This is why she was mentioned here as an example. A psychotherapeutic effect as described above could unfortunately not occur here, since the clinical history revealed life-threatening and chronic problems. Within a few weeks we had to readmit A. once more into an intensive care clinic.

In the attempt to bring order somehow into the spectrum of fear-sensations and disorders, one has a hard time in systematizing them within the framework of classical medicine. One distinguishes between

- panic disorders,
- compulsory disorders,
- post-traumatic stress,
- generalized anxiety disorder, and
- school phobia.

Then there are actual anxiety phenomena connected to situations or objects, so-called phobias:

- claustrophobia   fear of closed rooms or spaces
- agoraphobia   fear of large spaces
- acrophobia   fear of heights

- pnigophobia — fear of suffocation
- ergasiophobia — fear of writing
- taphephobia — fear of being buried alive
- erythrophobia — fear of blushing, of turning red
- animal phobias — fear, for example, of dogs, spiders, mice
- social phobias — fear of being alone, or being among people,

  fear of separation

Appearance and frequency

In one third of all child psychiatry cases, girls outnumber boys, and psychiatric cases are seen more frequently in cities.

The actual manifestations that predominate among teenagers are: fear disorders, compulsions, phobias, depressions.

In younger children, phobias predominate (animal, school, separation), dependent on the emotional life of father and mother. This happens in cases of constricting education or overprotection.

CHAPTER 10

Salutogenesis
Seeking the Source of Health

Promoting health or preventing illness

Materials collected for this book pertain to the activity of school physicians who want to promote the work of education both at school and at home. They point in the direction already suggested by Rudolf Steiner. Modern research into salutogenesis and resilience has also provided validation and corroboration for these ideas. The word salutogenesis is a combination of the Latin word *salus, salutis,* 'health' and the Greek word *genesis* 'origin' or 'calling into being.' Thus salutogenesis means 'inquiry into the origin of health.' This line of thinking represents a new paradigm, a new direction for research.

For the past 300 years, the accepted paradigm in medicine has been pathogenesis. This term is made up of the Greek words *pathein* 'to suffer' and *genesis* 'origin,' and indicates the search for the cause of suffering or illness. The concept of prevention has developed in this context. Based on pathogenesis, disease prevention means to prevent and eliminate disease-causing factors. The primary questions are how a disease arises and how it can be prevented by eliminating pathogenic factors.

People have a natural desire to care for and maintain their health. This can be done by avoiding contact with pathogenic microorganisms, poisons, and other health threats. This basic idea of preserving our God-given health is old, fine, and sound. However, enormous increases in health care costs made it necessary to create large organizations for cost-effective management. Many health maintenance organizations (HMOs) have been bought by profit-oriented corporations whose efforts to economize have resulted in unsatisfactory patient care and bankruptcy of the organizations. Members of these HMOs have limited choice of a primary care physician and of prescription medications. People feel managed and have little or no influence on their health care. The human contact and warmth got lost, and the spiritual aspects are completely absent. In spite of all this misunderstanding and mismanagement, there is a seed for change that can give us hope. In Ann Arbor, Michigan, an initiative has been founded to build up community supported anthroposophical medicine, a subscription service similar to the biodynamic movement's community supported agriculture. This innovative response to current health care needs can be a positive step in moving medicine from a pathogenic to a salutogenic approach.

Salutogenesis came into being as a concept in the 1960s in English-speaking countries. *Aaron Antonovsky* (1923–1994), the father of the salutogenic paradigm, investigated the health of elderly people in Israel and developed criteria for measuring both physical and emotional health. To his great surprise, he found that some of the healthiest older people were individuals who had survived the horror of the Holocaust.

Abraham Maslow (1908–1970)—a founder of humanistic psychology and psychotherapy, along with Carl Rogers and Erich Fromm—also made surprising discoveries in his research on emotional health. He studied healthy individuals to establish criteria for mental health. Those found to be the healthiest had all had inner breakthrough experiences, such as out-of-body events, spiritual encounters with God, or other mystical experiences. He found that there is a healthy center in every emotionally sick soul. If that core can be strengthened in the right way, the patient can learn to master his problems and can participate more fully in his or her human environment.

Rudolf Steiner (1861–1925) stated firmly in a lecture to medical professionals that physicians must consider the well-being of all of humanity if they want to help individuals. Why? Because each human being is part of the whole, consciously or unconsciously influencing it in one way or another by his or her way of relating inwardly to the self and outwardly to others. Every person is actively involved in the development of the earth and of all humankind. The more I as a physician succeed in acting out of an all-encompassing perspective— even in the smallest matters—the more I contribute to the benefit and progress of the whole. The more isolated I am, ignoring the larger social and spiritual context, the greater is the danger that I will be a pathological factor in the process of evolution. To become sound, healthy, and "whole" is a process of integration. Illness always results from isolation or disintegration of individual processes, functions, or substances in the organism. We are thus challenged to involve ourselves in the great goals of humanity in even the small things we do and to make sure that we do not lose sight of them.

Another aspect of salutogenesis is resilience research. Heredity and environment are found not to be the only determining factors in human development. A third factor that has been neglected is the centrally important matter of human relationships. The essential elements in a personal relationship are:

- honesty, truthfulness, and uprightness
- love
- respect for the autonomy and dignity of the other person, even if the individual is a young child or utterly dependent.

A child who has experienced such a good relationship—even if it was only with one individual and for one period of time—can develop in a healthy way even if conditions are otherwise poor, if the child is beaten every evening and not cared for properly during the day. In France, the book *Plus fort que la haine* [by T. Guénard] is a good example of this. "Much stronger than hate" was the experience of love and compassion received by a three-year-old child who had been severely traumatized and neglected before spending three precious months with foster parents. This positive experience set the tone for the rest of the child's life, making it possible to identify with the good and with a loving heart.

Was Kinder staerkt. Erziehung zwischen Risiko und Resilienz [What will make children strong: raising children between risk-taking and resilience] is the title of a book in which many studies on children's quality of life are evaluated. These studies lay out the factors that establish the foundation for good health for a whole lifetime. This publication provides further support for the theory and practice of Waldorf education. The contents should be documented in the coming years by our own research.

Not till the 1990s did salutogenesis become widely accepted in public health and academic discussions. Until that time, the pathogenic approach had still been financially viable. Explosive expansion of health care costs have led to international openness to the new concept of salutogenesis. Now the predominant questions are: Where does health originate? and How can we improve health? rather than: Where does disease originate and how can it be prevented?

What is the principal difference between the old pathogenic and the new salutogenic concept? The pathogenic concept starts—in the case of a contagious disease, for example—with the infection model. Thus we may ask: Who has infected me? What is the name of the virus or bacterium? Which antibiotic can help? The salutogenic concept requires different questions: Why does one person become ill while others in the area remain in good health? The question of why one person gets an infection and another does not is a salutogenic research question.

The consequences of the nuclear disaster in Chernobyl have shown, for instance, that a high percentage of the population contracted leukemia and other cancers. But why didn't every person with the same exposure get sick? What protected them? What part of the human organism supports health?

Psychosocial health—an economic perspective

It is not only politicians but also economists who are interested in the salutogenesis principle. In 1994 the General Agreement on Trade in Services (GATS) was signed during the Uruguay round of WTO consultations. 120 countries have since ratified the agreement; politicians are prepared to privatize services in the social sphere.

The consequence is that social services have to be given new and transparent structures. Quality management procedures have therefore been developed that allow services to be accurately described, for instance, how long it takes to carry out a particular nursing procedure in the best possible way. The problem with this is that services will not be paid for unless they are immediately effective and also cost-effective. Human warmth and time given to an individual patient who does not want to be taken to the toilet in efficient record time, for example, but who also has an urgent question that needs an answer, would still have to be included in the system as something worth paying for. But then there is the argument of being short of funds. Quality assurance does increase effectiveness in the economic sense, but it opens the way to regimentation of the entire social sector, and this will not meet people's actual needs. Important new questions arise here concerning the form of a truly modern health service that looks to the future and includes civic organizations and patients' associations.

In his book *Der sechste Kondratieff* [The sixth Kondratieff], Leo Nefiodov shows that economic development goes through long waves of growth and decline, called Kondriateff waves after the Russian scientist Nikolai D. Kondratieff (1892–1938). He found that completely new developments come every 40 or 50 years, with major innovations taking the world economy forward. [See Mager, *The Kondratieff Waves.*]

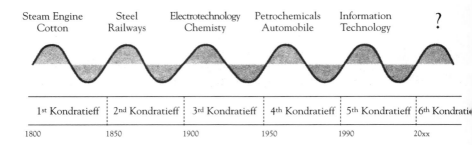

The steam engine was invented and cotton mills were mechanized around 1800. The steel industry and the railways followed, then the oil industry and plastics, and finally, information technology and the computer industry. Each of these developments brought an upswing in the economy. The computer industry boom may end sooner than expected. The fascinating question is: what will come next? We may well expect it to be psychosocial health or the social services market. According to WHO calculations, if dependence on drugs continues to increase the way it has over the last

330

20 years, every second citizen in industrialized countries will be dependent by 2100. About 50% of the world population will then be addicts to varying degrees. Economic figures show that work time missed due to psychosocial problems is seriously on the increase. People are no longer so resilient; they take more frequent sick leave and are progressively less able to cope with strain. There must be enough people who are healthy if the economy is to remain stable in the long run. This, then, is another reason why economists are interested in salutogenic concepts.

To prepare for a salutogenic approach, a system must be developed that will allow us to describe specific services in such a way that they can be put on the market and bought by customers. Social institutions such as retirement homes for the elderly, and also schools and day-care centers for children, are confronted with questions of quality assurance and quality management. On the one hand, this will—we hope—improve the quality of work and services; on the other, it will make them available for purchase in various different ways. The prospect of moving towards a 20:80 society, in which only 20% of the population is working and 80% depend on social services, makes it incumbent on all of us to do everything we can to reverse those numbers. The majority of the population should be so fit and active that they will be happy to work and to create new workplaces based on new comprehensive economic and social policy visions, in order to provide for those who are unable to work. With the enormous increase in health care costs, we now stand shoulder to shoulder with politicians, industrialists, and economists in the desire that human health may be promoted to the greatest possible degree.

Sources of physical, emotional, and spiritual health

The main points in Antonovsky's salutogenesis research and Maslow's studies on emotional health and resilience are:

At the physical level there is the principle of *heterostasis*. The word is made up of the Greek *hetero*, meaning 'different' or 'other,' and the Latin *stasis*, 'state' or 'condition,' together meaning 'different state.' The antonym *homoeostasis* derives from the Greek *homoios*, 'like' or 'similar' plus *stasis*, together meaning 'similar state.'

With the pathogenetic model, the organism aims to provide an environment that is as stable as possible, i.e. homeostatic. This is, of course, important, though the question is how the goal is to be achieved. With the salutogenic model, a healthy organism is not determined by homoeostasis but by a continuous sequence in which heterostatic processes are transformed into homoeostatic ones. This model has a high level of activity and adaptability.

The heart of the salutogenic principle is the human ability to deal with unfamiliar elements and conflict, gaining strength in doing so. The principle of heterostasis thus also means that we must learn to endure stress and not merely avoid it. We must get to know the limits of endurance in body and soul and learn to extend them. The salutogenic principle is in accord with advice that has always been given in anthroposophical medicine, for instance, that it is good for children to go through childhood diseases. This helps to develop the immune system and the capacity for self-regulation and self-healing.

That brings us to the question of immunization, which is advocated so strongly by the health authorities. We must, of course, always ask if the individual child is strong enough to cope with the disease, and it is mainly the physician's responsibility to judge this. If the constitution is so weak that one cannot expect the child to cope, it will, of course, make sense to immunize him or her or to treat the condition with antibiotics and with medicines that bring down the temperature. On the other hand it is important to make sure that mass immunization without considering the consequences does not block children from working through any of the childhood diseases. This would deprive them of the opportunity to develop new and more extensive powers of resistance.

The typical advice given in pathogenetic terms would be to get yourself vaccinated against all influenza viruses, avoid stress and trouble as far as possible, take sick leave or take tablets of some kind as soon as you feel the least bit sick. With salutogenesis, on the other hand, the key questions are: How do I learn to cope with life situations, and how can I remain inwardly and outwardly flexible? How do I develop stress and frustration tolerance and become more stable emotionally?

At the soul level, it is important in terms of salutogenesis to develop a *sense of coherence*, a sense that all things are related to one another. We need to find our place in the grand and small scheme of things before we can discover the meaning of our lives.

How does one develop a sense of coherence? Antonovsky says, very simply: Children should have an education that gives them a satisfying philosophy of life. They must be able to learn that the world is:

- comprehensible,
- meaningful, significant and of value, and
- manageable.

A philosophy of life is satisfying in this sense if it helps people to find themselves and cope with life in such a way that life makes sense.

After the Second Word War, for instance, many children bore a great burden of fear due to personal experiences during that war or because of what they had heard from adults about atomic bombs dropped on Japan, and so on. Here it is important to have at least one person close by who understands the children's situation, someone to whom they can talk and who will help them to develop a sense of coherence. This may at least make it possible to live with worries and anxieties of this kind and develop the hope that something can be done to overcome the fear and the causes of war. Many children and young people are now going through similar experiences after the events of September 11, 2001. Discussions, reports, and commentaries, and the widest possible range of information are needed so that they may understand the event and work through it. But, depending on the child's age, the most important thing is that there is someone—ideally a parent—who has lived through this all, is aware of it and yet has an aura of hope and confidence in life. It is truly helpful to know that people may go through dangerous situations and major problems and yet be cheerful, positive about life, and "normal."

There are many ways in which people can develop a sense of coherence, starting early in life. In Waldorf schools, for example, students and teachers say their "morning verse" together every day before the first lesson starts. This one, written by Rudolf Steiner, was recommended for students from the age of 11 or 12 onwards.

I look into the world
In which the sun is shining,
In which the stars are sparkling,
In which the stones repose;
Where living plants are growing,
Where sentient beasts are living,
Where human beings, soul-gifted,
Give a dwelling place to the spirit.

I look into the soul
That lives within me.
The world-creator moves
In sunlight and in soul light,
In wide world space without,
In soul depths here within.

To you, creator spirit,
I will now turn my heart
To ask that strength and blessing
May grow deep within me
For learning and for work.

A philosophy of life has nothing to do with presenting things from a particular point of view; that would be ideology. It is rather a process of inner growth in which the individual gains increasing insight and connection with all that goes on in the world.

Another important element in helping children to gain a sense of coherence is that at school, too, they have the example of grown-ups who are working on, and further developing, their own sense of coherence for themselves and the world. That is one of the most important tasks in our time, the fifth post-Atlantean period which, according to Rudolf Steiner, started in the fifteenth century. According to the German writer, poet, and scientist Goethe, our age is characterized by making a pact with evil, like the pact between Mephistopheles and Faust. There is every indication that coming to terms with the powers of and tendencies towards evil is our current task. No one who has awakened and gained self-awareness today can ignore this, for television and videos present us with the full picture of cruelty and destructiveness in the world.

Once we know and understand evil, we are not so much in danger of taking it up or falling victim to it. We have a better chance, as we recognize and overcome evil, of developing opportunities for doing things that are good, loving, and true. An ancient Chinese proverb says: There are only two ways of gaining wisdom—through insight or from painful experience.

The third vitally important, and also the hardest, thing people have to learn is to develop powers of resistance, *resilience in mind and spirit* by putting their trust in the progress and inherent meaningfulness of human evolution—especially today. Think of how many people grow depressed today because they have lost confidence in evolution, God, and humanity. The cruelties, violence, corruption, wars, and disasters about which we hear all the time are beyond the limit of what many people can bear. Sickness and abuse of drugs or medicines are the consequence—or acts of desperation and terror, also suicide. Here we must develop a philosophy of life that helps us to understand and work through things that are negative and destructive, so that meaning can be found.

Hans Jonas (1903–1984), physicist, philosopher, contemporary and colleague of Aaron Antonovsky, brought an important element into the twentieth-century ethics debate with his "responsibility principle." Responsibility based on humanism and human integrity is the heart of his philosophy. Hans Jonas's mother had died in the Auschwitz gas chambers. This was something he, an orthodox Jew, could not grasp. According to Jewish tradition, God lives in history—is active in it and goes through the historical process with humanity. God can be experienced through history and he does not punish upright people. After Auschwitz, Jonas could only ask: Where was God when the horror of Auschwitz happened? Had he turned away from the human race and abandoned them? Did he never exist, in fact? Or had God changed his relationship with the human race? Did God also develop his relationship with the human race further in the course of human evolution? Questions like these took Jonas to a living, evolutionary, changing concept of God. You can read about this in his book *Mortality and Morality*. The question he put there is: If such a thing as the Holocaust could happen, can God be almighty and all-wise? Jonas's conclusion is that God has shared his all-wisdom and omnipotence with humanity—giving them the opportunity to decide freely for the good, and at the same time also the possibility of being in error and going astray in the worst possible way. Human beings must now know what they are doing. *They* are responsible for their handiwork, not God. Jonas discovered the middle realm as the sphere of the truly human. It is the realm of the heart, of conscience and love, and it is compatible with human freedom and independently gained insight. This is the only sphere where a stable relationship between human beings and God has been and is possible from the first days of creation to the present time. Knowledge and power can be abused. They serve human beings to develop their abilities and self awareness. Love, however, simply *is*. It characterizes the eternal core of humanity, and God stays connected with this—even in Auschwitz. God *is* love. This God was able to be present at Auschwitz and help people in the gas chambers. This "concept of God after Auschwitz" saved Jonas's image of God. That concept is at the same time the most powerful salutogenic principle—the principle of the human spirit willed by the I itself. This mobilizes all powers of resistance in us. It provides the answer to the question: What enables me to resist attacks in body, soul, and spirit and stay healthy? Three important principles are involved.

The first principle is that we *consciously relate to God and the spiritual world*: I am in God and God is in me. I am whole and absolutely inviolable. Solzhenitzyn wrote in *The Gulag Archipelago* about lying on the ground, with a Russian soldier about to stamp on his face with a dirty boot. He lay there, seeing the boot come closer, and at that moment the thought came: You can only destroy my body, but you cannot touch my mind. The most powerful resource for resistance is knowing God, mystic experience, or being in touch with one's identity, experiencing our own I as eternal spirit.

The second principle of invulnerability that mobilizes resources for resistance is the *human relationship* principle. People who found themselves in extreme situations say again and again that they were only able to cope because they felt profoundly connected with one or more other people. We hear, for example, how Nelson Mandela coped with years of imprisonment because he knew that his wife was continuing the fight outside. Close, warm, reliable human relationships— with one's father, mother, grandparents, friends, people we love, marriage partners—have a protective effect. You no longer feel alone, never abandoned, but always surrounded or supported by love. This power can also come from a close relationship with someone who has died. Anyone who knows this power and is able to offer it to others will be able to maintain resistance in adverse circumstances. That person will know that life is worth living in spite of the nightmare he or she is going through at the moment. This will have its time and will then pass.

The third principle was found when statistics were established in salutogenesis research. It relates to *money and property*. People feel their resistance is strengthened if they have a villa on Mallorca, for instance, or lots of money in a Swiss bank. Knowing that I will be able to enjoy life to the full with such resources does also give me the strength to hold on in difficult times. I know that I can live my life after I get out of this bad situation. I will have the strength to carry on.

The three principles share the qualities of security, identification, or existential "being" experienced at the material, psychological, and spiritual levels.

Opening up the sources of health—a new task in medicine

The basic principle of salutogenesis, which rests on heterostasis and activation of the body's own defences, calls for utterly new approaches in all fields of modern medicine.

This includes proper *nutrition*, with vitality gained from natural foods. The organism has to make more of an effort to digest and transform these into body substance than it does with processed canned vegetables or synthetic vitamins. Anything offered on the market as precooked, pre-digested, substituted, or "instant" does not sufficiently challenge the organism to be active itself. Activation rather than making things easy is the basic principle for healthy nutrition. Anthroposophical medicines are also designed to strengthen a patient's own bodily defences. Such work should not be done for the body. Instead, the medicines help the organism to develop and mobilize its powers of resistance and self-healing.

Education that takes account of the essential nature of a child sets age-appropriate limits and helps children to know themselves and to develop. It is important for children to see people around them accepting challenges and coping with difficulties. They must be able to measure their own powers against those of adults they know, in order to know and stabilize their own abilities. The outstanding characteristics of good education are honesty, love, and respect for others. Honesty is fundamental. However important love and autonomy may be, they have no secure foundation without honesty, which we might call "love at the level of insight." Clear thinking, which signifies health at the level of mind and spirit, teaches children to see themselves as part of the world and get their bearings within it.

A child who has broken a toy will come to a grown-up, full of trust, and say, "Can you make it whole again?" "To make whole" is also the meaning of healing. Health is balanced integration of all organs and organ function. It also means wholeness and the holy in us.

Anthroposophy as a science of the human soul and spirit can relate to this new health concept of salutogenesis in every respect. This does, however, also mean that people—and especially anthroposophical teachers and physicians—must accept responsibility and make their own investigations, thus helping to make this concept widely known and applied. It is also important to bring the reality of the spirit into scientific medical discussions and not leave it aside as something "transcendental," nor leave it as the domain of theologians and philosophers. The health of modern people is essentially determined by how they see themselves as human beings and what path of inner development they take. For this reason, we will conclude with an approach to inner training.

Health for today and tomorrow—an inner path to the sources of personal development

Everyone can learn to be healthier and more human by bringing the divine spiritual spheres of existence to awareness in themselves. How this may be done has been shown by Rudolf Steiner, an experienced teacher in the field of self-development. In three of his books, *How to Know Higher Worlds, An Outline of Esoteric Science,* and *Theosophy,* he clearly showed, however, that gaining knowledge and impulses for higher development and doing exercises will only benefit us if we aim to let the results of our work bear fruit in daily life. Seen in this light, personal development means gaining life experience and getting to know all the facets—the heights and the depths—of life. After all, how are we going to develop such magnificent human character traits as reverence, inner calm, courage and confidence, hope, faithfulness, devotion, love and truthfulness, and finally also an autonomy that profoundly acknowledges the autonomy of others, unless these qualities are made part of everyday life? Steiner thus wrote:

> For some, ordinary life in itself provides a more or less unconscious process of initiation. . . . These are people who go through rich experiences of a kind that makes their self confidence, courage, and steadfastness grow in a healthy way and lets them learn to bear suffering, disappointment, and

the failure of anything they may have undertaken with greatness of soul and above all calmly and with their strength unbroken. Anyone who has gone through experiences of this kind will often be an initiate without knowing it, and it then needs only little more to open their ears and eyes of the spirit, so that they will be clairvoyant. [This and all following passages are from *How to Know Higher Worlds*.]

The anthroposophical approach to inner training is designed to make this process of initiation possible for those who seek it actively and in full awareness. It begins with thinking about a circumstance or a quality you want to acquire. You can consider it at leisure, measuring your own life by it, and reflecting when and how you have had experience of this quality and what conditions need to be created to develop it further. One possibility is to meditate regularly on such qualities of thought or feeling, another to decide to make it an exercise in everyday life for a set number of weeks or months—for example, practicing it when doing specific things in the course of the day, in specific kinds of conversation or when meeting particular people. You will learn that thoughts are reality, for you find that something that initially was just a thought will gradually become part of your own nature—part of your identity. You learn in this way how your own nature is awakened more and more clearly in spirit and thought, coming alive in clear thoughts and inner responses. You will, however, also find that self-serving and instinctive traits will grow stronger and present obstacles to your endeavors. On the one hand, this has to do with the fact that you become more sensitive and perceptive to anything negative and are more aware of the contrast to positive qualities. On the other hand, the soul and spirit grows freer with the exercises and more autonomous with regard to your own body, which can then be a more powerful opposing force because of its inborn instincts and drives.

It is important, therefore, to have certain conditions in life that will ensure a healthy balance and provide a basis for good habits that will support you in the heights and depths of life. These are the "seven conditions for inner training." They are given below, for they are also seven basic ethical attitudes that we may practice on our own or with others. They help us to develop the resource of a profoundly ethical and moral relationship to humanity and world on which we can draw for health in body, soul, and spirit. Rudolf Steiner's words on the subject are:

> It needs to be emphasized that with none of these conditions is it demanded that they should be met completely; one should merely endeavor to meet them. No one can fully meet them; but everyone can set out on the road towards meeting them. It is the will to set out on this road, the attitude that matters.

Seven conditions for healthy development

The first condition is to concentrate on promoting health in body and mind. How healthy someone is, will not in the first place depend on him, of course. But everyone can try to improve things in this direction.

We might well think that this would lead to health-egotism. Rudolf Steiner went on, however, to describe how we can find the right relationship to enjoyment—and to obligation. Body and soul are engaged in daily work, and it can happen that we have to disregard health for the sake of our obligations. Perhaps we'll skip a meal or work through half the night or a whole night to keep things going. This means that work often demands that we neglect our health. Anything that might make us ill needs to be balanced out by the right attitude to enjoyment. We can learn to enjoy things intensely, but in such a way that the enjoyment gives us the strength to persevere with our work in a better and more contented way. It is important never to look for enjoyment as an aim in itself—this will consume energy—but to learn to enjoy things in such a way that they give us strength and new motivation for life and development. For people who are unable to enjoy things, it is particularly important to realize that enjoyment is a basic condition for maintaining health in soul and body. The problem is merely to keep our heads and also know the right time to stop, just as it is said that we should stop eating when we are enjoying our meal the most. If we take enjoyment beyond its peak, or use drugs and stimulants that can damage health, we have to make up for this from other resources.

The second condition is that we must feel ourselves to be part of the whole of life. Much is required to meet this condition fully. But individuals can only meet it in their own way. If I am a teacher and my student does not come up to my expectations, I should focus not on the student but on myself. I should feel at one with the student to the point where I can ask myself: Is it because of something I have done that my student is not coming up to expectations? I would then reflect on changing my own approach so that the student will be better able to meet my demands in the future. With this attitude, our whole way of thinking will gradually change. This applies to the least as well as to the greatest things. For instance, I would see a criminal differently from the way I would have done without this attitude. I reserve judgement and say to myself: I am merely human, as he is. It may be that the upbringing and education I have had have preserved me from a destiny similar to his. I may then also come to think that this human brother might have been different if the teachers who took trouble over me had also done so for him. I would reflect that I was given something that was not available to him, and that I actually owe my good side to the fact that it was not given to him. From there it will be a short step to seeing myself as part of the whole of humanity, sharing the responsibility for everything that happens.

People who practice this will note—actually with some dismay—how much power they have because of their attitude. If someone annoys me and I react at the same level, the situation may easily escalate or lead to a persistently strained atmosphere. If, on the other hand, I do not allow myself to be trapped into responding in the same manner, but ask myself, as I leave the situation behind me: What should my attitude be so that this person, too, can show a better side? or What must have been going on internally, what happened at home, perhaps, to make his response so uncontrolled? Even if one does not find an answer, the very fact that the question is asked in all honesty, not condemning the other individual out of hand, marks an important step. It is not uncommon for the other person to have a change of attitude after a period of time.

The third condition for esoteric training is directly connected with this. One must come to realize:

> . . . that his thoughts and feelings have as much significance in the world as his actions. It has to be realized that it is just as pernicious to hate someone as to hit him. I then come to realize that I am not only doing something for myself in working to perfect myself but also for the world. The world benefits from my pure feelings and thoughts as much as it does from my good behavior.

Any of us who have other people around us whom we love, respect, and value will know how much good thoughts can influence other people. Children met with loving respect will grow up in such an atmosphere as if surrounded by a morally protective wall. This will allow them to cope with the usual daily upsets and things that might worry them with a completely different inner certainty than would be possible without such protection.

The fourth condition means to gain the view

> that our true human nature is inner rather than outer. Esoteric training will not get us anywhere if we see ourselves as entirely the product of the physical world. The essential basis for such training is to know ourselves to be of the spirit. Once we are able to feel this, we are capable of distinguishing between inner responsibility and outward success. We come to see that the one cannot be directly measured against the other. As esoteric students, we must find the right middle between things prescribed by external conditions and things we perceive to be the right way of behaving. We

should not impose anything on people around us that they are unable to comprehend; yet we should also be quite free of the desire to do only the things that other people will consider right. We must wholly and entirely look for proper recognition of our truths in the voice of our soul, a soul that is struggling to gain insight in all honesty. We should, however, learn all we can from others, so that we shall know what is of benefit and does profit our souls. We will then develop the "spiritual scales," as it is called in esoteric terms. A heart that is open to the needs of the outside world will be on one of the scales, inner firmness and unwavering endurance on the other.

The fifth condition is

steadfastness in adhering to a resolution we have made. Nothing should make esoteric students abandon a resolution once it has been made, except for the realization that we have fallen into error. Every resolution is a power, and even if it does not give immediate results where first applied, it does work in its own way. Results are only important if we do things out of desire. Anything done from craving or desire is, however, worthless where the higher world is concerned. Here it is only love for our actions that counts. Anything that drives us to perform actions should come to fruition in this love. Then we shall not flag, either, in acting on our resolutions, however often we may fail.

A sixth condition is to develop a feeling of gratitude for everything bestowed on humanity. We must know that our own existence is the gift of the whole universe. Just think of all that is needed so that each of us can have and maintain existence! People wanting to go through esoteric training must be inclined to think this way. If they cannot do this, they will be unable to develop the comprehensive love that is needed to gain higher insight. I must love something if it is to reveal itself. And every revelation must fill me with gratitude, for I grow richer with it.

Finally we read:

All the above conditions must come together in a seventh: To take life at all times the way these conditions demand. Students thus create the possibility for themselves to give their lives consistency. Individual things they do in life will then be in harmony and not contradictory. They will be ready to develop the inner calm that they must have for their first steps in esoteric training.

If we look at our own inner training, we realize that as human beings we are, of course, imperfect, but above all we are capable of development. We can learn to be more and more human if we are prepared to think it, feel it, practice it, and want it anew over and over again. In gradually opening up the source springs we progressively gain health at the three levels of our existence—in body, soul, and spirit. In addition we gain a sound basic ethical attitude, and this can further the development of true humanity in all spheres of life.[59]

Notes

1. Peter Paulig, "Aufruf zur Verwirklichung der Humanen Schule, Millionen unserer Kinder leiden an der Schule!" [Appeal for realization of a humane school. Millions of our children suffer at school!] in *Der Kinderarzt* [The pediatrician] 7 (1984). Peter Paulig is a professor of the Philosophical and Pedagogical Faculty at the Catholic University in Eichstätt. The Bundesverband der Aktion: Humane Schule [Federal Association for the Movement of Humane Schools], the Deutscher Kinderschutzbund [German Association for Child Protection], and the Bavarian Parents Association are responsible for the contents of the publication. A large number of prominent professors were cosigners of this appeal along with the Professional Association of Pediatricians in Germany and ten other associations and organizations.]

2. Meinrad Schär, *Leitfaden der Sozial- und Präventivmedizin* [Manual of social- and preventive medicine] (Bern, Stuttgart, Vienna 1984) 144.

3. *Salutogenese in der Onkologie* [Salutogenesis in oncology], edited by H.H. Bartsch and J. Bengel (Freiburg/New York: S. Karger Verlag, 1997), 1ff.

4. Rudolf Steiner, "The Nature of Humanity," chapter in *An Outline of Esoteric Science*. See also Steiner, *The Education of the Child in the Light of Anthroposophy*. For information on books by Rudolf Steiner, see bookstore@steinercollege.edu. For information on contemporary work inspired by Rudolf Steiner, see the website of the Anthroposophical Society in America www.anthroposophy.org.

5. See also Stefan Leber, *Die Menschenkunde der Waldorfpädagogik* [The view of the human being in Waldorf pedagogy].

6. This brief description of the metamorphosis of the activity of the human components into soul- and spirit-activity was taken from the chapter entitled "Wie die vier Wesensglieder des Menschen geboren werden" [How the four components of the human being are born] in *Begabung und Behinderung* [Gift and handicap] by Michaela Glöckler (Stuttgart 1997).

7. Armin J. Husemann, *Der Zahnwechsel des Kindes* [The child's change of teeth] (Stuttgart 1996).

8. As an introduction, the following primary and secondary anthroposophical works are recommended:

    Rudolf Steiner, *Education of the Child in the Light of Anthroposophy*.

    _____ , *Soul Economy and Waldorf Education*.

    _____ , *Foundations of Human Experience*.

_____, *Practical Advice to Teachers*.

E. A. Karl Stockmeyer, *Rudolf Steiner's Curriculum for Waldorf Schools*.

Michaela Glöckler, *Das Schulkind—gemeinsame Aufgaben von Arzt und Lehrer* [The school-age child: common task of physician and teacher].

Gisbert Husemann and Eugen Kolisko, articles in *Der Lehrerkreis um Rudolf Steiner* [The circle of teachers around Rudolf Steiner].

Eugen Kolisko, *Auf der Suche nach neuen Wahrheiten* [The quest for new truths].

Wolfgang Schad, *Erziehung ist Kunst* [Education is art].

Stefan Leber, *Die Menschenkunde der Waldorfpädagogik* [The understanding of the human being underlying Waldorf pedagogy].

Heinrich Wiesener, *Entwicklungsphysiologie des Kindes* [Developmental physiology of the child].

Friedrich Husemann and Otto Wolff, *Das Bild des Menschen als Grundlage der Heilkunst*, Bd. 1-3 [The image of man as basis of the art of healing, vol.1-3].

Herbert Sieweke, *Anthroposophische Medizin. Studien zu ihren Grundlagen*, Teil I, [Anthroposophical medicine. Studies on its foundations, part 1] (Dornach 1982) and *Gesundheit und Krankheit als Verwirklichungsformen menschlichen Daseins. Anthroposophische Medizin. Studien zu ihren Grundlagen*, Teil 2, [Health and illness as realization-forms of human existence. Anthroposophical Medicine. tudies on its foundations, part 2] (Dornach 1994).

This list of books could be expanded. Rudolf Steiner's lectures on education, as well as the hundreds of articles and books of the secondary anthroposophical literature, reflect the many facets of this perspective. The abundance of this literature should not discourage the reader. The study of an anthroposophical understanding of the human being is a lifelong quest. The prerequisite for a school physician's work at a Waldorf school is love of children and lively interest in all the expressions of their character. The children can be comprehended more and more deeply with the help of anthroposophical insights as a basis for therapy.

9. Rudolf Steiner, *Anthroposophy: A Fragment* and *Foundations of Human Experience*, lecture of August 29, 1919. A detailed description of the twelve human sense activities and their cultivation through education is found in Wolfgang Goebel and Michaela Glöckler, *A Guide to Child Health* (Edinburg: Floris, 1990). An illustrative description of the twelve senses is offered by Albert Soesman in *Our Twelve Senses* (Stroud: Hawthorn, 1990).

10. Cf. Thomas McKeen, *Wesen und Gestalt des Menschen* [The form of the human being] (Stuttgart 1996).

11. *Phänomene des Kinderlebens. Beispiele und methodische Probleme einer pädagogischen Phänomenologie* [Phenomena in a child's life. Examples and methodological problems of a pedagogical phenomenology], edited by Wilfried Lippitz and Christian Rittelmeyer (Heilbron 1990), pp. 52–69. See also Michaela Strauß, *Understanding Children's Drawings* (*Von der Zeichensprache des kleinen Kindes* [The small child's symbolic language]) and E.M. Kranich, et al., *Formenzeichnen* [Form drawings] (Stuttgart 2000).

12. Armin J. Husemann, *The Harmony of the Human Body: Musical Principles in Human Physiology* (Edinburgh: Floris 1994).

13. See also Walter Holtzapfel, *Auf dem Wege zum hygienischen Okkultismus* [On the way to hygienic esotericism] (Dornach 1988) and *Medicine and Mysteries* (Spring Valley: Mercury 1994).

14. See also Michaela Glöckler, *Das Schulkind—Die gemeinsame Aufgabe von Arzt und Lehrer* [The school-age child: common task of physician and teacher] (Dornach 1998).

15. See also Michaela Glöckler, Jürgen Schürholz, and Martin Walker, *Anthroposophische Medizin—Ein Weg zum Patienten* [Anthroposophical medicine: A path to the patient] (Stuttgart 1993).

16. See Robert Ader et al., *Psychoneuroimmunology* (San Diego, CA 1991).

17. See also Walter Holtzapfel, *Auf dem Wege zum hygienischen Okkultismus* [On the way to hygienic esotericism] (Dornach 1988).

18. Armin J. Husemann, *Der Zahnwechsel des Kindes. Ein Spiegel seiner seelischen Entwicklung* [The child's change of teeth: a mirror of soul development] (Stuttgart 1996).

19. See *Thieme Taschenbuch für Zahn- und Kieferheilkunde im Kindes- und Jugendalter* [Thieme pocketbook for dental hygiene in childhood and youth], and *Der Zahnwechsel* [The change of teeth], study material of the International Association of Waldorf Kindergartens, Stuttgart.

20. *The Problem of Lefthandedness*, compiled by Gerda Hueck, will be reissued by Rudolf Steiner College Press (*Zur Linkshändigkeit* [Concerning left-handedness], published by the Curative Eurythmy Training in Stuttgart). Wolfgang Goebel and Michaela Glöckler, *A Guide to Child Health*, chapter on left-handedness. Sally P. Springer and Georg Deutsch, *Left Brain-Right Brain*. See also Audrey McAllen, *Teaching Children Handwriting* (Fair Oaks, CA: Rudolf Steiner College Press, 2002) 104–106, and William Gaddes, *Learning Disabilities and Brain Function: A Neuro-psychological Approach* (New York: Springer Verlag, 1985), chapter 7.

21. See also Petra Kühne, *Zur Situation der Ernährung in Deutschland* [Nutritional conditions in Germany] and *Ernährungssprechstunde* [Nutritional counseling] (Stuttgart 1993).

22. Dietrich Wessel, *"Das Problem Hausaufgaben"* [The problem of homework] in *Erziehungskunst* [Art of Education], (June/July 1992).

23. *Balneologie und medizinische Klimatologie*, [Study of baths and medical climatology] vol. 1 of W. Amelung and G. Hildebrandt, *Therapeutische Physiologie. Grundlagen der Kurbehandlung*, [Therapeutic physiology. Foundations of health resort treatment] (Berlin/New York 1985).

24. Cf. Joseph Rutenfranz, "Kind und biologische Rhythmik" [The child and biological rhythms], charts on p. 359, in *Deutsches Ärzteblatt* [Publication for German doctors], Institute for Performance-Physiology, University of Dortmund (February 8, 1979).

25. Gunther Hildebrandt, "Zur Physiologie des rhythmischen Systems" [On the physiology of the rhythmic system], from *Beiträge zur Erweiterung der Heilkunst* [Contributions to an elaboration of medicine] (January 1986): 8f.

26. On page 83 of his book, Lindenberg states:

It becomes clear that we are not only concerned with the moral problem of the students' goodwill, their so-called pulling themselves together or some such thing, in classroom instruction, when we call to mind what goes on physically—physiologically—in the students while they are engaged in mathematics. Two decades of research in this field is available to us. Teachers should know about this. In the Physiological Institute of the University of Marburg at the end of the fifties, three physicians—Golenhofen, Blair, and Seidel—carried out experiments that investigated the physiological effects of doing arithmetic in the head. First of all, they found that blood circulation of the muscle in the left lower arm increased by 150 to 250% in comparison to normal blood circulation during intense mental arithmetic. In the right lower arm, the increase was not quite so significant. At the same time, blood flow in the skin of the hands was reduced.

All this indicates an increase of metabolic activity: the students work very hard. Further research dealt with the question of how such blood circulation of the muscles came about. At first, it was assumed that an increase of blood pressure was the cause of increased blood flow, but measurements indicated that blood pressure increased only slightly and did not come into consideration as the actual cause. Not until the radial nerve was blocked with novocaine in the left lower arm did it became apparent that the increase of circulation in the muscle of the lower left arm failed to appear and shifted to the lower right arm, where increased levels of blood circulation were measured. We are thus faced with the strange fact that blood circulation in the muscles has a relationship to the muscles' innervating nerve. The conventional presumption that mental calculation only takes place in the head and merely makes demands on the nerves is, in any case, false. Mental activity makes demands on the entire human being. Here we must naturally point out that the Marburg studies do not include any other demands placed on the body, because these investigations were limited exclusively to the blood circulation of both lower arms. But it is probable that other muscles, such as those of the legs and the back, are also affected. In addition, a teacher can determine, especially among younger children, that even the fluid balance, which is regulated by the pituitary gland, is more intensely stimulated by arithmetic than by other subjects. Mental calculation stimulates the urge to urinate—indeed, the motor nerves in general—more intensely than other subjects do.

27. Christoph Lindenberg, *Die Lebensbedingungen des Erziehens-von Waldorfschulen lernen* [Life conditions of education. Learning from Waldorf schools] (Reinbeck: rororoo-Sachbuch, 1981) 102f.

28. Gunther Hildebrandt, "Chronobiologische Aspekte des Kindes- und Jugendalters" [Chronobiological aspects of childhood and youth] in *Bildung und Erziehung* [Development and education], 4 (December 1994): 452-456.

29. For more details on this subject see Ernst-Michael Kranich, Rainer Patzlaff, Hartwig Schiller and Malte Schuchhardt, *Die Bedeutung des Rhythmus in der Erziehung* [The significance of rhythm in education] (Stuttgart 1992).

30. See the booklet on nurseries and daycare centers published by Internationale Vereinigung der Walorfkindergärten e.V. [International Association of Waldorf Kindergartens] (Stuttgart).

31. Cf. Stefan Leber, *Der Schlaf und seine Bedeutung* [Sleep and its meaning] (Stuttgart 1996); Stefan Leber, E. M. Kranich, J. Smit, H. Zimmernam and E. Schuberth, *Der Rhythmus von Wachen und Schlafen. Seine Bedeutung im Kindes- und Jugendalter"* [The rhythm of waking and sleeping. Its meaning for the age of childhood and youth] (Stuttgart 1990); and Audrey McAllen, *Sleep: An Unobserved Element in Education* (Stroud 1981) scheduled to be reissued by Rudolf Steiner College Press 2003.

32. *Foundations of Human Experience*. This book, also published under the title *Study of Man*, was the fundamental course for the teachers of the first Waldorf School in Stuttgart. Every morning for 14 days, Rudolf Steiner gave a basic lecture on the nature of the human being. In the course of each day he also gave lectures on methodology, as well as training sessions and lectures on the curriculum.

33. Cf. Jörgen Smit, *Der werdende Mensch. Zur meditative Vertiefung des Erziehers* [The developing human being. An aid to meditative deepening of the educator] (Stuttgart 1990).

34. E. A. Karl Stockmeyer, *Angaben Rudolf Steiners für den Waldorfunterricht. Eine Quellensammlung für die Arbeit der Lehrerkollegien* [Indications by Rudolf Steiner for Waldorf instruction, a collection of sources for the work of teachers], internal manuscript published by the Pedagogical Research Office, Stuttgart.

35. Cf. Friedrich A. Kipp, *Die Evolution des Menschen im Hinblick auf seine lange Jugendzeit* [The evolution of the human being in regard to the long period of youth] (Stuttgart 1991), and Wolfgang Schad, *Man and Mammals: Toward a Biology of Form* (Garden City, NY 1977).

36. See, for instance, Gerda Scheer-Krüger, *Das offenbare Geheimnis der Temperamente* [The manifest mystery of the temperaments] (Dornach 1996); Wolfgang Schad, "Zum anthroposophischen Verständnis der Temperamente" [Anthroposophical understanding of the temperaments] in *Erziehung ist Kunst* [Education is art] (Stuttgart 1991); M. Anschütz, *Children and Their Temperaments*; R. Wilkinson, *The Temperaments in Education*; and Rudolf Steiner, *Anthroposophy in Everyday Life*.

37. See "Das Kind in der mittleren Klassenlehrerzeit" [The child in the middle grades] in *Zur Unterrichtsgestaltung im 1. bis 8. Schuljahr an Waldorf-/Rudolf Steiner Schulen* [Forming of the curriculum from first through eighth grades], part 2, 97ff.

38. Horst Nickel, "Das Problem der Schulreife—Eine systematische Analyse und ihre praktischen Konsequenzen" [The problem of readiness for school—a systematic analysis and practical consequences] in Dieter Karch, Richard Michaelis, et al., *Normale und gestörte Entwicklung* [Normal and disturbed development] (Berlin/Heidelberg/New York/Tokyo 1989).

39. *Die Bedeutung des Zahnwechsels in der Entwicklung des Kindes* [The significance of the change of teeth in child development], published by the Association of Waldorf Kindergartens, Pedagogical Research Center of the Alliance of Waldorf Schools (Stuttgart 1988).

40. Kaspar Appenzeller, *Grundlagen für eine neue Art der Herzauskultation* [Foundations for a new form of heart-auscultation] (Basel 1989) 32ff.

41. Rudolf Kischnick, *Leibesübung und Bewußtseinsschulung* [Physical training and schooling of consciousness] (Basel 1989).

42. Caroline von Heydebrand, *The Curriculum of the First Waldorf School* (Forest Row, Sussex: Steiner Schools Fellowship Publications, 1966).

43. E. Weimann, H. Lorer, S. Schwidergall, W. Bohnert and H. J. Böhlers, "Pubertäre Entwicklungsverzögerung von Kunstturnerinnen" [Delay of puberty in top female gymnasts] in *Sozialpädiatrie und kinderärztliche Praxis* [Social pediatrics and pediatric practice], 2 (1996).

44. Gisbert Husemann, "Der Sport—ein Religionsersatz? Eine medizinisch/pädagogische Zeitbetrachtung" [Sports—a substitute for religion? A contemporary medical/pedagogical study] in *Der Merkurstab* [Staff of Mercury] (1996): 222-225.

45. J.P. Lin, J.K. Brown and E.G.Walsh, "Physiological Maturation of Muscles in Childhood," *Lancet* (1993).

46. Erhard Fucke, *Grundlinien einer Pädagogik des Jugendalters* [Basic principles for education of teenagers]. See also Betty Staley, *Between Form and Freedom: A Practical Guide for the Teenage Years*, and Dean Stark, *A Waldorf Approach to Coaching Team Sports*.

47. See J. Morais, et al., "Does awareness of speech as a sequence of phones rise spontaneously?" *Cognition* 7 (1979): 323-331, and K.E. Stanovich, ed., *Children's reading and the development of phonemical awareness* (1978), both cited in P. Zimmermann, "Lese-Rechschreib-Schwäche als Entwicklungsstörung. Untersuchung an Waldorfschülern der Klassen 4-6" [Reading and spelling weakness as developmental disorder. Examination of 4th–6th grade Waldorf school students] (unpublished manuscript, Herdecke, 1993).

48. R. Berlin, *Eine besondere Art der Wortblindheit* [A special kind of word blindness] (Wiesbaden 1887). M. Crithley, *The Dyslexic Child* (London: Heinemann Medical, 1970).

49. P. Zimmermann, see note 47.

50. W.S. Condon and L.W. Sander, "Neonate Movement is Synchronized with Adult Speech. Interactional Participation and Language Acquisition," *Science* 183 (11 January, 1974): 99-101. See also W.S. Condon, "Multiple Response to Sound in Dysfunctional Children," *Journal of Autism and Childhood Schizophrenia*, vol. 5, no 1. (1975).

51. J. Hein, "Wesen und Therapie der Raum-Lage-Labilität (Legasthenie)" [Nature and therapy of spatial and postural instability (dyslexia)], *Erziehungskunst* [Art of education] 7 (1977): 384ff.

52. R. Braumiller, "Der Gleichgewichtssinn und die Legasthenie" [The sense of balance and dyslexia] *Erziehungskunst* [Art of education] 6 (1975): 313ff.

53. G. Husemann, "Aufrechtbewegung, Sprachbewegung, Eurythmie und Turnen" [Upright movement, speech movement, eurythmy, and gymnastics] in *Sinnesleben, Seelenwesen und Krankheitsbild* [Sense life, soul nature, and description of illness] (Stuttgart 1998).

54. First published in *Beiträge zu einer Erweiterung der Heilkunst nach geisteswissenschaftlichen Erkenntnissen* [Contributions to an extension of the art of healing following spiritual scientific insights] (1986).

55. Markus Treichler, "Anorexia mentalis," in *Beiträge zu einer Erweiterung der Heilkunst nach geisteswissenschaftlichen Erkenntnissen* [Contributions to an expansion of the art of healing], 5 (1980): 172–180.

56. Johannes Bockemühl, "Behandlung der Pubertätsmagersucht" [Treatment of anorexic addiction in puberty] in, *Beiträge zu einer Erweiterung der Heilkunst nach geisteswissenschaftlichen Erkenntnissen* [Contributions to an expansion of the art of healing], 5 (1980).

57. See also Gisbert Husemann, "Der Liquor cerebrospinalis" [Cerebrospinal fluid], in *Sinnesleben, Seelenwesen und Krankheitsbild* [Sense life, soul being, and description of illness] (Stuttgart, 1998), and Monica Bissegger et al., "Die Behandlung von Magersucht—ein integrativer Therapieansatz" [The treatment of anorexia—an integrated effort at therapy] (Filder Clinic therapy team report, Stuttgart 1998).

58. Karl König, in Camphill Letter, Christmas 1965, quoted by Hans Müller-Wiedermann in *Karl König. Eine mitteleuropäische Biographie im 20. Jahrhundert* [Karl König. A central-European biography in the twentieth century] (Stuttgart 1992) 416.

59. The development of such a sound basic moral attitude is described in detail in Michaela Glöckler, ed., *Spirituelle Ethik* [Spiritual ethic] (Dornach: Verlag am Goetheanum, 2001).

Bibliography

Where possible, English language references have been added to the bibliography of the German edition of this book.

References by Rudolf Steiner
Publishers:
AP   Anthroposophic Press, Hudson, NY
BD   Bio-Dynamic Farming and Gardening Assn., Kimberton, PA
Garber   Garber Communications, Blauvelt, NY
Mercury Mercury Press, Spring Valley, NY
RSP   Rudolf Steiner Press, London
SBC   Steiner Book Centre, Toronto
SSF   Steiner Schools Fellowship Publications, Forest Row, Sussex

GA number refers to the volume in the complete works of Rudolf Steiner in German.

Agriculture BD 1993 GA 327
Anthroposophical Spiritual Science and Medical Therapy Mercury 1991 GA 313
Anthroposophy. A Fragment AP 1996 GA 45
Anthroposophy in Everyday Life. AP 1995 Lecture on temperaments GA 57
Art in the Light of Mystery Wisdom RSP 1996 GA 275
Balance in Teaching Mercury 1990 GA 302a
Being of Man and His Future Evolution, The RSP 1981 GA 107
Case for Anthroposophy, The RSP 1970 GA 21
Course for Young Doctors Mercury 1994 GA 316
Curative Eurythmy RSP 1983 GA 315
Deepening the Art of Healing (See *Course for Young Doctors*)
Discussions with Teachers AP 1997 GA 295
Education for Adolescents AP 1996 GA 302
Education for Special Needs (curative education course) RSP 1998 GA 317
Education of the Child AP 1996 GA 34
Education of the Child in the Light of Anthroposophy, The (in *Education of the Child*)
Faculty Meetings with Rudolf Steiner AP 1998 GA 300/a–c

Foundations of Human Experience (Study of Man) AP 1996 GA 34

Health Care as a Social Issue Mercury 1984 GA 314

How to Know Higher Worlds (Knowledge of the Higher Worlds) AP 1994 GA 10

Human Values in Education RSP 1971 GA 310

In the Changed Conditions of the Times AP 1941 GA 186

Introducing Anthroposophical Medicine AP 1999 GA 312

Kingdom of Childhood, The AP 1996 GA 311

Man: Hieroglyph of the Universe (See The Mystery of the Universe)

"Man's Connection to Spiritual Beings," April 28, 1923 lecture, in The Waking of the Human Soul and the Forming of Destiny SBC 1970 GA 224

Modern Art of Education, A RSP 1981 GA 307

Mystery of the Trinity and Mission of the Spirit, The AP 1991 GA 214

Mystery of the Universe—The Human Being: Model of Creation AP 2001 GA 201

Outline of Esoteric Science, An AP 1997 GA 13

Practical Advice to Teachers RSP 1976 GA 294

Renewal of Education, The AP 2001 GA 301

Roots of Education, The AP 1997 GA 309

Search for the New Isis, The Mercury 1983 GA 202

Soul Economy and Waldorf Education. AP 1986 GA 303

Spiritual Ground of Education, The Garber 1989 GA 305

Spiritual-Scientific Aspects of Therapy (See Anthroposophical Spiritual Science and Medical Therapy)

Theosophy AP 1994 GA 9

Theosophy of the Rosicrucians, The RSP 1981 GA 99

Three Perspectives of Anthroposophy, lecture of July 22, 1923, typescript GA 225

Truth Wrought Words AP 1979 GA 40

Universe, Earth and Man RSP 1987 GA 105

Waldorf Education for Adolescence (See Education for Adolescents)

Steiner, Rudolf and Ita Wegman, Fundamentals of Therapy AP 1999 GA 27

References by other authors

Ader, Robert, et al. Psychoneuroimmunology. San Diego, CA: Academic Press, 1991.

Aeppli, Willi. The Care and Development of the Senses. Forest Row, Sussex: Steiner Schools Fellowship Publications, 1993.

Amelung, W. and G. Hildebrandt, eds. Balneologie und medizinische Klimatologie, [Study of baths and medical climatology] vol. I. Therapeutische Physiologie. Grundlagen der

Kurbehandlung, [Therapeutic physiology. Foundations of health resort treatment], Heidelberg: Springer Verlag, 1985.

Anschütz, Marieke. *Children and Their Temperaments*. Edinburgh: Floris, 1995.

Antonovsky, Aaron. *Unraveling the Mystery of Health*. San Francisco: Jossey-Bass Publications, 1987. German title: *Salutogenese: zur Entmystifizierung der Gesundheit*. Tübingen: Dgvt Verlag, 1997. See also Antonovsky A., ed. *The Sociology of Health and Health Care in Israel*. Somerset, NJ: Transaction Publishers, 1990.

Apenzeller, Kaspar. *Grundlagen für eine neue Art der Herzauskultation* [Foundations for a new form of heart-auscultation]. Basel: Zbinden Verlag, 1989.

Bartsch, H.H. and J. Bengel, eds. *Salutogenese in der Onkologie* [Salutogenesis in oncology]. Freiburg and New York: np, 1997.

Baur, Alfred. *Healing Sounds*. Fair Oaks, CA: Rudolf Steiner College Press, 1993. In German: *Lautelehre und Logoswirken*. J. Ch. Mellinger Verlag, 1989.

Berlin, R. *Eine besondere Art der Wortblindheit (Dyslexia)* [A special kind of word blindness (Dyslexia)]. Wiesbaden: np, 1887.

Bissegger, Monica, et al. *Die Behandlung von Magersucht—ein integrativer Therapieansatz.* [The treatment of anorexia—an integrated effort at therapy]. Filder Clinic therapy team report. Stuttgart, 1998.

Bott, Victor. *Spiritual Science and the Art of Healing*. Rochester, VT: Healing Arts Press, 1984.

Braumiller, R. "Der Gleichgewichtssinn und die Legasthenie" [The sense of balance and dyslexia]. *Erziehungskunst* [Art of education] 6 (1975) 313ff.

Bockemühl, Johannes. "Behandlung der Pubertätsmagersucht" [Treatment of anorexic addiction in puberty]. In *Beiträge zu einer Erweiterung der Heilkunst nach geisteswissenschaftlichen Erkenntnissen* [Contributions to the expansion of the art of healing] 5 (1980).

Bockemühl, J., et al. *Toward a Phenomenology of the Etheric World*. Spring Valley, NY: Anthroposophic Press, 1985.

Bühler, Walther. *Living with Your Body*. London: Rudolf Steiner Press, 1979.

Condon., W.S. "Multiple Response to Sound in Dysfunctional Children." *Journal of Autism and Childhood Schizophrenia* vol. 5, no 1 (1975).

Condon, W.S. and L.W. Sander. "Neonate Movement is Synchronized with Adult Speech. Interactional Participation and Language Acquisition." *Science* 183 (January 11, 1974) 99–101.

Crithley, Macdonald. *The Dyslexic Child*. London: Heinemann Medical, 1970.

Fucke, Erhard. *Grundlinien einer Pädagogik des Jugendalters* [Basic principles for education of teenagers]. Stuttgart: Verlag Freies Geistesleben, 1998.

Glöckler, Michaela. *Begabung und Behinderung* [Gift and handicap]. Stuttgart: Verlag Freies Geistesleben, 1997.

_____ . *Gesundheit und Schule*. Dornach: Verlag am Goetheanum, 1998.

_____ . *Medicine at the Threshold of a new Consciousness*. London: Temple Lodge, 1997. *Medizin an der Schwelle* . Dornach: Verlag am Goetheanum, 1993.

_____ , ed. *Spirituelle Ethik* [Spiritual ethic]. Dornach: Verlag am Goetheanum 2001.

_____ , ed. *Das Schulkind—Die gemeinsame Aufgabe von Arzt und Lehrer* [The school-age child: common task of physician and teacher]. Dornach, 1998.

Glöckler, Michaela, Jürgen Schürholz, and Martin Walker, eds. *Anthroposophische Medizin—Ein Weg zum Patienten* [Anthroposophical medicine—a path to the patient]. Stuttgart: Verlag Freies Geistesleben, 1993.

Goebel, Wolfgang and Michaela Glöckler. *A Guide to Child Health*. Hudson, NY: Anthroposophic Press and Edinburgh: Floris, 1990. *Kindersprechstunde* . Stuttgart: Verlag Freies Geistesleben, 1998.

Guénard, T. *Plus fort que la haine*. Paris: Presse de la renaissance, 1999.

Hauschka, Rudolf. *The Nature of Substance*. London: Rudolf Steiner Press, 1983.

_____ . *Nutrition*. London: Rudolf Steiner Press, 1983.

Hein, J. "Wesen und Therapie der Raum-Lage-Labilität (Legasthenie)" [Nature and therapy of spatial and postural instability (dyslexia)]. *Erziehungskunst* [Art of education] 7 (1977) 384ff.

Heydebrand, Caroline von. *The Curriculum of the First Waldorf School*. Forest Row, Sussex: Steiner Schools Fellowship Publications, 1966. *Vom Lehrplan der Freien Waldorfschule* . Stuttgart: np, 1994.

_____ . *Childhood: A Study of the Growing Child*. Hudson, NY: Anthroposophic Press, 1995.

Hildebrandt, Gunther. "Chronobiologische Aspekte des Kindes- und Jugendalters" [Chronobiological aspects of childhood and youth]. *Bildung und Erziehung* [Development and Education] 47th annual set, #4 (December 1994): 452–456.

_____ . article in *Chronobiologische Grundlagen der Prävention und Rehabilitation*. np: np,1978

_____ . "Zur Physiologie des rhythmischen Systems" [On the physiology of the rhythmic system]. *Beiträge zur Erweiterung der Heilkunst* [Contributions to an elaboration of medicine] (January 1986): 8f.

Holtzapfel, Walter. *Auf dem Wege zum hygienischen Okkultismus* [On the Way to Hygienic Esotericism]. Dornach: Verlag am Goetheanum, 1988.

_____ . *Children with a Difference: The Background of Steiner Special Education*. E. Grinsted, Sussex and Launceston, Cornwall: Lanthorn Press, 1995.

_____ . *Children's Destinies*. Spring Valley, NY: Mercury Press, 1984.

_____ . *Children's Illnesses*. Spring Valley, NY: Mercury Press, 1989.

_____ . *Medicine and Mysteries*. Spring Valley, NY: Mercury Press, 1994.

Hueck, Gerda, comp. *The Problem of Lefthandedness*. Spring Valley, NY: St. George, 1986, to be reissued by Rudolf Steiner College Press. German title: *Zur Linkshändigkeit*

[Concerning left-handedness], published by Curative Eurythmy-Training Heubergstraße 15, DE-70188 Stuttgart, 1978

Husemann, Armin J. *Der Zahnwechsel des Kindes. Ein Spiegel seiner seelischen Entwicklung* [The child's change of teeth. A mirror of the soul development]. Stuttgart: Verlag Freies Geistesleben, 1996.

_____ . *The Harmony of the Human Body: Musical Principles in Human Physiology.* Edinburgh: Floris, 1994.

_____ . "Die plastisch-musikalisch-sprachliche Menschenkunde. Eine Methode des anthroposophischen Studiums." Sonderheft der *Beiträge zu einer Erweiterung der Heilkunst* [The Sculptural, Musical and Vocal Study of Man. A Method of Anthroposophical Study. Special edition of the magazine, Contributions to an Extension of the Art of Healing] 5 (1986).

Husemann, Friedrich, and Otto Wolff. *The Anthroposophical Approach to Medicine.* 3 vols. Spring Valley, NY: Anthroposophic Press, 1982. German title: *Das Bild des Menschen als Grundlage der Heilkunst.*

Husemann, Gisbert. "Aufrechtbewegung, Sprachbewegung, Eurythmie und Turnen" [Upright movement, speech movement, eurythmy, and gymnastics]. In *Sinnesleben, Seelenwesen und Krankheitsbild* [Sense life, soul nature, and description of illness]. Stuttgart: Verlag Freies Geistesleben, 1998.

_____ . "Der Liquor cerebrospinalis" [Cerebrospinal fluid]. In *Sinnesleben, Seelenwesen und Krankheitsbild* [Sense life, soul being, and description of illness]. Stuttgart: Verlag Freies Geistesleben, 1998;

_____ . "Der Sport—ein Religionsersatz? Eine medizinisch/pädagogische Zeitbetrachtung" [Sports—a substitute for religion? A contemporary medical/pedagogical study]. *Der Merkurstab* 49 (1996): 222-225.

_____ . article in *Der Lehrerkreis um Rudolf Steiner* [The circle of teachers around Rudolf Steiner]. Stuttgart: Verlag Freies Geistesleben, 1979.

Jonas, Hans. *Mortality and Morality: A Search for the Good after Auschwitz.* Northwestern University Press: 1996. *Der Gottesbegriff nach Auschwitz.* Frankfurt: Suhrkamp, 1987.

Kipp, Friedrich A. *Die Evolution des Menschen im Hinblick auf seine lange Jugendzeit*[[The evolution of the human being in regard to the long period of youth]. Stuttgart: Verlag Freies Geistesleben, 1991.

Kischnick, Rudolf. *Leibesübung und Bewußtseinsschulung.* [Physical training and schooling of consciousness]. Basel: Zbinden Verlag, 1989.

Kolisko, Eugen. *Auf der Suche nach neuen Wahrheiten* [The quest for new truths]. Dornach: Verlag am Goetheanum, 1989.

_____ . *Nutrition* Nos. 1 & 2. Bournemouth, England: Kolisko Archive Publications, 1978.

_____ . article in *Der Lehrerkreis um Rudolf Steiner* [The circle of teachers around Rudolf Steiner]. Stuttgart: Verlag Freies Geistesleben, 1979.

König, Karl. *Sinnesentwicklung und Leibeserfahrung,* [Development of the sense organs and experience of the physical body]. Stuttgart: Verlag Freies Geistesleben, 1995.

_____ . Camphill Letter, Christmas 1965, quoted by Hans Müller-Wiedermann in *Karl König. Eine mitteleuropäische Biographie im 20. Jahrhundert* [Karl König. A central-European biography in the twentieth century]. Stuttgart: Verlag Freies Geistesleben, 1992.

Kranich, Ernst-Michael, M. Jünemann, H. Berthold-Andrae, E. Bühler, and E. Schuberth. *Formenzeichnen* [Form drawings]. Stuttgart: Verlag Freies Geistesleben, 2000.

Kranich, Ernst-Michael, Rainer Patzlaff, Hartwig Schiller, and Malte Schuchhardt. *Die Bedeutung des Rhythmus in der Erziehung* [The significance of rhythm in education]. Stuttgart: Verlag Freies Geistesleben, 1992.

Kügelgen, Helmut von. "About Elementary Eurythmy in the First Seven Years." Stuttgart: 10th Circular Letter of the International Association of Waldorf Kindergartens, Michaelmas 1993.

_____ . *Child Dances.* Stuttgart: Study Material of the International Association of Waldorf Kindergartens, vol.10.

_____ , comp. *Spiritual Insights from the work of Rudolf Steiner.* Silver Spring, MD: Waldorf Early Childhood Association of North America, 1999.

Kühne, Petra. *Ernährungssprechstunde* [Nutritional counseling]. Stuttgart: Verlag Urachhaus, 1993.

_____ . "Zur Situation der Ernährung in Deutschland" [Nutritional condition of Germany]. Available through Arbeitskreis, Ernährungsforschung, Querweg 19 DE 75378 Bad Liebenzell.

Leber, Stefan. *Die Menschenkunde der Waldorfpädagogik* [The view of the human being in Waldorf pedagogy]. Stuttgart: Verlag Freies Geistesleben, 1993.

_____ . *Der Schlaf und seine Bedeutung,* [Sleep and its meaning]. Stuttgart: Verlag Freies Geistesleben, 1996.

Leber, Stefan, E. M. Kranich, J. Smit, H. Zimmernam, and E. Schubert. *Der Rhythmus von Wachen und Schlafen. Seine Bedeutung im Kindes- und Jugendalter* [The rhythm of waking and sleeping. Its meaning for the time of childhood and youth]. Stuttgart: Verlag Freies Geistesleben, 1992.

Lin, J.P., J.K.Brown, and E.G.Walsh. "Physiological Maturation of Muscles in Childhood." *Lancet,* 1993.

Lindenberg, Christoph. *Die Lebensbedingungen des Erziehens-von Waldorfschulen lernen* [Life conditions of education. Learning from Waldorf schools]. Reinbeck: rororo-Sachbuch, 1981.

Lippitz, Wilfried and Christian Rittelmeyer. *Phänomene des Kinderlebens. Beispiele und methodische Probleme einer pädagogischen Phänomenologie* [Phenomena in a child's life. Examples and methodological problems of a pedagogical phenomenology]. Bad Heilbronn: Klinkhardt, 1990.

MacLeod, Sheila. *The Art of Starvation: A Story of Anorexia and Survival.* New York: Schocken Books, 1982.

Mager, N.H. *The Kondratieff Waves*. London: Praeger, 1986.

Marti, Ernst. *Das Ätherische* [The Etheric Elements]. Basel: Verlag Pie Pforte, 1994. See also *The Four Ethers*. Roselle, IL: Schaumburg Publications, 1984.

Maslow, Abraham. *Motivation and Personality*. London: Longman Higher Editions 1987.

McAllen, Audrey. *Teaching Children Handwriting*. Fair Oaks, CA: Rudolf Steiner College Press, 2002.

_____. *Sleep: An Unobserved Element in Education*. Stroud, 1981. To be reissued by Rudolf Steiner College Press 2003.

McKeen, Thomas. *Wesen und Gestalt des Menschen* [The form of the human being]. Stuttgart: Verlag Freies Geistesleben, 1996.

Morais, J. Morais, et al. "Does awareness of speech as a sequence of phones rise spontaneously?" *Cognition* 7 (1979): 323-331.

Nefiodow, L.A. *Der sechste Kondratieff. Wege zur Produktivität und Vollbeschäftigung im Zeitalter der Information* [The sixth Kondratieff: How to achieve productivity and full employment in the information age]. Bonn: Rhein-Sieg Verlag, 2000. See Mager, *The Kondratieff Waves*.

Nickel, Horst. "Das Problem der Schulreife—Eine systematische Analyse und ihre praktischen Konsequenzen" [The problem of readiness for school—systematic analysis and practical consequences]. In Dieter Karch, Richard Michaelis, et al., eds. *Normale und gestörte Entwicklung* [Normal and disturbed development] Berlin/Heidelberg/New York/Tokyo: np, 1989.]

Opp, F., ed. *Was Kinder stärkt. Erziehung zwischen Risiko und Resilienz* [What strengthens children: education between risk and resilience]. Basel: Reinhardt Verlag, 1999.

Paulig, Peter. Peter Paulig, "Aufruf zur Verwirklichung der Humanen Schule, Millionen unserer Kinder leiden an der Schule!" [Appeal for realization of a humane school. Millions of our children suffer at school!] in *Der Kinderarzt* [The pediatrician] 7 (1984).

Pfeiffer, Ehrenfried. "Rudolf Steiners landschaftlicher Impuls" [Rudolf Steiner's agricultural impulse] in *Wir erlebten Rudolf Steiner. Erinnerungen seiner Schüler* [We Experienced Rudolf Steiner: Recollections by His Students]. Stuttgart, 1988.

_____. "New Directions in Agriculture" in *A Man Before Others: Rudolf Steiner Remembered*. Bristol: Rudolf Steiner Press, 1993.

Rutenfranz, Joseph. "Kind und biologische Rhythmik" [The Child and Biological Rhythms]. *Deutsches Ärzteblatt* [Publication for German doctors], February 8, 1979. Institute for Performance-Physiology, University of Dortmund.

Sattler, Johanna Barbara. *Der umgeschulte Linkshänder*, [Reeducation of left-handed children]. Donauwörth: Auer, 2000.

Schad, Wolfgang. *Man and Mammals: Toward a Biology of Form*. Garden City, NY: Waldorf School Publication, 1977. *Säugetiere und Mensch*. Stuttgart: Verlag Freies Geistesleben 1985.

361

_____. "Zum anthroposophischen Verständnis der Temperamente" [Anthroposophical understanding of the temperaments]. *Erziehung ist Kunst* [Education is art]. Stuttgart: Verlag Freies Geistesleben, 1994.]

_____. *Zur Organologie und Physiologie des Lernens. Aspekte einer pädagogischen Theorie des Leibes* [Organology and physiology of learning].

Schär, Meinrad. *Leitfaden der Sozial- und Präventivmedizin* [Manual of social- and preventive medicine]. Bern/Stuttgart/Vienna: np, 1984.

Scheer-Krüger, Gerda. *Das offenbare Geheimnis der Temperamente* [The manifest mystery of the temperaments]. Dornach: np, 1996;

Schmidt, Gerhard. *The Dynamics of Nutrition.* Wyoming, RI: Bio-Dynamic Literature, 1980.

_____. *The Essentials of Nutrition.* Wyoming, RI: Bio-Dynamic Literature, 1987.

Sieweke, Herbert. *Anthroposophische Medizin. Studien zu ihren Grundlagen, Teil I* [Anthroposophical medicine. Studies of its foundations, part 1]. Dornach: Verlag am Goetheanum, 1982. *Gesundheit und Krankheit als Verwirklichungsformen menschlichen Daseins. Anthroposophische Medizin. Studien zu ihren Grundlagen, Teil 2* [Health and illness as realization-forms of human existence. Anthroposophical Medicine. Studies of its foundations, part 2]. Dornach: Verlag am Goetheanum, 1994.

Sixel, Detlef. *Rudolf Steiner über die Temperamente* [Rudolf Steiner on the temperaments]. Dornach: Goetheanum Pedagogical Section, 1990.

Smit, Jörgen. *Der werdende Mensch. Zur meditative Vertiefung des Erziehers* [The developing human being. An aid to meditative deepening of the educator]. Stuttgart: np, 1990.

_____. *Spiritual Development: Meditation in Daily Life.* Edinburgh: Floris, 1991

Soesman, Albert. *Our Twelve Senses: Wellsprings of the Soul.* Stroud: Hawthorn Press, 1990.

Solzhenitsyn, Alexander. *The Gulag Archipelago.* Translated by T. P. Whitney. n.p.: Collins/Fontana, 1974.

Springer, Sally P and Georg Deutsch. *Left Brain—Right Brain.* New York: W.H. Freeman, 1993. German title: *Linkes/Rechtes Gehirn.* Berlin/Oxford: n.p., 1995.

Staley, Betty. *Between Form and Freedom: A Practical Guide for the Teenage Years.* Stroud: Hawthorn Press, 1988.

Stanovich, K.E., ed. *Children's reading and the development of phonemical awareness* . 1978. Cited in P. Zimmermann 1993.

Stark, Dean. *A Waldorf Approach to Coaching Team Sports.* Fair Oaks, CA: Rudolf Steiner College Press, 1999.

Stave, Uwe. *Die Umwelt des Kleinen Kindes.* Stuttgart: Verlag Urachhaus, 1990.

Stockmeyer, E.A. Karl. *Angaben Rudolf Steiners für den Waldorfunterricht. Eine Quellensammlung für die Arbeit der Lehrerkollegien,* (Indications by Rudolf Steiner. for Waldorf instruction, a collection of sources for the work of teachers). Internal manuscript publication by the Pedagogical Research Office, Stuttgart. Available through DRUCKtuell, Postfach 10 02 22, DE-70827, Gerlingen. *Rudolf Steiner's Curriculum for Waldorf Schools.* Third edition. Forest Row, Sussex: Steiner Schools Fellowship, 1991.

Strauß, Michaela. *Understanding Children's Drawings.* London: Rudolf Steiner Press, 1988. German title: *Von der Zeichensprache des kleinen Kindes* [The small child's symbolic language]. Stuttgart 1994.

Thieme *Taschenbuch für Zahn- und Kieferheilkunde im Kindes- und Jugendalter;* [Thieme pocketbook for hygiene of teeth and jaws in childhood and youth].

Treichler, Markus. "Anorexia mentalis" in *Beiträge zu einer Erweiterung der Heilkunst nach geisteswissenschaftlichen Erkenntnissen* [Contributions to the expansion of the art of healing]. 5 (1980) 172-180.

Twentyman, Ralph. *The Science and Art of Healing.* Edinburgh: Floris, 1989.

Weimann, et al. "Pubertäre Entwicklungsverzögerung von Kunstturnerinnen" [Delay in puberty in top female gymnasts]. *Sozialpädiatrie und kinderärztliche Praxis* [Social pediatrics and pediatric practice] vol. II. np., 1996.

Wiesener, Heinrich. *Entwicklungsphysiologie des Kindes* [Developmental physiology of the child]. Berlin/Göttingen/Heidelberg: n.p., 1964.

Wessel, Dietrich. "Das Problem Hausaufgaben" [The problem of homework]. *Erziehungskunst* [Art of Education] (June-July 1992).

Wilkinson, Roy. *The Temperaments in Education.* Fair Oaks, CA: Rudolf Steiner College Press, 1977.

Zimmermann, P. Lese-Rechschreib-Schwäche als Entwicklungsstörung. Untersuchung an Waldorfschülern der Klassen 4-6 (unveröffentlichtes Manuskript [Reading and spelling weakness as developmental disorder. Examination of Waldorf School students of classes 4-6 (unpublished manuscript)], Herdecke, 1993.]

Booklet on daycare centers published by Internationale Vereinigung der Walorfkindergärten e.V. [International Association of Waldorf Kindergartens], Stuttgart.

Die Bedeutung des Zahnwechsels in der Entwicklung des Kindes [The significance of the change of teeth in the child's development]. Stuttgart: Association of Waldorf-Kindergartens, Pedagogical Research Center of the Alliance of Free Waldorf Schools, 1988.

Der Zahnwechsel [The change of teeth], study material of the International Association of Waldorf Kindergartens, Stuttgart.

"Zur Unterrichtsgestaltung im 1. bis 8. Schuljahr an Waldorf-/Rudolf Steiner Schulen" [Forming the grade 1–8 curriculum] in *Das Kind in der mittleren Klassenlehrerzeit* [The child during the middle grades], part 2. Joint project of the Goetheanum Pedagogical Section and the Waldorf Schools Association. Dornach (1996).

Index

Altmeier, Marianne 111

anemia
in girls 48–49

anorexia nervosa 304–310

Antonovsky, Aaron 326, 336

arithmetic, geometry
arithmetic and morality 212–215
effect on ego 184

art
as expression of the human being 27
importance of performances for life after
death 112–113
interaction of science, art, and religion
220–224
related to human components chap. 3
therapy for anorexia nervosa 310

astral body 17–20
artistic judgment 179
in classroom instruction 49–58
in girls and boys 194
permeates etheric body in 12th–13th
year 174
related to music 29–31
secondary gender characteristics 20
teacher's, effect on etheric of students
42–43
teacher's, sympathy and antipathy 43

Baur, Alfred 295

Bengel, J. 16

biodynamic compost preparations 103

blood, overactivity in 75

Bockemühl, Johannes, M.D. 227, 242, 269,
310, 311

breathing 163–166

comprehension transmitted through
rhythmic system 186
experience of 208–209
works with nervous system 204–207

Bücher, Ernst 290, 302

central nervous system 18
cramps in 74–75

change of teeth 57–58
and memory 56
and transformation of body form 272–273
astral body begins to play on nerve
fibers 205
birth of the etheric body 19–20, 101
speech before and after, 188–189

child study in faculty meetings 58–75,
225–244

circulation in adult
related to play in childhood 46

components of the human being 17–20
and classroom instruction 49–58
physician's relationship to 33
related to arts chap. 3
rhythms of 116–117
teacher's relationship to 33
See also physical body, etheric body, astral
body, ego/ego-organization

constitution of the child
earthly/cosmic 82–84
fantasy-rich/fantasy-poor 85–87
large-headed/small-headed 76–82
types of 240–241

craniotabes 78

Deutsch, Georg 87

dexterity exercises
for educating practical life experience
100–103

digestion in adult
 related to play in childhood 46

drawing
 effect on the ego 184–185
 motifs in children's pictures 279–280

drug consumption 25

dyslexia 290–303

education
 and game rules 281–282
 and goals of team games 282–283
 artistic instruction and faculty of judgment
  179–180
 as healing 15, 226, 268, 339
 between preexistence and postexistence
  109–114
 effect of instruction on ego 183–186
 humane school 11
 instruction raised to the level of art 185
 joyous atmosphere 152
 lifting unconscious questions into
  consciousness 182–183
 nonverbal, in kindergarten 266
 physiological effects of chap. 7
 sports instruction 287–288
 with the goal of well-being 15
 See also Waldorf

Ege, Arvia MacKaye 119

ego/ego-organization 17–20
 birth of 20
 daily engagement strengthens personality
  120
 drawing conclusions 180
 effect of instruction on 183–186
 in classroom instruction 49–58
 in eurythmy with small children 154–155
 in young child 159
 influenced by astral body in teenagers
  194–196
 presence of mind 43
 related to poetry 30–31
 relationship to language 188–190
 self-discipline of adult 267–268
 teacher's, effect on astral of students 42
 voice of conscience 159

Egyptian temple-sleep
 healing in 35–36, 40

etheric body 17–20
 day and night activity 38–39

dual function of 37–38
 in classroom instruction 49–58
 influenced by astral body in teenagers 196
 lawfulness applied in eurythmy 30
 mental images, forming 171–172
 metamorphosis of growth forces into
  thought forces chap 4, chap 7, 271–280
 permeated by astral body in 12th–13th year
  174
 related to sculptural-pictorial arts 27–29, 31
 tends to practice eurythmy 210
 teacher's, effect on physical of students 42
 vitalizing processes in 43

eurythmy, a 20th century art 30–31
 and singing 211–212
 clutivating imagination through 86
 etheric body tends to practice 210
 healing benefits of doing and watching 211
 in first seven years 154–157
 lawfulness of the etheric applied in 30–31
 quiet time important after 211–212
 required subject all through school
  207–211
 sequence of school subjects 128–132
 soul-spiritual form of gymnastics 287
 spiritualizes an earthly child 83
 therapeutic 71, 261–264
 for dyslexia 297–299
 for right- or left-sidedness 88
 yearly rhythm 146

faculty meeting
 child study in 58–75, 225–244
 heart of the school 72–73
 questions about children 111–112

fear, overcoming 311–324

feeling 18, 30, 83–84, chap. 7
 related to archangelic world 170
 rhythmic ability in speech 276
 sense of rhythm and beat 275–276
 space awareness 274
 stimulates rhythmic system 164

festivals, yearly rhythms 149–151

first grade, readiness for 20

foreign language, yearly rhythm 146

Freinet 13

Fucke, Erhard 287

366

Galen 16

genetic esotericism 40

geography, geology
effect on ego 184–185
effects of teaching 172–179

Goebel, Wolfgang, M.D. 238

Greif, Daniela 290, 299

gymnastics
quiet time important after 211–212
yearly rhythm 146

Heidebrand, Caroline von 169

Hildebrandt, Gunther, M.D. 117, 123, 136

Hippocrates 16

homework 67, 106–109

history
effect on ego 184–185
effects of teaching 172–179
relation of impulses in humanity and in
nature 216
rhythm of lessons 132–135
sequence of school subjects 128–132

human organism (threefold nature of)
and interaction of science, art, and religion
220–224
polarities in 230, 240–241
treating imbalances in 76–82

Husemann, Armin, M.D. 31, 57, 290, 297

Husemann, Gisbert, M.D. 31, 304

hygienic esotericism 35, 41

illness
childhood diseases 266-267
love for 73–74

imagination
and thinking 276–280
imagining, judging, concluding 132–135
painting and writing for 85
reading and observation for 85
instrumental music or singing for 86,
308–309
eurythmy for 86

immune system
depends on soul and spirit 37

intelligence, stimulation of 186–187

Jonas, Hans 336

Kayser-Springorum, Marina, M.D. 265

Kersten, Wolfgang, M.D. 245

Kischnick, Rudolf 289

Kolisko, Eugen, M.D. 14, 21, 62, 68, 152

Kondratieff, Nikolai 330
Kondratieff waves 330

König, Karl, M.D. 23, 289

Kügelgen, Helmut von 154, 158

Kummer, Karl-Reinhard, M.D. 269, 281

larynx 189–190, 294–297

learning disabilities 25

left-handedness
left-handers learning to write with the right
hand 90–99, 265
treatment of 87–99

life body 31

limb system 17–19
See also metabolic-limb system

Lindenberg, Christoph, M.D. 126–128

liver 47

love, lack of 75

MacLeod, Sheila 304

Mandela, Nelson 338

Marti, Ernst 271

Maslow, Abraham 326

mathematics
in healing 40

mechanical esotericism 41

memory
and change of teeth 56
and pictorial thought 276–277
in the main lesson 127–128
linked with metabolic-limb system 186
memorization 69
pictures disappear or stay 85
sleep improves memory 187

metabolic-limb system 17, 19
linked to memory 186
judgment connected with arms and hands
179
related to willing 164
sleep improves metabolism 187

Montessori, Maria 13

movement
children's need for 67
developing intelligence through 102–103
eurythmy in the first seven years 154–157
healing influence on the head 203
in school schedule 125–126
personal qualities from the ego 17
soccer, effects of 281–289
synchronizing several activities 279
See also eurythmy, and gymnastics

Müller-Wiedemann, Hans, M,D. 261

music, singing 201–207
imagination and 86, 308–309
effect on ego 184
effect on life after death 112
eurythmy and singing 211–212
mood of the fifth 157
quiet time important after singing 211–212
sequence of school subjects 128–132
spiritualizes an earthly child 83

Nefiodov, Leo 330

nerve-sense system 19
how breathing works with 204–207
perception through 186
related to thought 164

neuritis
in boys 48–49

neurophysiology
thinking stimulated by dexterity exercises
100–101

Nietzold, Jochem 289

nutrition
and health, teaching of (7th grade) 142
one source of health 339
questions of 265
related to interest and consciousness
103–106
sugar 47–48

painting
cultivating imagination through 85

pathogenic, pathological 15
causes of disease 16

Paulig, Peter 11

Pehm, Maria Teresia 90

Peterson, Peter 13

Pfeiffer, Ehrenfried 103

physical body 17–20
change in heart sounds 273
games played with feet 283–285
hindrance to supersensible components
60–61
in classroom instruction 49–58
joy nurtures 151–152
music in the form of the 202–203
related to gravity and architecture 27, 31
reflex-organization 272–273
result of vitalizing process in etheric 43
transformation of body form 272–273
See also change of teeth

physics
and intellectuality 215–219
rhythm of lessons 132–135

play
related to circulation and digestion in old
age 46

preschool, nursery
medical and pedagogical questions in
153–160

Pressel, Simeon 289

preventive medicine 40
paradigm change 15
specialist 15
See also salutogenesis

Prömm, Peter 289

punishment 67

quiet child
 well-behaved or ill 67

quiet time
 needed after eurythmy, gymnastics, and
  singing 211–212

reading
 and observing 190–192
 cultivating imagination through 85

remedial instruction
 dexterity exercises for 101–102
 for dyslexia 300–302

resonance of processes as therapeutic impulse
 231

rhythm
 4-week 115–116, 141–146
 5-day week 135–136, 140–141
 7-day healing rhythm 136–139
 cure rhythms 143–145
 daily course of arithmetical speed 120
 daily course of physiological performancce
  readiness 121
 day and night 119–135, 167–168
 imagining, judging, concluding 132–135
 importance of for health 117–118
 in the main lesson 126–128
 monthly 141–146
 school schedules chap. 6, 122, 124–126
 sequence of school subjects 128–135
 sleeping and waking 168–169
 structure of lesson supports proper
  breathing 165
 weekly 135–140
 yearly, care of physical body 146–152
 yearly, festivals 149–151

rhythmic system 18
 comprehension transmitted through 186
 connected with music 202–203
 feelings stimulate 164
 human rhythmic function periods 123

Rutenfranz, Joseph 122

salutogenesis, salutogenic 40, chap. 10
 concept 16–17
 definition of health 265

inner path to source of personal
  development 340–346
 psychosocial health 329–331
 resilience research 327–328

Sattler, Barbara 87

school physician
 and learning to write with the right
  hand 88
 and therapeutic education 261–264
 child psychiatrist 311–324
 compensation according to social law 263
 help develop healthy school schedule 115
 joy and health 152
 know importance of art in curriculum 113
 knowledge of human constitution 20–21
 medical exam for school entry 269–280
 on homework 107
 public work of 265–268
 role of 14–15, chap 5, 245–260
 role in child study 227–237, 238–244
 survey of German Waldorf schools
  255–260
 translate medical knowledge into
  instructional measures 307

science
 interaction of science, art, and religion
  220–224
 rhythm of lessons 132–135

senses
 education of 25
 ego experiences itself through 24–25
 of sound 291–297
 twelve 23–24

sleep 166–170
 ideas of Descartes and Bergson 178–179
 improves metabolism and memory 187
 unformed questions in 182

soccer, effects of 281–289

Solzhenitzyn, Alexander 337

soul
 functions 17
 immune system depends on 37
 influence on body through repeated earth
  lives 44
 never ill 70–72
 observable in sick child 62
 soul activity 18

speech
  children reachable through 280
  effect on ego 184, 188–190
  instruction 187–190
  related to breathing 166
  rhythmic abilities in 276

spirit
  activity 17
  never ill 70–72
  observable in sick child 62
  participation with creator force 158–160
  path of spiritual development 340–346

spirit-self 31
  teacher's, effect on ego of student 42

Springer, Sally 87

Steiner, Rudolf 13
  arts as expression of the human being 27
  consider all humanity in order to help
    individuals 327
  education is healing 15
  hygienic esotericism 35
  salutogenic concept 16–17
  soul influence on body through repeated
    earth lives 44

  quoted passages by
    arithmetic and morality 212–215
    biodynamic compost preparations 103
    blood, overactivity in 75
    body-free and sense bound thinking
      39–40
    boy who was hydrocephalic 63–64
    breathing 163–164
    breathing, how works with nervous
      system 204–207
    case of 8-yr-old who stopped growing
      33–35
    central nervous system, cramps in 74–75
    child as revelation of divine-spiritual
      laws 113–114
    child study in teachers' meetings 59–75
    children in spiritual world more recently
      than teacher 110
    clear speech 166
    compassion 311
    craniotabes 78
    dexterity exercises 100–102
    education, relation to healing and health
      226, 253
    earthly/cosmic child 82–84
    Egyptian temple-sleep 35–36
    eurythmy and singing 211–212

eurythmy compared with gymnastics
  207–210
eurythmy, healing benefits of doing and
  watching 211
faculty of judgment 179–181
feeling as preparation for thinking
  164–165
health and nutrition (7th grade) 142
homework 67, 107–108
human being as a musical instrument
  201–203
hygienic esotericism 41
illness, love for 73–74
imagination and music 308–309
imagination, cultivating 85–86
imagining, judging, concluding 132–135
instruction based on understanding of
  human components 49–58
instruction, effect on ego 183–186
intellectual study based on earlier
  pictures 215–216
intelligence, stimulation of 186–187
joy nurtures physical body 151–152
language, personal relationship to
  188–190
large-headed/small-headed child 76–82
left-handedness 88–89
love, lack of 75
medical training 55
memorization 69
music, effect on life after death 112
music, healing influence on the head
  203
nutrition, related to interest and
  consciousness 103, 105–106
physical body reveals other components
  225
punishment 67–68
quiet child 67
quiet time important after eurythmy,
  gymnastics, and singing 211–212
reading and observing 190–192
rhythms of human components 116–117
school physician, role of 14, 46
school schedules 115–116, 124–126
school subjects chap 8
science, art, and religion 220–221
sequence of school subjects 128–135
sexuality 200–201
sleeping and waking rhythm 168–170,
  178–179
social law, salary according to 263
speech and truth 187
spiritual development 341–346
spiritual, political, and economic life
  221–224

teacher training 55, 68
teacher's inner life, effect on students
    42–43
teacher's work, effect on child's physical
    development 45–49
teaching geography 176–177
teaching history (9th–10th year)
    173–176
teaching historical relationships
    (12th–13th year) 174–175
teaching physics 216–219
teaching zoology 192–193
teenagers, differentiation of sexes
    193–199
temperament, classroom seating for 69
temperament, sugar in diet for 69–70
temperament, treating children according
    to 160–162
therapeutic nature of a Waldorf school
    75
treating imbalances in the threefold
    human organism 76–82
unconscious questions 182–183
verse given to doctors and medical
    students 252–253
verse given for Waldorf school children
    119, 334
Waldorf school, a growing organism
    72–74

Stockmeyer, E.A. Karl 171

teacher training 55, 68

teacher's work
    effect of inner life on students 41–43
    effect on child's physical development
        45–49

teenagers
    differentiation of the sexes in 193–201
    importance of moral and aesthetic
        196–197
    need for privacy 197–199
    puberty, questions of 265

temperament
    classroom seating for 69
    extreme disposition of 47–48
    in cosmic and earthly child 83
    sugar in diet for 69–70
    teaching history through 175–176
    treating children according to 160–162

thinking 18–20, 30
    developed through dexterity exercises

100–101
    imagination and 276–280
    metamorphosis of growth forces into
        chap 4, 101, chap 7
    related to angelic world 170
    related to nerve-and-sense system 164

Treichler, Markus 306

Waldorf school/education
    dyslexia in, case study 290–303
    effect of curriculum on physical
        development 15
    growing organism 72–74
    soccer at 288
    therapeutic nature of 76

Wessel, Dietrich 109

will/willing 17–20, 30, chap 7
    forces, changes in 273
    in eurythmy with small children 155
    learning led to 165
    related to archai 170
    related to metabolic-limb system 164, 187

writing
    cultivating imagination through 85
    effect on ego 185

zoology (14- or 15-yr-olds) 192–193